CAMBRIDGE LIBRAR

Books of enduring sch

Literary Studies

This series provides a high-quality selection of early printings of literary works, textual editions, anthologies and literary criticism which are of lasting scholarly interest. Ranging from Old English to Shakespeare to early twentieth-century work from around the world, these books offer a valuable resource for scholars in reception history, textual editing, and literary studies.

The Stage

The librettist and theatre manager Alfred Bunn (1796–1860) published these memoirs of his career, giving a view 'both before and behind the curtain', in 1840. He professes not to be fond of autobiographies, is clearly irritated at the not always flattering walk-on role he is given in the memoirs of some of the greatest contemporary performers, and regards this three-volume work as a way of settling a number of scores. His account cannot therefore be said to be unprejudiced, but it is written with a verve which makes it very readable, and – allowing for bias and exaggeration – provides a fascinating account of the period when Bunn was running both the Theatre Royal at Drury Lane and the Opera House at Covent Garden, providing libretti for some of the best known British composers of the period, and quarrelling with almost everyone he worked with in the course of his career.

Cambridge University Press has long been a pioneer in the reissuing of out-of-print titles from its own backlist, producing digital reprints of books that are still sought after by scholars and students but could not be reprinted economically using traditional technology. The Cambridge Library Collection extends this activity to a wider range of books which are still of importance to researchers and professionals, either for the source material they contain, or as landmarks in the history of their academic discipline.

Drawing from the world-renowned collections in the Cambridge University Library and other partner libraries, and guided by the advice of experts in each subject area, Cambridge University Press is using state-of-the-art scanning machines in its own Printing House to capture the content of each book selected for inclusion. The files are processed to give a consistently clear, crisp image, and the books finished to the high quality standard for which the Press is recognised around the world. The latest print-on-demand technology ensures that the books will remain available indefinitely, and that orders for single or multiple copies can quickly be supplied.

The Cambridge Library Collection brings back to life books of enduring scholarly value (including out-of-copyright works originally issued by other publishers) across a wide range of disciplines in the humanities and social sciences and in science and technology.

The Stage

Both Before and Behind the Curtain, from
Observations Taken on the Spot

VOLUME 3

ALFRED BUNN

CAMBRIDGE
UNIVERSITY PRESS

CAMBRIDGE
UNIVERSITY PRESS

University Printing House, Cambridge, CB2 8BS, United Kingdom

Cambridge University Press is part of the University of Cambridge.

It furthers the University's mission by disseminating knowledge in the pursuit of
education, learning and research at the highest international levels of excellence.

www.cambridge.org
Information on this title: www.cambridge.org/9781108081665

© in this compilation Cambridge University Press 2017

This edition first published 1840
This digitally printed version 2017

ISBN 978-1-108-08166-5 Paperback

THE STAGE:

BOTH BEFORE

AND

BEHIND THE CURTAIN,

FROM

" OBSERVATIONS TAKEN ON THE SPOT."

BY ALFRED BUNN,

LATE LESSEE OF THE THEATRES ROYAL DRURY LANE AND
COVENT GARDEN.

' I am (NOT) forbid
To tell the secrets of my prison-house."
HAMLET, ACT 1. SC. V.

IN THREE VOLUMES.

VOL. III.

RICHARD BENTLEY, NEW BURLINGTON STREET,
Publisher in Ordinary to Her Majesty.
1840.

LONDON:

PRINTED BY IBOTSON AND PALMER,
SAVOY STREET, STRAND.

CONTENTS

OF THE THIRD VOLUME.

CHAPTER I.

CHAPTER II.

CHAPTER III.

CHAPTER IV.

CHAPTER V.

CHAPTER VI.

CHAPTER VII.

CHAPTER VIII.

ERRATA IN VOL. III.

Page 31, 5 line from top, *for* application *read* applications.
  39, 16 — top, *for* sound of fury *read* full of sound and fury.
  65, 6 — bottom, *for* or *read* for.
  81, 7 — top, *for* qui *read* que.
  82, 6 — bottom, *for* pedier tout ceci je le saurai *read* pedier. Tout ceci je le savais.
  97, 22 — top, *for* Mr. Allen, Mr. Balfe *read* then Mr. Balfe, Mr. Allen.
  120, 3 — top, *for* whose of *read* of whose.
  152, 9 — top, *for* assuredly *read* speedily.
  153, 9 line of Contents, *for* Scrope *read* Scribe.
  217, 9 line from top, *for* communiquée *read* communiqué

THE STAGE:

BOTH

BEFORE AND BEHIND THE CURTAIN.

CHAPTER I.

Mr. C. Kean's appearance in London—A lecture on bad habits—Garrick's villa—Mems of a Manager—A change of AIR—Ferdinand Ries—Italian Opera at Paris—Severini—Mrs. Bland and Mrs. Jordan—what is *in* Bishop, and how to extract it—Stanfield and Macready—Murphy praised, *whether* or no—John Reeve and the Lord Mayor—Dimond ——— his life and death—His many trials—LENT, not paid for—The Lord Chamberlain *again!*—Mrs. Glover's fall from the stage—C. Kean's Hamlet and Richard—Three hundred guinea's worth of lectures—A Shaksperian prophecy—Seguin and Talleyrand—Unpublished letter from Lord Byron—Barclay and Jackson—Magic Flute—a Roman Nose—Persiani—Boisragon—Morton—C. Kean and his father contrasted—Dinner and dessert.

I REMEMBER few instances of greater excitement than that which preceded, and attended, the return of Mr. Charles Kean to the metropolitan boards. The *hiatus* occasioned by the death of his father, the

futile attempts made from the period it occurred up
to the moment in question to find a fit successor; and
the written and oral reports which had run through
all dramatic circles for several seasons, that " the son
of the man " (the appellation of the late King of
Rome) was the only one by whom such *hiatus* could
be filled up; the acknowledged vast distinction of
habits * between the offspring and the father, more

* Do you desire an occasional day's retreat, good reader, from the
turmoils of business, and for the enjoyment of " all-powerful nature "
in the company of those who feel with yourself? Then do what I do
sometimes—drive down in the cool of the day to Hampton, dine and
sleep there, and come up in the morning. [N. B.—any day but Sunday.] I went there on one occasion with two friends "learned in the
law," and another sinful boy, " learned " in everything ; and while
dinner was being prepared, we paid a visit to Garrick's Villa, and
were kindly shown every part and parcel of it by Mrs. Carr, an intimate
companion of Mrs. Garrick, and who at this time, and since her death,
had resided there. We talked of course of Garrick, after that of Kean ;
when on the old lady inquiring how Drury Lane went on, and my
replying in a tone somewhat devoid of enthusiasm, she observed,
" Ay, ay, you should do as Davy did — Davy never kept no bad
company—have nothing to do with people of BAD HABITS !" Now
whether she referred to the habits of poor Kean, or to those of my
three friends whom she wistfully eyed, as she thus delivered herself,
this deponent sayeth not. I cannot dismiss the worthy tenant of this
delightful abode, without letting the reader into a secret Mrs. Carr
let us into. On inquiring how long the communication, passing under
the high road between the gardens of the house and the lawn facing the
river had been made, she answered, " Oh, Janson, he did that—
Janson said to Davy, ' if you can't get over it, you must get under
it,' and so Davy, he made the hole :' " and as her reply referred to
Dr. Johnson and Mr. Garrick, we received the information with becoming homage.

especially made manifest in the extraordinary instance of the protection bestowed by one on the mother, compared with the protection withheld by the
other from the WIFE ;—all these considerations combined to warm up the dramatic spirit, as far as it
was capable of resuscitation, of the dormant British
public.

Mr. C. Kean, during his long sojourn in the provinces, had established one of the first principles by
which the success of public aspirants is tested,
which consists of being invariably attractive wherever he went and played. Unaided by any of the
obvious advantages of a metropolitan fame, Mr. C.
Kean could fill the principal country theatres, while
others in possession of those advantages could not
attract people enough to pay for lighting them. His
detractors argued that all this was only trading in the
name of the father and in the amiable qualities of
the son, and had no connexion whatever with the
personation of the drama; while his friends more
reasonably maintained that such adjuncts might be
useful in a first instance, but that the repetition of
such great success could only be obtained by the
possession of great talents. To solve the question,
to mortify or to gratify his opponents, (consisting, after
all, only of those who were foolishly trying to uphold
another,) and to carry out the judgment of his
admirers, Mr. C. Kean entered into an engagement
with me to perform a limited number of nights, at a

salary of 50*l*. a night. Laying aside the fact, insisted upon in another part of these volumes, that " there is no harm in a guinea," there was an immense importance attached to the fact of a young man, bearing the name and having in his veins the blood of KEAN, being able to command a salary hitherto only given to him who first bore it. Leaving out of the question whatever quality of talent Mr. C. Kean possessed, there cannot be a doubt, had his salary been but fifty shillings a night, it would have been asserted that he possessed none ; as, on the other hand, he had the credit for the gift of an unusual quantity, from the unusual terms he stipulated for.

My principal object being rather to chronicle the sayings and doings of other people, than to set down any opinions of my own, I shall leave any discussion on Mr. C. Kean's general performance to those whose business or pleasure it is to deal in the same ; and shall content myself with such extracts from my own journal of memoranda, kept at the time, as may be illustrative of the season 1837-38. Mr. Kean had arrived in town to fulfil his engagement, while I was labouring under severe indisposition, and one of his visits to me I perceive thus referred to, which I take the liberty of classing amongst a great many others, under the designation of

MEMS OF A MANAGER!

January 7, 1838.—Charles Kean called on me to-

day, during one of my paroxysms of intense suffering—he's in an established funk about the result of
to-morrow: it is momentous to him and all of us;
but " funking" will only make it more so. He has
good qualities in him, with a very gentlemanly mind;
Eton has done that part of the business for him—
he'll get well through—doing much himself, and we
helping him with the rest. I liked some of his
Hamlet when I saw it at Brighton in September last.
" Is it the king?" will hit others, " I guess," as it hit
me. Miss Charles, whose real name is Pettingall, has
thrown up her engagement, because, at Mr. Kean's
suggestion and request, I put Miss Romer into the
part of *Ophelia,* instead of her sweet self—*she*'ll be
sorry before *I* shall.

January 8.—Charles Kean makes, what may be
termed his début in *Hamlet,* prepared with new scenes,
dresses, and paraphernalia. His appearance and his
performance elicited a degree of enthusiasm never
heard of but in the case of his father; for he might
truly say, as his sire said before him, " the pit rose
at me"—receipt of the house, despite reduced
prices, and without taking annual boxes into account,
453*l.* 10*s.* Though suffering from the effects of
severe illness, I flannelled up, and went down to see
the sight. A very earnest actor, with most of the
peculiarities, (not the intenseness, mind,) and all the
faults of his renowned papa. By perseverance, talent,
and conduct, he has at length managed

" To climb
" The steep where Fame's proud temple shines afar."

His fencing perfect—plenty of *foils* provided by the
rest of the company. This play will run, and like
some other things that *run*, will *draw ;* which two
isolated words are part of the favourite slang of a his-
trio's vocabulary.

January 10.—The Royal Exchange burnt down
—the " whereby" not yet known—a thorough dis-
may in the city, but it will open the purses of many
which are at present too full. " Blood, Iago, blood,"
—your citizen wants bleeding occasionally, at least
in his pocket. The wags say that a " solid change is
gone to take a " change of air"—Kean fidgety, lest
the attraction of his second night should suffer by
the event.

January 13.—Ferdinand Ries, the composer, died
at Frankfort-on-the-Maine. The last time I met
Ries, was at the house of his friend Mr. Sharpe,
North End, Fulham. Tom Welsh was present, and
we sat in divan on an opera, by the aforesaid Ries,
'yclept *A Night on Lebanon.* Ries was a profound
musician, but had no melody in him. He married
Miss Mangeon, sister to the lady of that name,
who appeared (and disappeared) at Drury Lane
some years since. Ries was an agreeable, gentlemanly man, but not equal to an opera; his last,
The Robber's Bride," was a miserable failure.
He was an excellent teacher, but an indifferent

imparter of sound, and there is a wide distinction therein.

January 15.—The Italian Opera House in Paris burnt down, the cause originating in some over-heated flue There was a performance yesterday, (Sunday,) which accounts for it. Poor Severini would *per-severein* jumping from a window, and met that death he would have escaped had he remained quiet. It will serve for talk to the Parisians for at least one entire month. Mrs. Bland died this day, aged 73; she married the brother of Mrs. Jordan; but the chances are, that those who never aided her living, are not likely to mourn for her dead! Bravo—" O world, thy slippery turns"— what a ballad singer!—in appearance like a fillet of veal on castors—it was " vox et preterea nihil"—but *what* a vox!

January 16.—Ferdinand Ries buried at Frankfort on the Maine.

January 18.—I met Bishop at Mackinlay's dinner-table, and agreed to write an opera with him—two of the three to write, and t'other to publish. If he will but be HIMSELF, the stuff is still *in* Bishop ; but trying first to be Rossini, and after that to be Weber, knocked it all *out* of him. The composer of *When the wind blows*, and the *Chough and Crow*, and *The Indian Drum*, and *Mynheer Von Dunk*, and such like things, cannot afford to copy any one. Bishop has a classical and gentlemanly mind, which is as rare as it is pleasant to meet with in any one whose back has once rubbed against the scenes of a theatre.

January 20.—The people are Murphy-mad, as well as Kean-mad. This, it was foretold, would be the day on which the lowest degree of the thermometer would be experienced; and it was so. They tell me that Macready has sent Stanfield 300*l.* for painting a diorama in the pantomime of *Peeping Tom*—that Stanfield has retained one-half and has returned the other, and that Macready has caused the said other half to be expended in a piece of plate, to be presented to the said Stanfield. The two reasons why *I* doubt this report are, that I never yet heard of Macready giving away money, nor of Stanfield refusing it. This scene-painter's salary with me was 16*l.* per week; and although his present work has certainly been the salvation of the pantomime and the season, there is some difference between *this* SALARY and *that* SUM—still, what with silver and salver, assistants, timber, canvass, paint, foil, flattery, and other ingredients necessary for the completion of a work by Stanfield, Macready must have paid pretty dearly for his Christmas pudding. Stanfield is a first-rate artist,—but—but, is it not *Richard* who says,

"A little flattery sometimes does well?"

His taking up a brush, in opposition to the interests of Drury Lane Theatre, the cradle of his reputation, betrayed bad taste and bad blood, methinks; he was made too much of there, and others, equally deserving, made too little of.

January 22.—Murphy, the new almanac wonder, as true as holy writ, thus far; if he continue to be so, his discovery will equal that of the longitude.

January 24.—John Reeve died in the evening of this day, at his house in Brompton. He was a diverting mountebank, but a confirmed drunkard. His great favouritism with the public enabled him to take great liberties with them: he was only fitted for the Adelphi Theatre, where a fine salary and a funking manager completely spoiled him: he was born in 1799, and was therefore in his fortieth year. His acting was a striking illustration of the vast difference there is between a *farceur* and a comedian. Poor John was the *Bottle Imp* of every theatre he ever played in. The last time I saw him, he was posting at a rapid rate to a city dinner, and on his drawing up to chat, I said, "Well, Reeve, how do you find yourself to-day?" and he returned for answer, "The Lord Mayor *finds* me to-day!"

January 26.—Her Majesty visited Drury Lane Theatre to see Charles Kean in *Hamlet*—the house was a choker—463*l.* 3*s.* 6*d.* The Queen looked well, and, better still, was received well. Charles improveth by practice and patronage, and the loss of fear—it is literally a relief to see a *Hamlet* not resorting to the vulgarism of having a stocking dangling at his heel, to prove the distemper of his mind; and a greater one yet to find the grave-digger omit what was " a custom more honoured" in the *waistcoat* than the " observance ;" they must be bad actors indeed, who resort to such trickeries to achieve a triumph over the language of Shakspeare.

January 27.—Heard of the death of William Dimond, which took place at Paris more than three months ago, and has been kept a secret by his friends, who, though they rejoiced at his decease, were ashamed of his existence, and *ergo* were silent. He possessed great knowledge of the stage, as his pieces of " The Foundling of the Forest," " Doubtful Son," " Conquest of Taranto," " Lady and Devil," and some twenty others, attest. His last piece, I believe, was the *Novice*, brought forth the beginning of this season at Covent Garden Theatre. His enormities are said to have broken his mother's heart, and to have been the cause of his father cutting his throat. He succeeded that most respected parent in the management of the Bath Theatre ; but was compelled by General Palmer, the larger proprietor, to relinquish it altogether in 1823 ; since which period he has been in many jails, (in Horsemonger Lane, under the name of James Bryant,) and tried in many courts, (he was tried at Croydon assizes under the name of William *Dimer*,) under many names, for heinous crimes—out of all of which he escaped by mere miracles ; his deeds at Bath, the early and great scene of his profligacy, would fill a volume in the narration.

January 30.—By an absurdity in the legislation of the country, every theatre on one side (the Surrey) of the Thames is open this day; but every one on the other (within what is called the jurisdiction of the Lord Chamberlain) shut. Imagine any functionary having the power to take the bread out of some hundreds of mouths on a day when the chances are, he puts an extra quantity into his own. Well may they say, "the times are *out* of JOINT"—the actors are, at all events. "The smallest force constantly applied" will produce some effect, and I will never cease using *my* "small force," until some relief is obtained by the abolition of this absurd bit of mummery. Buckstone has published a very silly letter in this day's *Herald*, to endeavour to prove that poor John Reeve was not a drunkard—he might much more easily have proved that he was seldom sober.

I break off my mems for a few minutes to introduce the following communication, upon this day's prohibition, which took place at the time :

> "Theatre Royal, Drury Lane,
> "January 31, 1838.

"Mr. Bunn presents his compliments to the mem-
"bers of his company, and informs them, that with
"the view of giving them full salary during Lent, a
"bill was brought last year into Parliament, at a cost

" to himself of 145*l.*, which was put an end to by
" the king's death.

" He this year, with the same object in view, ap-
" plied to the Lord Chamberlain to give the per-
" mission the said bill would have carried, and sub-
" joins a copy of the answer to his application
" received from the Lord Chamberlain :

" Lord Chamberlain's Office,
" January 24, 1838.

" Sir,

" In answer to the question contained in your
" letter of the 20th instant, I am directed by the
" Lord Chamberlain to acquaint you, that any per-
" formance of dramatic entertainments on the Wed-
" nesdays and Fridays in Lent, or in Passion week,
" will be objected to.

" I am, Sir,
" Your obedient servant,
" WILLIAM MARTINS.

" A. Bunn, Esq."

It has been seen already that Mr. Charles Kemble,
Captain Polhill, and myself, advertised, in different
seasons, performances for this day, and that we were,
one and all, prohibited from giving them. Having
paid pretty dearly in the last session of parliament
for the introduction of some subsidiary law, any
similar course this year appeared to me a ridiculous
measure ; and I therefore preferred simply putting

the question to " the powers that be," to prevent
either unpleasantness or expense. The reader has seen
the result, and has, I presume, laughed it to scorn; it
is hardly to be believed that, in such an enlightened
land as this, an ancient usage of Romish customs
should be kept in full force at the very time the
parties who enforce it are endeavouring, in other
respects, to make the people believe they are abolish-
ing every trace of such formalities. The Lord
Chamberlain will allow any gallimaufry to be exhibited in the minor theatres, on the Wednesdays
and Fridays in Lent; but a reasonable and inoffen-
sive performance must not take place at either Drury
Lane or Covent Garden Theatres: but then, to be
sure, as hath been already remarked, there is some
consolation in their being *Patent* THEATRES !! a
patent theatre, where it is supposed you may do
anything and everything you please! I presume
there will be a time come when we shall have
another Lord Chamberlain with other and juster
views; until we do, we must follow up the present
one, until common reason—to say nothing of justice
—be called in to his aid, and this foolish prohibition
altogether abandoned—*mais revenons à nos moutons:*

February 1.—John Reeve buried at Brompton
New Church. Thalberg, " le pianist monstre," as
poor Malibran used to call him, visited me to-day—
he is a handsome, unassuming, young man, and a
giant at his trade ; he was one of the many of her

successful swains, and probably the one she was most attached to—for the time! Macready sick " of thick coming fancies, that keep him from his rest;" he was leeched this evening, I hear, after playing—he'll be bled more than that, if he remain much longer a manager.

February 3.—Mrs. Glover, the best living actress by many degrees, has had a fall from one of the Coventry stage-coaches, and is much smashed— sorry for it indeed—when she falls in reality *from the* STAGE, she will not leave a successor behind her— her line will be extinct. The Serpentine like a fair to-day ; skating is surely giving away a chance—a worthless mode of closing one's career, conferring no honour on the ONE, and extracting no kind of regret from the MANY ; and yet some eight or ten to-day had " *too much of water* "—here break we off again.

It is a strange truth, but " truth *is* strange, stranger than fiction "—that, ever dissatisfied with what we do possess, we are panting to gain more—passing over the sacred injuction handed down to us, " In whatever situation of life you are, learn therewith to be content." Mr. Charles Kean had, up to this day, played *Hamlet* twelve nights without interruption, producing a receipt, exclusive of annual boxes, of 3,858*l*. 12*s*. 6*d*., which makes a nightly average of 321*l*. 10*s*.; but, as if discontented with such produce, we prepared *Richard the Third* with becoming pomp. We stand so far excused from the charge of dissatisfaction, that the applications for Mr. C. Kean's appearance in that character were incessant at the box-office, and the result will prove that the public were earnest in their solicitations, and we were wise in our compliance. The recollection of the interest taken from the first, and maintained to the last, in the performance of *Richard the Third* by Mr. Kean's father, materially added to that which manifested itself for the introduction of the son in it; and viewed altogether, the almost incredible personal resemblance, the same peculiarities, many of the same tones, the same action, hereditary and not copied, all conspired to instil and to retain in the public mind the same degree of admiration.—*Nous verrons.*

February 5.—Charles Kean appeared in *Richard the Third,* which tragedy was produced with great care and expense; house 409*l.* 5*s.*; he will do fully as well, if not better, in this part, as he has thus far done in *Hamlet.* Her Majesty was present from the rise to the fall of the curtain, and commanded me to express to Master Charley how delighted she was with his performance.

February 6.—Received the subjoined note from Charles Kean ; shall do all in my power to aid him, for two sufficient reasons ; firstly, because I like him, and secondly, because I hate the pretenders who *dis*like him :

" Dear Bunn,

" I cannot allow a day to pass without expressing
" my sincere acknowledgments to you for the great
" assistance you have rendered me, in producing
" ' *Hamlet*' and ' *Richard the Third* ' in so splendid
" and magnificent a manner, which has been so con-
" ducive to any success I may have obtained ; and
" my only hope is, that in the course of our future
" connexion, I may be enabled by my exertions to
" repay the obligation I feel myself under to you.

" I remain
" Very truly yours,
" Charles Kean.

" Feb. 6, 1838, 30 Old Bond-street."

February 7.—Rejoice in the good fortune of - my
young friend Georgiana, Lady Lyndhurst, daughter
of my old friend Lewis Goldsmith ; she has just
obliged me with a call, on her arrival from France.
Though an accomplished and deserving lady, it is
not always that desert is so crowned, as to place on
the brow the coronet of such an illustrious statesman
and lawyer as my Lord Lyndhurst. I am a complete Murphy man as yet, for his Almanac has not
been out as yet—rain again, and it is so.

February 9.—Saw Charles Kean's *Richard* again
—a stirring performance from first to last—the rest
I leave to the critics. Murphy right again, " rain
and wind, and it is so ! I shall ferret him out

to-morrow, for the prosecution of a thought just entered into my cranium.

The thought in question, to which reference has just been made, was an offer conveyed to Mr. Murphy, through his respected publisher Mr. Whittaker, of three hundred guineas, to deliver ten lectures on " Meteorology," at Drury Lane Theatre ; and for making this offer I was assailed with every species of abuse by the opposition party—on a pretence of my having proposed the same terms for a catch-penny affair that are given for a classical drama—the inference to be gathered from which is, that I would not encourage the production of such a drama, but was ready and anxious to give encouragement to a matter of temporary excitement. If this proposal had been made with the view of displacing more regularly dramatic material, I might have been blamed with some degree of justice ; but, inasmuch as astronomical lectures have been delivered on both the patent stages, and on many other London stages, on the Wednesdays and Fridays in Lent, and as it was only on those days, when no dramatic performance was allowed, that such lectures were to be given, the manager must have been a fool indeed who did not try to make them as attractive as possible. But the trash and the nonsense, the folly and the falsehood, which party spirit leads to, is inconceivable. I would not, however, have feared wagering any sum I could pay, that had Murphy lectured at Drury Lane Theatre on any night any drama was represented at the other house, by the united talent of all the London theatres, the receipt to his lecture should have doubled that of the performance. The reader has been already reminded of Doctor Johnson's celebrated line,—"Those who live to please must please to live," and the more he keeps it before him, the surer will he be to go right in his judgment upon London theatricals. Now to our journal again:—

February 12.—They hiss Mr. King nightly for his performance of *Richmond* ; and yet, I have Shakspeare's authority for putting him in the part :—

> " Henry the Sixth
> " Did prophesy that *Richmond* should be KING !"

A friend of mine called on me to-day, who met Mr. Lambton, Lord Durham's brother, at dinner yesterday, and Lambton told him that he was dining at the palace on Thursday last, and was talking with Lord Melbourne over Lord Mulgrave's " Private theatricals," when, the royal attention being attracted, her Majesty was pleased to ask what sort of an actor Lord Mulgrave was ? " Oh, very bad, very bad indeed," was the premier's reply. And " So I should think," was her Majesty's gracious rejoinder. Her Majesty ought to be, and *is*, a good judge. Murphy out—so he was in not accepting my offer ; but he gave me two reasons for declining

it : his great timidity was one, and then the obvious
necessity of letting out the secret of his science, another.   A scribe by the name of Fox is belabouring
Charles Kean in a morning paper—to judge by his
writings, his name *should* be GOOSE !

February 18.—Seguin, senior, dined with me to-
day ; the opera lost the premier of its cabinet when
it lost him.   In terseness of remark, in biting,
shrewd, and wherewithal polite, irony, he has no
equal but—TALLEYRAND.   He is a complete theatrical diplomatist.   Murphy, the " weather gauge,"
paid me a visit ; he is an extraordinary man, and
though he has been out occasionally, my faith is not
yet shaken in the principles he lays down—he is
right to-day.   As he came into the room all of a
shiver, and exclaimed with genuine Hibernian ac-
cent and emphasis, " Gracious God, what tirrible
weather !" he seemed very much astonished at my
replying, " It's your own fault, for predicting it !"

February 26.—Met Captain Barclay—"a thousand
miles in a thousand hours"—hey, and as fine a fellow
now as ever,—and our " dearly beloved " Jackson,
too, " the corporeal pastor and master " of the great
poet, Lord Byron, at dinner to-day—he gave *us* the
sublime chant (immortalized in Don Juan),

" On the high toby spice flash the muzzle,"

in his very best manner ; and he gave *me* a letter
addressed to him by the mighty lord, of which the
following, hitherto unpublished, is a copy, and which

I mean to keep as a prize, as long as " all this flesh keeps in a little life :"

"Cambridge, Oct. 30, 1803.

" DEAR JACK,

" My servants, with their usual acuteness, have " contrived to lose my swordstick. Will you get me " such another, or as much better as you like, and " keep it till I come to town. I also wish you to ob- " tain another bottle of that same Lamb's-Conduit- " Street remedy, as I gave the other to a physician " to analyse, and I forgot to ask him what he had " made of it. Keep that also till we meet, which " I hope will be soon, and believe me ever yours " truly,

" B."

" P.S. I am this far on my way north, and will " write to you again on my arrival."

February 28*th.*—Attended a meeting of those foolish people called " the Renters" of the theatre— clamorous for their dividends, and as abusive as if I had them in my pocket. Their chief claim to such lies in the fact of the former holders of their deben- tures having sold to the proprietors their claim to Killigrew's patent ; but as almost every purpose of that patent has been vitiated by the acts of govern- ment, the purchase may be considered a sort of fraud. They talk of meeting again on the 21st of next month, and if they do,

" Then I'll speak a little."

March 1.—Her Majesty having been pleased with Mr. Charles Kean's *Richard III.*, was pleased to come and see it again.

March 3.—Charles Kean appeared in *Sir Giles Overreach*, and, to my poor way of thinking, it is the best thing by far he has done. I see now the reason why Macready stipulated, in his last article of engagement with me, not to be called upon to act this character!

March 10.—We brought forward, for the first time in an English garb, Mozart's opera of *The Zauberflote;* and as a mere matter of opinion, regardless of what others do think, and not at all affecting what *I* do *not* think, I deem it to be one of the most perfectly "*got up*" affairs our stage has seen, being long and properly studied in every respect, and elaborately prepared in every department. That kindest of all kind contributors, Murray, presented me with a copy of Wilkinson's extraordinary work—one of the *most* extraordinary ever published in this or any other country— "THE MANNERS AND CUSTOMS OF "THE ANCIENT EGYPTIANS," which was of infinite service to me. Who would be without it, that could attain to it by gift or purchase?

I bethought me at this time of the repeated and unjust attacks levelled at me for neglecting the legitimate drama, and the fulsome compliments paid the rival lessee for his support of it; and I could not but contrast the causes which led to so much illiberality, falsehood, and injustice; for while Covent Garden

was exhausting its resources in the preparation of
Auber's opera of the *Domino Noir*, which proved an
utter failure, Drury Lane was giving some one of
Shakspeare's plays every night, backed by this celebrated composition, Mozart's *Magic Flute*, which
completely filled the theatre! A perseverance in
such reckless partisanship recoils at last upon the
perpetrators of it—a lie too often repeated is detected at last, although it appear in print; because
there are yet left in the world people who prefer the
evidence of their own eyesight to the assertions of
all the scribes in Christendom.

With a view, however, of redeeming past errors, a
very praiseworthy, but not very prudent, step was now
taken by the Covent Garden Manager; for the admirable manner in which *Coriolanus* was produced
was worthier of far better acting than it met with.
When the principal character in this noble play was
represented by the late Mr. John Kemble, the people
flocked in shoals to see it, notwithstanding it was
unable to boast of any such excellent preparation.
" Blessed is he that expecteth nothing, and he can
never be disappointed !" Nothing was expected
from Mr. Macready's personation of the noble Roman,
and no disappointment was experienced at nothing
being achieved. The play, therefore, brought Mr.
Macready a great deal of credit, but very little ready
money—it is preferable to have the two, if possible;
but the latter is more useful in a theatre. There is
no leading the public taste; the people are almost as

cunning upon the subject of theatres as the persons
engaged in them, know a good thing from a bad one,
and will not allow their judgments to be perverted.
James Smith put down a very amusing couplet on
this preparation of *Coriolanus* :

> " What various wonders does each scene disclose
> " Where all is Roman, save the Roman's nose!"

But disclaiming all personalities, and indulging in no
predilections, I cannot deny, and I will defy any one
to deny, that Coriolanus was put upon the Covent
Garden stage in a manner worthy of any theatre and
any manager. As there has been a little hole made in
the journal, we may as well take the liberty of filling
it up.

March 24.—The Italian Opera—" I cry ye mercy"
—Her Majesty's Theatre opened this evening, and
introduced an exquisite singer in the person of
Madame Persiani. She has a true but thin voice,
with an altogether unequalled style of execution ; and,
but that she is infernally ugly, she would go a great
way towards pushing Giulietta Grisi from her stool.
Boisragon (son of the popular Cheltenham physician)
appeared in the part of *Rodolpho,* and succeeded well :
he has an excellent voice, and is altogether *bien
organisé.* Last season my worthy friend Knowles,
with his usual good judgment and good heart, sent
me this letter in Boisragon's behalf:

"Wednesday night,

"29, Alfred Place, Bedford-square.

"My dear Sir,

"I want you to *prove* to-morrow a vocalist, whom
"I think it would be to your interest and his to hear;
"as to his merits I say nothing more. Pray, by the
"kindness you have shown me—substantial—pray ap-
"point an hour to-morrow, when he may present him-
"self, and give you a taste of his quality. I am not
"trifling—I would not trifle with you. The more
"private the better, perhaps with a sprinkling of the
"orchestra. I request that you will send me your
"sweet response to-night.

"A piano will do. I am, as always, in earnest.

"Your debtor and friend,

"J. S. KNOWLES."

And in compliance with Knowles's wish, I had the
pleasure of hearing Monsieur Boisragon. If his prejudice had not run in favour of a *debút* on the Italian
stage, I should have been most happy to have introduced him on that of Drury Lane; and whenever
Monsieur Boisragon thinks of English music, and I
can give him the trial, I will, for he has an excellent
organ—Tati the most forbidding tenor in existence I
should say—a very common *'taty* indeed.

March 28.—Morton, the dramatist, died at five
minutes past three in the afternoon—never spoke
after six the preceding evening—the water on the

chest choked him. The last official letter I received from Morton, was on his retirement from the office of reader to Drury Lane in 1833 ; and, in returning me his pass-key and all MSS. then in his possession, he slipped in with them these few words :

> " Eyes, look your last—
> " Arms, take your last embrace."

" DEAR BUNN,
" This packet clears my cupboard and conscience. " That the clearance may be mutual, pray send me " a farce entitled *Love* and *Agility*.
                    " Yours, &c.
                              " THOMAS MORTON.
" 15, Store-street, July 3, 1833.
" A. Bunn, Esq."

Morton was a worthy and honourable man, and " a " fellow of infinite jest." I liked him living, and I was truly sorry to hear of his death: Colman and Morton—well, we have but one or two more left of their school and times, and I hope they may yet be spared to us.

Mr. Charles Kean's engagement was now drawing to a close, and not merely for the vast contribution his exertions had been the medium of bringing to the treasury, but as a mark of good fellowship to the man, and admiration of the artist, his admirers were bent upon giving him a dinner, and something more substantial by way of dessert. I had the pleasure of undertaking it, and the pleasure of carrying it through; and the recollection at this present moment is as great a pleasure as either of the two former ones. Before entering, however, upon the reward he received, beyond his salary, for his exertions, let us examine the extent to which he deserved it. In the first chapter of the first of these volumes will be found a recapitulation of the receipts attracted by Mr. Kean senior on his *debût* before a London audience ; and it will be a matter of theatrical curiosity to contrast them with those attracted by his son on the present occasion. The difference, when all things are considered, will be found to be so trifling, as to be scarcely worth noticing ; and the result will prove that while the generally high salaries of performers are, beyond any doubt, the cause of the total decay of the drama, there are instances when the payment of an exorbitant salary is not merely a justifiable, but a prudent measure ; and if ever there was one instance more than another when it *was* justifiable, it was the present one. Between the 8th of January and the 3rd of March, Mr. Charles Kean played forty-three nights—twenty-one of them in *Hamlet*, seventeen in *Richard the Third*, and five in *Sir Giles Over-reach ;* and the following is a general recapitulation of the receipts, and the nightly average of them as well :

21 nights of *Hamlet* produced	£6,236 0*s*.,	nightly average	£296 19*s*.
17 nights of *Richard the Third*	5,516 14	do.	324 10
5 nights of *Sir Giles*	1,536 8	do.	307 5
43 nights,	£13,289 2	do.	£309 10

The nightly average Mr. Charles Kean's father played to was 484*l*. 9*s*., exhibiting an apparent nightly excess over that his son played to, of 174*l*. 19*s*. But it must not be forgotten that the prices of admission in 1814 were, 7*s*. to the boxes, 3*s*. 6*d*. to the pit, 2*s*. to one gallery, and 1*s*. to the other, and the half-price was in proportion; whereas, in 1838, the prices were 5*s*. to the boxes, 3*s*. to the pit, and 2*s*. and 1*s*. to the galleries, with a proportionate reduction in the half-price. That the reader may judge of the difference such reduction makes, a statement shall be submitted to him. The largest receipt Mr. Charles Kean played to was 464*l*. 3*s*. 6*d*., on which occasion seven hundred and seventy people paid to the boxes —which number, at 5*s*. each, makes the sum of 192*l*. 10*s*.; but had the prices been 7*s*., the amount would have been 269*l*. 10*s*., a difference of itself of 77*l*. Then seven hundred and sixty-eight people paid to the pit—which number, at 3*s*. each, makes a sum of 115*l*. 4*s*.; whereas, at 3*s*. 6*d*., the amount would be 134*l*. 8*s*. In these two items alone arises a difference of 96*l*. 4*s*., which, added to 3*l*. 18*s*.—difference in the half-price to boxes and pit, makes a total of 100*l*. 2*s*. In addition to this, is to be taken into consideration that the father played only three

c 2

nights per week, and the son played four nights during the greater part of this engagement; and that consequently, by a more frequent repetition, the attraction becomes somewhat lessened. Between the 8th of January and the 3rd of March the son played forty-three nights, as just stated, whereas, in a corresponding period of 1814, following his *debût*, the father played between the 26th of January and the 21st of March, only twenty-two nights. The father in that period played *Richard the Third* ten times, *Shylock* ten times, and *Hamlet* twice; whereas the son played *Richard the Third* seventeen times, *Hamlet* twenty-one times, and *Sir Giles Overreach* five times. Thus, in the same period of two months, though each of them played only three characters, yet, barring one night, the son played twice as often as the father. Weighing, therefore, all these things together, it will be found that in the outburst of their London career, there was but a slight difference in the attraction of either—a coincidence without any parallel in the annals of the stage. The management reaped the greater advantage from the exertions of the elder Mr. Kean, because his salary, for three nights' performance, was 20*l.*; whereas the salary of Mr. Charles Kean, for three nights' performance, was 150*l.* But, as I said before, the demand of such an enormous salary is justifiable, when the attraction is such as herein made manifest : and while Mr. Charles Kean was thus highly remunerated himself, I never knew a performer more anxious that his manager should be equally so. It is a matter of notoriety, requiring little authority to insure belief, that good houses produce a good understanding, and a good dinner leads to its continuance ; and as other good things were the result of the dinner in question, the reader shall have " a right, true, and particular account " of all that was said and done at it.

CHAPTER II.

IT having been suggested that a dinner should be given to Mr. Charles Kean, and at that dinner a vase should be presented to him, in testimony of the high opinion entertained towards him by the subscribers to it, I set to work with the view of carrying the object into effect. Having, on my application to

Lord Morpeth, obtained the consent of that highly gifted nobleman to take the chair, the difficulty of filling the tables and the subscription list instantly vanished; and long before the day of festivity arrived, the application for tickets were sufficiently numerous to fill a room twice as large. The day fixed for the celebration was Friday the 30th of March; two days previous to which, when every preparation was believed to be complete, the receipt of the following letter threatened to derange the whole plan:

" Wednesday Evening,
"March 28, 1838.

" Sir,

" It is with extreme regret and disappointment " that I find myself compelled to announce to you, " that, in consequence of a new arrangement of the " business of the House of Commons, and the cer- " tainty of the debate upon Negro Emancipation, from " which I cannot absent myself, extending over Fri- " day, it will be wholly impossible for me to attend " the dinner to be given on that day to Mr. Charles " Kean.

" I ought, perhaps, to have guarded myself more " strictly against such a contingency, when I agreed " to discharge the honourable office of chairman on " this auspicious occasion. I was misled by the an- " ticipation of other business in the house, and by my " anxiety to bear a part in the tribute which I thought " so well deserved.

" I am conscious, however, that almost all there is

" of privation in this matter belongs to myself. I
" beg to enclose my contribution to the vase, which
" it is intended to present to Mr. Kean, as a humble
" mark of my admiration for his talents, and of my
" regret that I am debarred from this occasion of giv-
" ing it oral expression.

" I have the honour to be,

" Sir,

" Your most obedient servant,

" MORPETH.

" To A. Bunn, Esq., &c. &c. &c."

With that consideration, however, which is a distinguishing ornament in the character of Lord Morpeth, he recommended and aided my application to
the Marquis Clanricarde, who promptly consented
to supply the place of his noble friend ; and, with this
understanding, things went on smooth to their end.
The dinner was the best public one I remember to
have sat down at ; and being given in the saloon of the
theatre, it was necessary, in order to insure its being
served up " hot, all hot," to convert the spacious
painting-room, with its large fires, into a kitchen.
When the smoking viands had been disposed of,
and a moderate quantity of choice wines, well iced,
had been imbibed, the noble chairman, turning round
to Mr. Charles Kean, who sat on his right hand, addressed him something after the following fashion—
indeed, I may say, word for word :

" MY DEAR FRIEND,

" I sincerely regret that our mutual friend, Lord
" Morpeth, is not able to attend here to perform that
" task which, in consequence of his absence, has
" devolved upon me, because I know that he would
" perform it in a manner more honourable to you, more
" satisfactory to the gentlemen whom I represent,
" and more worthy the occasion ; and that he would
" adorn the subject with those flowers of rhetoric
" with which his highly cultivated intellect and his
" classical mind are amply stored, but which I regret
" to say I cannot command. But I know your kind
" ness will overlook any deficiency, and you will not
" measure the depth of my feeling, and that of the
" gentlemen I represent, by the deficiency of my lan-
" guage, or by the value of the offering which is before
" you. At the same time, I trust you will receive
" that cup with satisfaction, because sure I am there
" is no tribute which you can receive, either from
" your friends or the public, which you may not
" attribute to your own merits and your own abilities.
" Perhaps one source of the high position to which
" you have attained, is the fact of your having entered
" upon your professional career with no circumstance
" of advantage that I can recollect or call to mind.
" The name you bore, the similarity in form, in
" feature, and in voice, which nature had impressed
" you with, and which proved to every beholder that
" the genius of the father was transmitted to the son,

" counteracted the indulgence usually manifested to a
" youthful beginner; but you have overcome all
" obstacles. You knew the toil, the study, and the
" diligence that it would require to attain to emi-
" nence in your profession—by study, I mean that
" diligent examination of the variety of delicate and
" almost imperceptible shades and tints of character,
" which our mighty bard has infused into all his
" heroes, so as not only to create corresponding ideas
" in your own mind, but to be able to convey those
" ideas to an audience, and make them feel and
" recognise the character which Shakspeare drew.
" In this you have succeeded, and you have raised
" the character of the stage, while you have earned
" the admiration of your friends and the public.   It
" is a circumstance not only singular, but I believe
" unprecedented, that a performer should have
" appeared forty-three nights in one season, and
" played only three parts, and those old stock parts,
" so well known to the public that they would receive
" no gratification from them, except in the way they
" were performed." The noble chairman then referred
to the estimation in which actors had been held
in ancient Greece and Rome, and to the low condition of the stage in this country until its character
was vindicated by Garrick, and sustained by the
Kemble family, names with which that of Kean was
well calculated to stand associated; and having
acknowledged, as one of Mr. Kean's principal claims

upon the respect and admiration of his friends, his unblemished integrity, high honour, and refined taste in private life, he concluded by expressing a hope that his honourable friend would long continue the ornament of the stage, the delight of his friends, and, above all, the pride of that surviving parent, who lived to bless him as the joy, the stay, and the comfort of her declining years.

The presentation to Mr. Kean consisted of a massive silver vase, of exquisite workmanship, the lid to which was surmounted by a model in miniature of Roubilliac's celebrated statue left by Garrick to the British Museum, a cast from which stands in the rotunda of Drury Lane Theatre. It is not a little singular that, on the day of the dinner, Garrick's as celebrated cup (made from the even more celebrated Shakspeare-mulberry) which had long been in the possession of the late Mr. Zachary, was sold by public auction, at Christie's rooms in King Street; and the enthusiasm and good taste of Mr. Murray pointed out this relic as a fitting present to Mr. Kean on the occasion. But from the expense of the other having been incurred, and from its being at the identical moment in the theatre, the purchase of another was not feasible; and having been bought by Mr. Owen of Bond Street, he obligingly sent it to the theatre for the inspection of the company during their repast, as a matter of peculiar interest under existing circumstances. In the front of the vase that

was presented to Mr. Kean were inscribed these
words:

PRESENTED
to
CHARLES KEAN, Esq.,
By the admirers of his distinguished talent,
at
A PUBLIC DINNER,
Given to him in the Saloon of the
THEATRE ROYAL, DRURY LANE,
March 30th, 1838;
The Right Honourable
LORD VISCOUNT MORPETH, M.P.,
in the Chair.

The complimentary address of the noble marquis,
and the gift with which it was followed up, was thus
acknowledged by Mr. Charles Kean:

" MY LORDS AND GENTLEMEN,
" The situation in which your kindness has at this
" moment placed me is the most arduous and difficult
" I have ever yet encountered.   It would be un-
" becoming affectation were I to pretend that I was
" not in some measure aware of the high and un-
" merited compliment you intended to confer on me.
" I had thought and hoped that when the proper
" time arrived, I should have been able to express

" myself in terms suited to the occasion. The
" opinions and wishes of the distinguished company
" by which I am surrounded have been conveyed to
" me by the noble chairman in a manner so unex-
" pectedly kind, so flattering, and so overwhelming,
" that even a practised orator might falter in his
" reply; but lest I should appear cold and ungrateful,
" while my breast is throbbing with contrary
" emotions, let me entreat you to receive the language
" of the heart, in place of set phrases of studied
" eloquence ; and believe in the sincerity of those
" feelings which, by their own intensity, have deprived
" me of adequate expression. The distinguished
" honour I am now receiving at your hands is one
" which artists of the highest name and pretensions
" have hailed with delight, when in the decline of
" life, and at the close of a long and brilliant course,
" as the climax of their honourable exertions. How,
" then, must I appreciate your kindness, young in
" years, standing almost on the very threshold of my
" professional life, my pretensions untried by the puri-
" fying test of time, the station I am ultimately to fill
" unascertained, upheld by the partial judgment of en-
" thusiastic friends, and, above all, by a name which has
" been my most powerful introduction to the notice
" and favour of the public ? I cannot and do not wish
" to blind myself to my true position ; but I feel that
" an affectionate remembrance of the father has in
" your eyes invested the son with attributes to which
" he has no personal claim, and has placed him in a

" situation, brilliant indeed, and dazzling, but full of
" difficulty and danger. I shrink from the conscious-
" ness of my own inability to realise the expectations
" of those friends who have so kindly committed
" themselves in my favour ; yet, to the latest hour of
" my existence, the remembrance of this, the proudest
" day of my life, will serve as a stimulus to unre-
" mitting exertion, and make me feel as if I had given
" a pledge which it is my duty to redeem.   My
" Lords and Gentlemen, the place where we are now
" assembled is associated in my mind with feelings
" of hereditary interest; within these walls the name
" of Kean first became known to the British public,
" and the success of my father formed an epoch in
" the history of the drama which will not soon be
" forgotten. After an interval of twenty-five years, on
" the same boards, and by the same public, my
" humble efforts have been received with a degree of
" favour and indulgence far, indeed, beyond my
" merits and expectations, and which has engraven
" on my heart one paramount feeling of lasting
" gratitude.   My Lords and Gentlemen, I will oc-
" cupy your attention no longer.   What I have said
" is totally unworthy of the occasion, and conveys
" but faintly what I feel.   The conduct of my future
" life can alone convince you how I estimate the
" honour I have received."

The polite reference to the health of the manager,
which called that individual upon his legs, enabled
me to have a slap at the pretenders who had been

using their utmost exertions, during Mr. Charles Kean's engagement, to underrate him in public opinion. I told them that the reason of my having incurred the charge of neglecting the works of our immortal poet arose from the fact of my having been unable to find any talent, until the present time, qualified to support the honour of the mighty bard; and the enthusiasm with which that observation was received, convinced me that my hearers were entirely of my way of thinking. It was the more necessary to make these observations, from the incessant though vain attempts that were made by the partisans of Mr. Macready to disprove the truth of them. In addition to the coxcombical ignorance displayed by Mr. Forster, and the pompous nothingness of Mr. Fox, and the "sound of fury" yells of other barking and biting dogs, the cudgels were taken up by a writer of far greater ability in other matters than he displayed in this, and in an hebdomadal paper, whose general reputation for sterling wit should not have admitted into its columns any baser matter.

I will trouble the reader with but one short specimen, by a perusal of which he may estimate the rest. The subjoined few lines made their appearance in that Sunday authority, March 4, 1838, professing to be a criticism on Mr. Charles Kean's performance of *Sir Giles Overreach* the preceding evening :

" Drury Lane Theatre.

" Massinger's play of *A New Way to pay Old*
" *Debts* was brought out last night, in order to intro-
" duce Mr. Charles Kean in the character of *Sir*
" *Giles Overreach.* Not going with high expecta-
" tions, we were not disappointed. We have already
" recorded our opinion of this gentleman's talent, and
" see no reason to retract it. Would we did : the
" public did not seem to go with him, as the phrase
" runs, until the last act, and then they were as up-
" roarious as we were silent. The reason of the
" difference must be sought for in the ' strange pas-
" sions' into which we are told *Sir Giles* has thrown
" himself about his daughter. It is only justice
" to own, that the audience relished the strangeness
" of these passions, as much as we marvelled at
" them. They shouted and hurraed—we sorrowed ;
" sorrowed that Mr. Kean should lend himself to
" mere melo-dramatic display, where a genuine lover
" of his art would be absorbed in the serious and
" passionate, and leave them to speak for themselves
" in the effective.

" The house was crowded, and Mr. Kean was vo-
" ciferously summoned to receive its congratula-
" tions."

It would not be a task of much difficulty to analyse the fustian contained in the foregoing remarks ;
but it would be difficult to do so with the acuteness
which distinguished the annexed piece of criticism
on a piece of criticism altogether unworthy of the

name. It was written at the time, and placed in my hands; but not having been used, I have availed myself of the writer's permission to insert it, conceiving it is scarcely necessary to name the eminent author of *Orlando in Roncesvalles*, and the reviewer of Grimm's correspondence in the *Quarterly Review*, as the author of the diatribe in question. Mr. Merivale may not be offended, but cannot be exalted, by any encomium of mine.

" A paragraph has appeared in one of our most
" popular weekly journals, by way of criticism on
" Mr. Charles Kean's performance of *Sir Giles*
" *Overreach* on Saturday night, of which it is difficult
" to pronounce whether the malice or the ignorance
" be most conspicuous. What was the exact measure
" of expectation with which the critic went to attend
" that performance—whether he did or did not meet
" with disappointment — whether having already
" recorded his opinion of this gentleman's talent,
" he saw any or no reason to retract or alter it,—these
" are questions about which, it may be presumed, few
" people care; but when he goes on to assert that
" the public did not seem to go with him, as the
" phrase runs, until the last act, and 'then they
" were as uproarious as *we* (meaning the aforesaid
" critic) were silent;' when he further states that
" 'the reason of the difference must be sought for in
" the *strange passions* into which *we* are told *Sir*
" *Giles* has thrown himself about his daughter;' that
" it is only justice to own that the audience relished

" the strangeness of these passions, as much as we
" marvelled at them, that 'they shouted and hur-
" raed, *we* sorrowed: sorrowed that Mr. Kean should
" lend himself to mere melo-dramatic display, where
" a genuine lover of his art would be *absorbed* in the
" serious and passionate, and leave them to speak for
" themselves in the effective;' when such hyper-
" transcendental-germaine trash as this is attempted
" to be made pass for the language of sound and sober
" criticism, to the great disparagement, and eventual
" serious injury, of a most deserving young actor,
" such strong evidence of the existence of a set de-
" sign to detract and calumniate, it is worth while, for
" the sake even of the public taste, to expose the
" malice of an attack disguised under the veil of such
" shallow criticism.

" Now, in the first place it must be obvious to all
" who are acquainted with Massinger's comedy, that
" during the four first acts, the character of *Sir Giles*
" *Overreach* (destined to burst upon the audience at
" last with an effect overwhelmingly terrible) is so
" artfully and judiciously *kept under* by the author,
" that, except for the announcement in the play-bills,
" and except for that marked superiority in attention
" to costumes and demeanour which (at least on the
" English stage) is sure to denote the presence of the
" principal actor, the *Star* of the evening—it would
" be impossible for a spectator, unprepared for the
" catastrophe, to conjecture that this mean, proud,
" grovelling, heartless, rapacious, sordid, bold, un-

" principled upstart is, in fact, no less than *the hero*,
" as it is termed, of the play, the very title of which
" is derived from the fortunes of another, who ap-
" pears at the outset to be the leading personage.
" It is only by slow and almost imperceptible de-
" grees that the character of this most exquisite
" of dramatic villains completely unfolds itself,
" and that rather by occasional words and speeches,
" at long intervals, than in the form of con-
" tinuous dialogue; and, during the whole of this
" (somewhat tedious) process, the attention of the
" audience is so closely kept to the developement of a
" rather intricate plot, and the display of the several
" other characters by which the piece is diversified,
" as necessarily to excite something like a feeling of
" disappointment at the comparative littleness of the
" main agent, and the even subordinate part which
" he seems to occupy. Whether Mr. Kean did not,
" with the design of giving more force and effect by
" contrast to the hurricane of passion which forms the
" catastrophe, rather *underact* these previous passages
" of the character, so as to sacrifice some points which
" ought to have been rendered more prominent with a
" view to dramatic consistency, may be made the sub-
" ject of fair and honest inquiry; but without pronounc-
" ing either 'ay' or 'no' on this question, we have
" only to observe, that, in the preceding sketch of what
" the actor had to personate, there is enough to furnish
" an answer to the sneer of our *Zoïlus* about ' the
" public not seeming to go with him, *as the phrase is*,'

" during these four-fifths of the performance. Yet
" even through this least prominent and least effec-
" tive part of the exhibition, to deny that he displayed
" much of the actor's most consummate talent—as,
" for instance, in his dialogue with *Lord Lovell*, and
" in that scene of monstrous and almost unnatural
" depravity where he tutors his daughter as to the
" mode in which he would have her receive his
" right honourable lordship's addresses, or to assert
" that it did not draw down the loudest but de-
" served plaudits of an overflowing and (what is
" better) a most attentive and discriminating audi-
" ence, strikes us as the extreme of injustice and
" falsehood.

" We now come to the catastrophe itself, as to
" which we will merely remark, in the outset, that if
" the critic be at all well guarded in his criticism, then,
" not only is Mr. Charles Kean false to nature and
" probability, but every performer who within our
" remembrance has attempted the character, (including
" the father of our present tragedian, whose *chef
" d'œuvre* it was generally reckoned,) was equally un-
" true to both, and the poet himself, too, the first and
" foremost of all the wrong-doers. If the ' passions'
" into which WE ARE TOLD that *Sir Giles* had thrown
" himself about his daughter, are, with reference to
" NATURE and PROBABILITY, fitly to be designated
" ' strong passions,' who is chargeable with the viola-
" tion thus insinuated as having been committed ?
" the actor ? or the author, whose plain and not to be

"mistaken stage directions he to the very letter has
"followed? What is the actor to do, when the
"author tells him to ' enter *with distracted looks,*
" driving in *Marrall* before him, telling him that he
" is a subject only fit for beating, and so to cool my
" choler,' suiting the action to the word, it is more
" evident by the context, drawing his sword upon his
" nephew *Wellborn* in the right honourable presence
" of lords and *ladies,* starting, ' overwhelmed with
" wonder,' at the discovery of the blank parchment
" which has suddenly frustrated one of his deepest
" laid and fondly cherished schemes of plunder and
" villany; rushing on his daughter to kill her, with
" the words — ' Thus I take the life, which
" wretched I gave to thee,'—when she kneels to ask
" his blessing and forgiveness for her stolen marriage ;
" defying to single combat the ' Lord,' whom he had
" designed for his son-in-law, with the courteous
" challenge, ' Lord ! thus *I spit at thee,* and at thy
" counsel ;' then hurrying off the stage with an in-
" vocation of ' hell,' to add, ' if possible,' to his
" afflictions, and finally re-entering in a state of des-
" perate lunacy, flourishing his sword in the belief
" that he is engaged in battle with a host of devils ;
" ' rushing forward and flinging himself on the ground,'
" where he ' foams' and ' bites the earth,' till
" ' forced off' by the attendants. And all this scene
" of detected or baffled guilt, passion or frenzy, thus
" marked for performance in characters the broadest
" and strongest that poets ever penned, our clever

" critic, in his complacent self-idolatry, bids us ob-
" serve that ' a genuine lover of his art' would enact as
" one ' *absorbed in the serious and passionate, leav-*
" *ing them to speak for themselves in the effective'*—
" words, the true sense and meaning of which we will-
" ingly leave to comprehensions far more refined and
" sublimated than our own to develope; while we are
" quite content to have our ears split, like the ' ground-
" lings,' even though the action may be termed ' melo-
" dramatic,' since we are too old to be frightened by
" nicknames, when it is at the same time such as is
" absolutely required in order to embody and give life
" to the poet's conception.

" To conclude—it is not the object of the writer of
" this article either to praise Kean, or vindicate
" Massinger, but simply to correct a piece of most un-
" just and malevolent criticism. Nevertheless, we
" must not do our young actor so great an injustice
" as not to record our own deliberate opinion—which
" is, that, whether the character of *Sir Giles Over-*
" *reach*, as designed by Massinger, be, or be not, true
" to nature and probability, no performer within our
" recollection, not excepting the actor's father him-
" self, has ever more successfully and completely ex-
" ecuted the task assigned him."

But the dinner honours we have been recording,
and the engagement which led to them, passed away
with the utmost harmony, and Charles Kean left
London for Edinburgh, full of good report. It gratified me to be of the slightest use to one with so much

talent, so absurdly abused by those who had so little—it gratified me to see the domestic virtues displayed by an excellent son to an invalided mother so amply rewarded, and the receipt of these few lines gratified me as much as any other part of the business :

"MY DEAR BUNN,

"I cannot leave town without gratefully acknow-
"ledging the manner in which you have upheld me
"during my present engagement; and conscious as
"I am how dependent my success was upon the
"prudence and liberality of the manager under whose
"auspices my re-appearance in London should be
"conducted, I feel that you have not only done all
"that was necessary, but more than my most sanguine
"wishes could have anticipated.

"I am aware that this is not a very substantial
"mode of proving my sense of your very great kind-
"ness; but fear that any other at the present moment
"would give to the enemy an opportunity of miscon-
"struing the real feelings which actuated me to adopt
"that course.

"Most truly yours,
"CHARLES KEAN.

"April 5, 1838. 30, Old Bond-street.
"A Bunn, Esq."

March 31.—Heard Persiani again : would that her voice were not so thin! but what a singer! The house looked very much like a meeting of creditors—

jews, attorneys and their clerks, bailiffs and their
followers, cyprians and their swains, occupying every
other box, and full half the pit.

April 8.—Birthday—42! Plenty of room for reflection, but not plenty of time to make it. Passion
week—no play, no pay; and if a man may not have
a lark then, he had better " incontinently drown himself"—went for one on a visit to the best of all good
companie, Allen, of Vache Park; met there the renowned Jackson, (Byron's pet,) and others who have
more than once "heard the chimes at midnight." This
seat did belong to Sir Hugh Paliser, who, it will be
remembered, caused Admiral Keppel to be brought to
a court-martial on charges of misconduct (pro-
nounced by the court to be " malicious and ill
" founded") in the action off *Ushant*, on the 27th
and 28th July, 1778. On the admiral's honourable
acquittal, Sir Hugh resigned his offices and command,
and vacated his seat in parliament. It was HE who
ought to have been tried; yet some people have their
own and the devil's luck too; for, two years after this
rascality, Lord North made Sir Hugh governor of
Greenwich Hospital, and in 1781 he took his seat in
the house as member for Huntingdon — Rowe's
right:

> " Heaven that made me honest, made me more
> " Than ever king did when he made a LORD !"

April 9.—Visited *Chenies*, the burial-place of the
Russell family. William the headless lies here, and

I could name those of his descendants who will follow him, for whom nature has since done what for him the law did on the fatal 21 July, 1683; but I must be respectful at least in their own resting-place, because the representative of that house is ground landlord of the patent theatres—especially at a time when they are worth very little more than the ground they stand on.

April 10.—By way of passing an intellectual day, we breakfasted first—then dragged the fish-ponds, shot at the Guinea fowls with rifles, then lunched, hunted a cat in a cherry tree, pistol fired, then had a drive, dined, played billiards, smashed some grilled bones, demolished some beakers of punch, and then to bed. What a rascally mess of " good entertainment for man and horse"—but one didn't come into the country to read plays or to hear 'em, and if you had, TOM would have very properly put his veto thereon.

March 14.—Kitty Stephens married to the Earl of Essex, 82 *versus* 45. I do remember me that my lord was a member of the Drury Lane committee in the year 1815, when I first rubbed my back against the walls of their theatre. Kitty has waited with the most exemplary patience for her coronet, and it would be hard indeed if the " finis *coronat* opus" had not come at last.

April 23.—Invited to the Shaksperian anniversary at Stratford-on-Avon. Oh! the delightful days that

I have passed in this delightful place, and with dear
Mathews, and the dear fellow whom Hook wove
into one of his memorable impromptu songs:

" And there's Captain Saunders
" Just seized with the jaunders,
" For fear that the monument should not be built,"

when we were all intent on building the said monument, the homage of the mortal to the immortal, as I
think Sir Walter saith in *Kenilworth*—and they are
both long since set out for the undiscovered country,
and I am left crawling between heaven and earth—
Saunders had in his possession, and I have had in
my hand, a letter that must have been opened by the
hand of Shakspeare. It was found by Saunders in
the archives of the Stratford corporation, of which
he was chamberlain, and was addressed, " To my
" loving friend and countryman, Mr. William Shak-
" speare, at the Bell, Doctors' Commons, deliver
" these"—'twas written by Richard Quiney, sealed with
the same seal that is affixed to the bard's will, and its
object was to pray him for the loan of £30, to relieve
him from all his worldly difficulties ; there can be no
question of its authenticity. We were, during this
sojourn, paying a visit to the resting-place of the
poet, when the darling old rector, Dr. Davenport,
observed, " I was standing here with a party some
" months since, when one of them, a foolish, and,
" thank heaven, a very distant relation of mine,
" sprang up to the monument of Shakspeare, and,

" with the view of possessing himself of a relic
" thereof, snatched the pen out of the right hand—it
" snapped in two, and I fell senseless on the floor."—
Associations equal in gratification to those this unpretending town affords, are not to be indulged in, in
any other spot under the sun.

March 26.—On duty to-day at the palace, and
could not avoid a little reflection.—Alas! to think
that the mighty realm, once the terror and the pride
of the fair world, should for a moment be jeoparded
by the foolish, prejudiced, and utterly incapable people who daily infest the presence-chamber of Albion's
Queen : but the Lady of the Isles, in the pride of her
bloom and her beauty, and the joyousness of her own
innocent heart, is too young to be enabled to fathom
the world's villany.

April 28.—Favoured with a long chat by Lord
Adolphus Fitzclarence, who is one of the very best
hearted "gentlemen of England" to be found in her
broad and free land, and full of all good qualities.
His habitual respect for the good old king, his excellent father, and the fondness with which he clings to
the minutest recollection of his gifted mother, would
serve as a bright example to most of the aristocracy
amongst whom he daily breathes.

April 30.—Lord Londonderry abused Lord Melbourne in the House of Lords, in a manner something
between Saint Giles's and Saint James's, for curtailing
the CORONATION of its fair proportions. The Marquis

is quite right; in all such matters the people think nothing of expenditure, being perfectly sure of having,
or of believing they have, their fun for their money.
If it *should* cost an extra £200,000, divide that sum
in the shape of an additional tax amongst the tax-
paying population, and it will be found to amount to
about three pence a head!!

In this month, the 19th, I had the pleasure of introducing to the public an opera, replete with beauty,
from the pen of a composer whose retiring habits had
too long withheld his high talent from being duly
appreciated. No modern opera contains more choice
morceaux (a grand disideratum for the English
market) than " *The Gipsy's Warning*," by Mr. Benedict, and his instrumentation may compete with most
of his predecessors. Though originally produced in
this unmusical country, as some varlets call it, a work
must have claims of a very superior order which,
like this, has gone through the honours of translation
and adaptation to a foreign stage. Mr. Benedict sent
me this letter the day after the production of his
opera:

" MY DEAR SIR,
" I am exceedingly gratified by your kind note of
" to-day. Such a testimonial is more valuable to me,
" as the success of my opera has been chiefly
" attained by your kind exertions, and the splendid
" and unrivalled manner with which, by your judi

" cious management, everything has been conducted.
" I seize this opportunity to thank you most cordially
" for all the proofs of friendship you have evinced to
" me during its progress.

" I remain, my dear Sir,

" Very truly yours,

" J. BENEDICT.

" 93, Piccadilly, Friday.
" To Alfred Bunn, Esq."

—not inserted, in testimony of any compliment the
writer was pleased to pay the manager, but to prove
that there are those to be found in the world who
appreciate the slightest attention that is paid to them.
I shall know no greater gratification than in bringing
forward on a future occasion any composition of so
able a professor, feeling well assured that the pleasure I shall derive from so doing will be participated
in by the community at large. Mr. Benedict is to the
fullest extent what Sheridan * called Elliston, the
first time he saw him, ' a promising young man"—
indeed far more than this.

* It was on the occasion of Elliston's appearance in *Charles Surface*
at Drury Lane Theatre. Sheridan sat in his box, Sam Spring, the box-
keeper, standing behind him; and when Elliston, at the sale of the
family pictures, said, "This is painted by Sir Godfrey Kneller after his
" best manner, and is esteemed a formidable likeness," Sheridan exclaimed, " Pooh ! pooh ! what does the fellow mean ? I wrote *in* his
" best manner, and not *after* it—a man can't paint AFTER HIS OWN MAN-
" NER—but he's a promising young man, Sam—promising young man.'
I had this from Spring's own lips.

May 9.—Charles Kean returned to his re-engagement—he has been absent but five weeks, but in that time he has allowed those who *have* seen him to forget him, in the folly and fashion of a London season —after Easter—and those who have *not*, want to know if he is a fine actor, and keep back until *they're told.* There comes a new world into Babylon when this period of the year arrives—at the same time, nothing can be more injudicious than to break the thread and too often the chain of anything, particularly if connected with public life. I doubt me if he will rouse up the Cockneys to any great extent until next Christmas hath waned, and then much will depend upon whose hands he gets into. He will, however, at all times do more than any of the dogs who venture to snarl at him.

May 17.—Talleyrand died in Paris.

> " It is impossible that ever Rome
> " Should breed thy fellow."

Heard an average anecdote of him five minutes ago. A creditor to whom the prince was indebted in a heavy sum, waited upon him as he was setting off on his last departure for this country—not to take so great a liberty as to ask for his money, but merely to ascertain any time, however remote, when he might presume to ask for a part of it. The diplomatist's only reply to the inquisitive intruder was, " Mon-" sieur, vous êtes bien curieux"—and no one but the diplomatist could have made *such* a reply. Balfe's new opera of *Diadeste*, though possessing much graceful melody, had better have lain by, than lain in, for a smaller theatre—it is not stirring enough for this huge building—the people can't pronounce the name or understand the game, and the music does not much enlighten them.

May 22.—Talleyrand buried with great pomp in Paris. Another century will not produce another Tallyrand. I am not quite sure that our secretary of state for foreign affairs does not at this moment tremble even at his memory. Phillips' new opera appeared—to be repeated "never another evening until further notice," say the wags.

May 30.—Went to the "Derby," as a *matter of* COURSE, wherein there appeareth no alteration since I first attended the said "annual," some five-and-twenty years ago:

> " Out upon time! it will leave no more
> " Of the things to come, than the things before:
> " Out upon time! who for ever will leave
> " But enough of the past for the future to grieve ! "

The "Derby" is more of an Englishman's holiday than any other celebration he cultivates—there be more of equality in it—the men who drive

> " Carts with two-and-twenty in 'em,"

are as good as my lord's "four-in-hand" on this day, at all events—four horses are of *some* importance; but one donkey obstructing the road is of much greater.

June 2.—Present at the Drury Lane Theatrical Fund Dinner. Lord Glengall did the honours of the chair, Harley did the duties of the master, and the stewards did—the company out of about 900*l.* The annual nonsense written by good Master Daniels, and delivered by good Master Harley, had this year a slap at Ducrow, and through Ducrow at me. Knowles took up the cudgels, and left the master prostrate; albeit Harley, in all the relations of private life, is an exemplary character, and an old ally of mine, whose excellencies it rejoiceth me to respect. These funds are now-a-days little else than inducements for performers to be more improvident and impertinent than their ordinary nature and avocation make them, and that " *more* " was not wanting.

June 4.—There was a time when one used to venerate this day, and that was when " George the Third was king;" but alas! all these pleasantnesses are passing away from us; and the worst of it is, they are replaced by nothing as good. The king's birth-day was wont to be a jubilee; but there are no kings now left to earth, that earth need care about commemorating. Kean's benefit—worth and talent well rewarded.

June 6.—Saw a piece called *One Hundred and Two*, in which Davidge played a part called *Philip Gabois* as well as Munden or Farren ever played *any* part. " Natur, father, natur! "

June 7.—Mr. Lodge's opera of *Domenica* won't do ; he is a good musician, but not equal to writing for the stage—perhaps holds himself above it.

June 10.—Dined at Topham's New Hotel at Richmond, to celebrate Ducrow's matrimonial honours, participated in by Miss Woolford. Slept there at Ducrow's particular request.

June 19.—Lord Castlereagh and Grisi's husband, De Melcy, fought at Wormwood Scrubs ; Castlereagh maintaining his ground, and maintaining at the same time the lady's honour like a *preux chevalier* of the olden time. How little do his political assailants know Lord Castlereagh ! who, in addition to a finished specimen of a nobleman, has ten times the intellect of all the fellows put together that descend to vituperate what they cannot aspire to imitate. During the rehearsals of *Ildegonda*, last year, at the Opera House, Melcy, the husband aforesaid, called Marliani, the composer of the work, to account for apparent familiarities during the rehearsals with his wife. Marliani assured him that nothing of the kind had taken place since their separation, (and this was previous to her marriage with De Melcy,) but that he was quite ready to fight, concluding his expression of willingness thus, " Si je vous tue, vous serez un cocu mort ; et si vous me tuez, vous serez un cocu vivant !" Monsieur De Melcy retired, and no more passed thereon ; he is the veriest puppy extant, and the one he affects to love will bolt from him

as sure as he deserves that she should.   I was in the
paddock at Epsom at the time that the elopement of
the *ci-devant* Miss Paton made so great a sensation,
and Robinson, the jockey, delivered a very appropriate opinion upon such subjects : " I'm not at all
astonished at it," said he, " for these strange fillies
were always terrible bolters."

June 18.—Invariably make a point of peeping into
Apsley House on this day, to see the spread of plate
in the dining-rooms, where the chiefs of Waterloo
assemble on its anniversary, to drink to *their* CHIEF,
the hero thereof.   What a scene for a man to be
proud of !—the world's annals hold record of no such
character as Duke Wellington, who, with more to be
ostentatious about, has less ostentation than any man,
perhaps, that ever existed.

June 22.—What odd things happen in this life !
Soult, who, the republicans of France say, and the
republicans of England are half disposed to admit,
won the battle of Toulouse on the 14th of April
1814, met the Duke of Wellington (who happened in
REALITY TO win it) at the Queen's Concert !!   Those
who doubt it, may refer to the duke's despatch,
brought by Lord William Russell to Lord Bathurst,
and dated Toulouse, April 12—true to a shaving.

June 22.—Dined at the Pitt Club in Merchant
Tailors' Hall.   To mention Pitt with the same
breath you name some certain ragged rogues now
in office is a disgrace to him who does it.   The best

general character I have read of Pitt is to be gleaned
from the life of Wilberforce, recently published.

June 24.—Feasted at Greenwich. What a glorious
place! the waters and all *they* bear, the hospital and
the associations *it* bears; but then the heat, that
nobody *can* bear. The *Trafalgar* is now the best
house in Greenwich, and is worth going to, if only
for the name. The stewards! (in plain English the
actors) of the Drury Lane Theatrical Fund dined at
the Star and Garter, Richmond (not a bad house to
pick out) on the monies of the said fund. So, the
public is to be taxed for a dinner, and subscription
afterwards, to find these mummers an annual jaunt
into the country, and a feast into the bargain! It is
high time this humbug was blown into " thin air," or
greatly reformed.

June 27.—At the time I am chronicling these
loose thoughts, I do wonder what are those of the
Queen of England, who is to be crowned as such
to-morrow? Our first maiden Queen worshipped
Shakspeare, our lord of the drama, and our second
one dees all she can to suppor this temples. God
speed her with the gift of that earthly crown she will
be in the morning presented with, upon the due and
becoming wearing of which will entirely depend its
exchange for that- heavenly crown " which fadeth
not away."

June 28.—On duty at the coronation of Queen
Victoria, in

      ——" the temple where the dead
      " Are honoured by the nations !"

as well as the living. As a mere sight, it is imposing
enough,—the crown, the sceptre, the star, the dove,
the robe, the ermine, are all smart gewgaws. But
"uneasy lies the head that wears a crown," is written
down by our dramatic prophet, and I bethought me
of the truth thereof, as I saw that hollow bauble
placed on the forehead of our lovely and beloved mistress. My Lady Essex, who was but some yesterday
or two back Miss Kitty Stephens, in walking up the
aisle, coronet in hand, looked for all the world as she
was wont to look in *Mandane.* " *Tempora mutan-
tur ;*" *her* change was in the fashion of her robe—
that's all.

    It having been the custom, before any of the present
generation came into " this breathing world," to
open the theatres gratuitously to the public on the
day of their sovereign's coronation, that custom was
adhered to on the present occasion, but with a somewhat important deviation from such antecedent
celebrations : for 600*l.* *used* to be given, but in the
present patent cheese-paring days a deduction of one
third was made, and the two royal theatres were
required to open their doors for 400*l.*, or to keep them
shut ! The management of this affair was entrusted
by some treasury trick to a Mr. Lane, a very civil
and obliging person; but as I presume his own
emolument depended to a certain extent upon his

making the most moderate bargain possible, he naturally exercised all his ingenuity to effect a serious reduction. Like the fleas Horne Tooke dilated upon,
the managers could not be brought to jump together,
or a much larger payment would have been given to
all. It is not to be denied that the sum in question was
far beyond the evening's expenses ; but it must not
be forgotten that great damage is done to the theatres
on such occasions by the introduction of much
doubtful company ; and that the general festivities
attendant upon the period, both before and after the
one grand ceremonial, are very detrimental to the
exchequer of all places of public amusement. As
one of my objects in putting these volumes together
is to make them serve as a book of reference, the
whole process of this petty STATE AFFAIR shall be
submitted, particularly as there can be little doubt
but it will be looked upon as a precedent.

Mr. Lane having waited upon me, and given me to
understand the amount that would be granted, re-
quested I would send it in the shape of a tender,
that he might formally submit it to the reigning
authorities. I did so, and received the subjoined
reply :

"London, 16th June, 1838.

" ALFRED BUNN, ESQ.

" Sir,—I am commanded by the Lords of the
" Treasury to acknowledge the receipt of your tender
" and agreement to open the Theatre Royal Drury

" Lane, free to the public, on the coronation day of
" her Majesty Queen Victoria, for the sum of four
" hundred pounds, and to signify their Lordships'
" approbation thereof; and I am further commanded
" to request you to submit to me, by Friday the
" 22nd instant, the entertainments you propose to
" give on that occasion.

" I am, Sir,
" Your obedient servant,
" J. V. LANE.

" 4, Adam Street, Adelphi."

In compliance with the request contained in the
foregoing communication, the entertainments proposed to be given on the occasion were named
through this gentleman to the general manager of the
coronation affair, and their approval was conveyed
by him the next day :

" No. 4, Adam Street,
" 23rd June, 1838.

" SIR,
" Having submitted to the Lords of her Majesty's
" Treasury the entertainments you propose on the
" coronation day, I am commanded by their Lord-
" ships to signify their approbation thereof.

" I am, Sir,
" Your obedient servant,
" J. V. LANE.

" To A. Bunn, Esq."

The *Belles' Stratagem* and the *Youthful Queen* were the entertainments selected for the important occasion, on which every crevice of the building was occupied. The affair passed off as such things generally do ; and on the 18th of July the subjoined letter came to hand, and on the 19th the business was wound up by the receipt of the money at the Treasury :

" No. 4, Adam Street, Adelphi,
" 18th July, 1838.

" SIR,

" By command of the Lords Commissioners of her
" Majesty's Treasury, I have to request your personal
" attendance at my office as above, on Thursday or
" Friday morning next, from ten to twelve o'clock, to
" receive a certificate according to your tender, for
" having opened your theatre gratuitously to the
" public on the coronation day of her Majesty Queen
" Victoria.

" I am, Sir,
" Your obedient servant,
" J. V. LANE.

" To A. Bunn, Esq.
" Theatre Royal Drury Lane."

June 29.—What fools the people are making of poor Soult and themselves, shouting after him wherever he goes, because we thrashed him wherever we found him ! Why don't they read the memorable manifesto issued March 8, 1814, by the old hound

against Wellington and this country—" the saviour
and the saved," instead of coursing his heels through
every alley of the metropolis, while he and his master
(Louis-Philippe) are laughing in their sleeves at the
helpless Lord ————, who has got it all up, in the
absence of any knowledge of foreign diplomacy.
The venerable ballad comes in again : —

> " Ri tum ti titherum fit ;
> " I beg you'll never mention it.
> " Not forgetting titherum high,
> " A tailor's goose can never fly !"

And talk for a century, this is what in the long-run it
will come to !

CHAPTER III.

The end of a Season illustrated by Mr. Ducrow—Mr. Bunn sick—
All sorts of Fishing—Spontini—Patent for opening, and Patent for
destroying Theatres—Windsor Castle—Ducks and Drakes—Mr.
Const and Mr. Munden—Walton and Johnson—Mr. and Mrs. Staf-
ford—Lord Byron and the Dean of Westminster—Suborning—
Infant's Death—Harrow on the Hill—An Extraordinary Feat of
Reynolds the Dramatist—Brighton—Mr. Charles Kean and Mrs.
Charles Kemble—The Lord Chamberlain and the German Opera—
Value of a Patent, and of a Chamberlain—Shakspearian Hoax —
Wright's Champagne—Madame Albartazzi—The *Tempest* a mere
puff—Horses and Asses.

THE season of 1837–38 having drawn to a close
with so unsatisfactory a result to the treasury of
Drury Lane Theatre, I was anxious to bring my
connexion with that establishment to a termination.
My rival seemed pretty much of the some turn of mind
as respected Covent Garden Theatre, or he had relinquished the management towards the latter end of
the season, which wound up, if I remember rightly,
under the direction of the proprietors. The fag end
of the season of a metropolitan theatre is literally disgraceful ; arising from the total neglect of business

by the performers, and the shameful mode of conducting it by all the mechanics and operatives.
Ducrow once gave me a much more graphic description of the finale of one of his seasons than I have
the power of transcribing. " I don't know how you
" find it," said he to me, " but as soon as I once
" announce the last few nights of the season, the
" beggars begin to show their airs. I went into the
" theatre t'other night, and seeing a prime little
" roasting pig on a nice white napkin in the hall, I
" told 'em to take it up to Mrs. D———. The fellow
" said it warn't for me—'twas for Mr. Roberts." I
naturally inquired who Mr. Roberts was, and Ducrow as naturally replied :—" Why, he's the chap as
" orders the corn, and I'm the chap as pays for it ;
" so he gets the pig, and I don't. Then those b——
" carpenters sneak in of a morning with their hands in
" their breeches pockets, doubled up as if they'd got
" the cholera, and at night they march out as upright as
" grenadiers, 'cause every one on 'em has got a deal
" plank at his back, up his coat. Then the super-
" numeraries carry out each a lump of coal in his
" hat, and, going round the corner, club their prig-
" gings together, and make the best part of a chal-
" dron of it. As to the riders, they come into
" rehearsal gallows grand, 'cause they've had all the
" season a precious deal better salary than they were
" worth ; and at night they come in gallows drunk,
" from having had a good dinner for once in their
" lives ; and forgetting that they may want to come

" back another year, they are as saucy as a bit of
" Billingsgate." This is about the case with all
theatres : and while the manager is blamed for all
these ill doings, and most assuredly is the only
sufferer by them, the real criminals escape unpu-
nished. Scenes such as this add to the disgust a
manager must perpetually feel, if he has any feeling
at all; and in the state of mind arising from such
sensation, I addressed this letter to the Sub-Committee
of Drury Lane Theatre :—

" London, June 30, 1838

" MY LORDS AND GENTLEMEN,

" From circumstances to which it is now unneces-
" sary to refer, and which no one can regret more
" than myself, I am induced to request that you will
" take such steps as you may deem necessary to
" obtain another tenant for Drury Lane Theatre ; and
" to state, that I shall be ready to surrender the
" remainder of my term whenever called upon so
" to do.

" I have the honour to be,
" My Lords and Gentlemen,
" Your obedient humble servant,
" A. BUNN.

" To the Sub-Committee of
" Drury Lane Theatre."

The committee went to work immediately fishing
for another tenant, and I went to Hampton fishing
for something else, as appears by my journal.

July 7.—Fished and slept at Hampton. Oh! how I envy the calm retreat purchased by our great Drury Lane predecessor, Garrick, in this quiet village! From Richmond to Hampton is one continued route of association. Pope's Villa, Strawberry Hill and Horace Walpole, Clive's Cottage, Woffington's Grave, Bushy Park and Mrs. Jordan, &c. &c., crowd upon the memory, and make one in love with by-gone days, and disgusted with the present ones. Garrick's Villa (owing to Carr's death) is to be sold, but, being in the hands of the law, will be kept there until half of its value at least is eaten into by 6s. 8d. and 13s. 4d.! Mademoiselle Blassis, the Italian singer, defunct at Naples, according to newspaper report—back to Babylon to-morrow, Monsieur Bunn, if you please.

July 8.—Spontini, (composer of *La Vestale, Fernando Cortez*, &c. &c.) who brought me letters of introduction from Berlin, dined with me to-day. He is intelligent and gentlemanly *out* of his profession, and gigantic *in* it. His object in coming to England is to make an arrangement with me for the introduction of a first-rate German company here. If I should re-open a London theatre, I would concert with him.

July 17.—The Vaudeville Theatre in Paris burnt to the ground. If *we* have a patent here for the annihilation of the drama, *they* seem to have one there for the annihilation of its temples.

July 18.—Mr. Charles Mathews and Madame

Vestris became man and wife at the parish church of Saint Mary Abbott's, Kensington.

July 20.—Went down to Brocket, on a fishing excursion with that pleasant and gentlemanly brother of the rod, and patentee of chop-suppers, Mr. Duruset.

July 21.—Fishing all day from cock-crow until sun-down. Is it not passing strange, that a man possessing so delightful a domain as Brocket, to sustain which he hath ample means, should consent to take upon himself the government of a country for which he hath NO means ? But Brocket is a fine place, and Byron, my Lord, hath been here, and poor Lady Caroline ! ! And then its waters have noble fish in them ; and it is too bad to abuse the man who allows you to pull them up—but alas ! while *I* am catching fish, HE is catching men—men—men. England is going to the devil—let my lord go too, (an' he like it,) but let him leave my land behind him.

July 30.—In for it, once more. The committee have advertised again and again, and as they cannot convert any other reasonable being into a jackass, they are willing to continue to make one of me, and I to be made one of :

" I am in blood
" Stept in so far, that should I wade no more,
" Returning were as tedious as go o'er ;
" Strange things I have in head, that will to hand."

But what fearful odds one has to fight against ! Macready re-opens Covent Garden, and his followers have clubbed together a large sum of money, to prevent, if possible, his becoming a loser by his speculation.

August 7.—Went to Windsor, and over the wonders of the Castle. There are few things amongst its " show" that have riveted my attention more than Sir Joshua Reynolds' portrait of Queen Charlotte nursing her first-born with the forefinger of the right hand extended, signifying " hush !" At this day it hangs in the drawing-room, where (then a bed-room) the said " first-born" (George IV.) died, and in the vault of the chapel, some rood or so off, the ashes of the nurse and the child lie together;

> " And mourned and mourner lie united in repose."

Here's a pretty lesson for kings, and subjects too, if you come to that—and the blackguards will not profit by it. Look on that child's roseate face, think on his career, reflect how he lived, where he died, and where his ashes now repose! And doth no wisdom spring herefrom ? No; we have all been roseate, lived, and shall die; and if we have not a royal vault to envelope our worms-meat, its remains will still be found, at the last day, as well in one place as another—when, as Addison says, " we shall all be contemporaries."

August 3.—Dined at Blackwall with the London Directors of the West of England Insurance Office, and, in a room adjoining one in which we were assembled for the purpose of undergoing the same opera-

tion, her Majesty's ministers! After dinner, the illustrious individuals came out and played at the old
school-boy amusement of " Who can throw a stone
farthest on the water?" Nice employment for England's guardians. Imagine Pitt and Fox and Burke,
and Sheridan and Tierney and Chatham, and even
Grey, playing at " Ducks and Drakes" on the
Thames; and this, with France having its own way
in Africa, Mr. Van Buren with his eye on the Wind-
ward and Leeward Islands and Canada, and Russia,
with a sigh for India, backing them both. But if
something be not speedily done, they will make
" ducks and drakes" of this once " Right little, tight
little island."

August 12.—Went for a day or two to Rickmansworth—dined with my respected friend Mr. Const—
he is a fine octogénaire, " full fourscore years and
upwards," but neither, as Lear says, " a foolish nor a
fond old man;" he *hath* been the latter in his time—
he is now " a fine old English gentleman," hospitable and entertaining at table, and has always been a
great follower and lover of the *ars dramatica*. He
originally, on authority from Mr. Harris, senior, engaged Munden — THE Munden— at Covent Garden
Theatre, for three years, on a rising salary of 4*l.*, 5*l.*,
and 6*l.* per *week ;** and now the vagabonds multiply
these figures by ten, and then demand them per
night.

* I have Mr. Const's authority for this now-a-days incredible instance.

August 13.—Angled the greatest part of the day—
love the sport, preferring the opinion of Isaac Walton
to the sarcasm of Samuel Johnson—one can fish and
reflect at the same time—*id est*, have a fly at the end of
your line, without having a fool at the end of your
rod. Glorious weather—and did we know HOW, we
should return thanks to the GIVER for the GIFT. In the
churchyard of this good parish of Rickmansworth
lieth interred Stafford, so long chief clerk of Bow
Street ; and, among other virtues enumerated on his
tombstone, he is stated to have made " the widow's
heart to sing for joy." Dunn, therefore, proposed to
" call on Mrs. Stafford for a song."

August 15.—Returned to town—pretty situation
for a manager to be in, not to know that you *are* one
until a few weeks before you are to open house, and
your rival having all the time beforehand to prepare "a
rod your to-*by* to tickle." Motions made in the two
houses of parliament to obtain some means of com-
pulsion or of inducement, to make the dean and
chapter of Westminster admit Thorwaldsen's statue
of Lord Byron into the Abbey, hitherto negatived by
them. This mummery of the dean and his dogs out-
rages common sense. Whatever doctrines have appeared in Lord Byron's works, tending, or so said,
to impeach revealed religion, are but the imagined
sentiments of those characters drawn by him, who
would be likely to entertain them. But hear him
when he speaks in his own person :

" My altars are the mountains, and the ocean,
" Earth, air, stars, all that springs from that great WHOLE
" Who hath produced, and will receive the soul! "

or if that won't satisfy the blackguards, who are the
real sceptics after all, let them turn to the description
of St. Peter's at Rome:

" Enter—its grandeur overwhelms thee not,
" And why ? it is not lessened, but thy mind,
" Expanded by the genius of the spot,
" Has grown colossal, and can only find
" A fit abode, wherein appear enshrined
" Thy hopes of immortality ; and thou
" Shalt one day, if found worthy, so defined,
" Meet thy GOD face to face, as thou dost now
" His Holy of Holies, nor be blasted by his brow !"

or a hundred such splendid instances, wherein his
writings breathe a pure and deep sense of religion.
How truly does Moore say, " Few are there of his
" passages, taken at hazard, that would not by some
" genial touch of sympathy with virtue, some glorious
" tribute to the bright works of God, or some gush
" of natural devotion more affecting than any homily,
" give him a title to admission into the purest temple
" of which christian charity ever held the guardian-
" ship." This sad *entêtement* of bigotry is only
swelling the vastness of his lordship's renown.

August 19.—Met and chatted with the noble and
obliging Viscount Allen, who recommendeth for spe-
cial inquiries into their vocal abilities, the Misses Cun-
dell who, his lordship reports, are now singing at the
Hague. Heaven knows that operatic, and every other

sort of talent, is much wanted at this present writing.

Perhaps the reader is not aware of the importance it is to a manager, his being enabled to take time by the forelock. During the entire month of July in this year, (1838,) my position was in a state of abeyance, for I asked the committee of the theatre to provide themselves with another tenant, and they were trying to do so. The interval between my declaring off and their declaring me on, was assiduously turned to account by the lessee of the rival theatre; and his efforts being directed rather to the impoverishment of me than to the enrichment of himself, the system of suborning was carried on in full force. Considering that, at the time, in reality I had no theatre, whatever might be the general opinion as to what theatre I *should* have, no performer could be blamed for making for himself the best possible provision. But there is a way of doing things which marks the character of him who does them; and although no one who has the pleasure of knowing TOM COOKE would think him capable of other than the noblest conduct, few of our craft adopt it to the extent he has carried all our dealings for a series of long years. At this time I received the subjoined letter from him, which speaks for itself:

" 6th July 1838.
" 92, Great Portland Street.

" MY DEAR SIR,

" An offer has been made to me from Covent Gar-

" den Theatre of such a nature as (under existing
" circumstances) it would be most imprudent to re-
" fuse; the duties required of me being so very light,
" as to be in every respect compatible with other
" branches of professional pursuits which I have long
" meditated adopting, and which the responsibility
" of my station at Drury Lane Theatre has hitherto
" prevented my entering into.

" I beg to assure you that *not the slightest feeling*
" *of hostility towards you* has induced me to this
" change, which, in all probability, you may not care
" about; still I wish you *to be first informed of it*
" from myself.

" Wishing to be explicit, I may as well add, that
" one of the undertakings alluded to in the beginning
" of this letter is a vocal academy on a large scale,
" the necessity of my attendance on which would
" render it impossible for me to command anything
" like the time I have hitherto devoted to a theatre.

" Believe me to remain

" Very truly yours,

" T. COOKE.

" To Alfred Bunn, Esq."

A man must have been a blockhead who could have
raised a point of objection to so straightforward an
intimation ; and I wished him then, as I shall ever
continue to wish him, the reward which high merit
and high character are pre-eminently entitled to.
What possible chance could there be for a manager

E 2

entering upon his duties at the eleventh hour, previous to the arrival of which his adversary had been
making ahead by every exertion he was capable of,
and those exertions backed by a private subscription
to defray his contingencies, or, in the event of a loss,
to pay his deficiencies. I beg not to be understood as
seeking to impeach, for one moment, my rival's pecuniary punctilio; for knowing one instance in the
case of a member of parliament where his contribution of 50*l.* was ultimately returned, I have not the
shadow of a doubt that every *sou,* whether in the
shape of service or hard cash, which was tendered to
Covent Garden Theatre, was scrupulously paid back
again. Still such aid is very timely, especially when
the experience of a past season does not make a man
very much in love with this kind of undertaking.
But I must see what my journal is registering all this
while.

August 20.—Lafont, the French tenor singer, defunct at Paris—it was *his* talent that used always to
keep Nourrit in check. He was a remarkably gentlemanly man, and when he and I used to pistol-shoot
in the *Champs Elysées*—two years are now departed
—I little thought he was so soon to set out on " the
long journey."

August 21.—Went on a pilgrimage to Harrow on
the Hill, to sit on the tombstone (Peachey's) under
the elm where Lord Byron " used to sit for hours and
hours when a schoolboy," as he himself expresses it.
The wife of the sexton, who has been there thirty-

seven years, saith she knew the poet well, and often
brought him hot water for his tea under the said
elm. Allegra, his illegitimate daughter, is buried
where he wished, inside the church ; but the vicar
would not allow the tablet the bard desired to be put
up, because it was setting an immoral lesson to the
boys ! ! The old sextoness showed me, inside the
west door, (it having been blown by a recent storm
from the grave it long presided over,) the monumental
wooden rail of one " Isaac Greentree, who departed
" this life in August 1800," on which, when a school-
boy, the noble bard wrote as follows :

> " There'll be a time when the green trees shall fall,
> " And Isaac Greentree rise above them all !"

His after writings have no finer thought in them,
despite every Dean that Westminster ever spermed.

August 22.—My old and valued friend, my reader
of plays and thinker-general, Reynolds the " dramatic
wight," dined with me at Brompton—a feat I believe
he has not accomplished elsewhere these dozen or
fifteen years past. Reynolds' humour is undying—
neither age nor infirmity having impaired its brilliancy one iota ; and I look upon this day with more
real delight, and shall anticipate a recurrence of that
delight with more satisfaction, than most others in
the kalends.

August 24.—Left town for Brighton, which one
had better do, even with Drury Lane on your shoulders, than crawl about the tenantless streets and
empty parks of the metropolis ; besides, I mean

Mr. Mahomed and his baths to open their batteries
on my kidneys, and to *gravel* the enemy therein con-
gregated; another "besides," which is, that I mean
to produce *Guillaume Tell* as Rossini wrote it, and
I mean Monsieur Bunn to adapt it.

August 25.—Domiciled at Brighton, where to-day
the rain and wind are "wild and high," but there is
a charm in their "fierce and far delight" which a
brace of tempests and double as many hurricanes
could not display in human city.

August 27.—When one thinks what Brighton *was*,
and what it now *is*, it is difficult to reconcile to the
mind the idea of Queen Elizabeth's "goode fyshinge
"towne of Brightelmstone, contayninge seventeen
"houses and thereanent." The sea has made it;
and what is there that man is suffered to gaze upon,
which can be compared to

"The sea, the sea, the open sea?"

so nobly and boldly sung by Barry Cornwall, whom
I long to immolate whenever I see him, for allowing
his dramatic laurels to repose on the monument of
Mirandola. Always, if possible, when at Brighton,
or elsewhere in the vicinity of the sea, contrive to be
housed in front of it. In storm or sunshine, it is beautiful to look upon; and though all reflection thereon
makes us more and more convinced of our own in-
significance, it inspires us with the wish to exalt
ourselves. It occurreth to me I shall never swim
therein again, unless this malady of mine mendeth.

Cigar'd upon the chain-pier till moon-down, praising man for his ingenuity, and thankful to his Maker for permitting him to exercise it. Charles Kean called on me, and says the people patronise him here to the tune of £300 clear in seven nights, which is at least three times as much as the mummery of his opponents can collect together in that same time.

August 30.—Saw Charles Kean perform *Claude Melnotte* in Sir E. Bulwer's drama of *The Lady of Lyons*. A more red-hot Port St. Martin, Surrey, Coburg, or what you will, melodrama was never seen. It contains, amidst some good situations unskilfully worked up, and amongst some admirable ideas bombastically expressed, as much sheer nonsense as was ever palmed on reader or spectator. A man who writes a bad play, and yet asks £500 for it, should be avoided (at all events by managers) by public proclamation.

September 3.—Mrs. Charles Kemble died at Chertsey, in a cottage left to her husband—I believe—by his sister Mrs. Whitelock. Went back to town in Ducrow's phaeton, and arriving at Astley's by half past eight, staid there to see the lion exhibition of Mr. Van Amburgh, which, incredible as it may appear, has brought to pass the words of the prophet, " And the lion, and the lamb, and the leopard, " shall lie down together."

Having some pages back introduced my reader to the Chevalier Spontini, I shall have the pleasure of making him better acquainted with that celebrated

composer; and having all along made him acquainted
with the peculiar pleasures of a *patent* theatre, I
will exemplify them a little more. I readily fell into
Spontini's view of the subject of a German opera,
from the success it met with at Drury Lane in the
year 1833; and during his sojourn in London he
employed his time in making many necessary and
preliminary arrangements. He had interviews with
some members of the royal family, with the representative at this court of the court he was employed
by, Baron Bulow, and with the Lord Chamberlain;
and he then addressed me a business letter, in reply
to a proposition I had made him, in which I laid
down the expense of introducing such a company
as he pointed out, at £6,000—five hundred of which
was to be his own remuneration:

" MONSIEUR,

" Sans pouvoir vous le dire *au juste*, votre plan
" me semble pouvoir s'executer avec succès, moyen-
" nant ce que nous pourrons y ajouter de facilités
" pour aplanir toutes les difficultés et le meilleur
" moyen pour tous les Allemands sera celui de leur
" assurer l'exactitude des paymens par une garantie
" qu'il exigent tous. Quant à moi, vous m'offrez
" sans doute ce que vous pouvez, qui vous semblera
" peut-être beaucoup; mais moi, je le trouve modique !
" Il faut mieux nous expliquer sur ce sujet, si outre
" *la direction générale* dont je serai chargé, je don-
" nerai encore en representation trois grand operas

" de moi, inconnu à Londres, et dont un connu seule-
" ment à Berlin, *Nourmahal*, parceque je n'ai jamais
" voulu le donner en partition à aucun autre théâtre ;
" il est par consequent nouveau pour l'Angleterre,
" la France, l'Italie, &c.

" Comment voulez-vous donc que ces trois grands
" operas ne me rapportent rien, et qui je ne sois recom-
" pensé que comme *simple directeur* de musique et
" des operas, comme tous vos directeurs d'orchestre
" des théâtres de Londres ?

" Je partirai d'ici Mardi matin ; demain, di-
" manche, et lundi, je serai à vos ordres, si vous voulez
" m'écrire l'heure *au juste* à laquelle vous *pourriez*
" *vous rendre chez moi,* ne pouvant plus m'absenter
" de mon logement par les grands preparatifs de
" mon départ.

" Mille complimens et amitiés,

" SPONTINI.

" 24 Août, 1838."

On the evening preceding his departure, we
finally settled our terms, by my making an advance
of just double in the remuneration allotted to himself,
for the privilege of bringing forth his three operas in
question.   At this last interview he told me that the
Marquess Conyingham had promised him a license
for the German operas ; and therefore, notwithstanding I conceived myself to possess, in the patent of
Drury Lane, the power to give such entertainments.
(having so done without let or hindrance in 1833)

E 5

I deemed it advisable to see the Lord Chamberlain,
that the interests of one party might not clash with
those of another. His lordship wished me to define
in writing my views relative to the Chevalier Spontini,
and, on my doing so, a letter was despatched to him
instanter to Paris from the Chamberlain's office,
saying that all performances otherwise than English
were prohibited at Drury Lane, as will be shown by
the Chevalier's own letter:

No. 1.

" Paris, 18 Août, 1838.

" Monsieur,

" Une lettre du 8 courant que j'ai reçu ici de la
" part du Lord Chambellan de Conyngham, vient
" paralizer toutes mes operations rélatives à l'éta-
" blissement à Londres de l'opera Allemand, ainsi que
" nous en étions convenus. L'on m'annonce que
" tout spectacle autre que l'Anglais est expresse-
" ment prohibé à votre théâtre de Drury Lane ; et que
" toutes les démandes faites pour des spectacles
" étrangers, notamment l'Allemand, ont été refusées,
" et que s'il y aura une communication quelconque
" à me faire à ce sujet, l'on s'empressera de me l'ex-
" pedier tout ceci je la saurai d'avance, et il me semble
" que c'est un refus decisif. Par consequent, j'atten-
" drai encore de votre part, Monsieur, une *réponse*
" *definitive* ici à Paris jusqu'au 30 courant, et après
" je partirai pour l'Italie. Si vous obtenez la dite
" permission pour l'opera Allemand, suivant nos

" conventions, vous pourrez vous entendre avec moi
" ici à Paris, rue du Mail, No. 13, jusqu'au 30
" du courant, et avec M. Röckel, qui correspond en
" mon nom avec Madame Devrient ; et avant mon
" départ de Paris je vous écrirai encore, si vous
" répondez promptement à la presente. Jusques à
" une décision et à la permission obtenue pour
" l'opera Allemand à Londres, je suis forcé de sus-
" pendre toutes les operations, afin de ne pas com-
" promettre. J'attendrai donc votre réponse.

" J'ai l'honneur d'être, avec une parfait estime,

" Monsieur,

" Votre très devoué,

" SPONTINI.

" Entendez-vous donc avec Mr. De Begnis pour
" mettre ensemble l'opéra Italien et l'Allemand. Les
" gazettes annoncent qui'l prendrai l'opéra Italien à
" la place de Laporte.

" Paris, rue du Mail, No. 13."

This letter came duly to hand on the 20th, on
which day the following communication was made
to Mr. Martins on the subject of its contents :

No. 2.

" Theatre Royal Drury Lane,
" Aug. 20, 1838.

" MY DEAR SIR,

" Previous to the departure of the Chevalier
" Spontini for Paris, he gave me to understand that
" the Lord Chamberlain had given him express per-

" mission to establish a German opera here for the
" ensuing season, and that, in the event of my con-
" cluding any engagement with him, such permis-
" sion would be transferred to me. I consequently
" completed one with him, and authorised him to
" form a company, agreeably to the plans we had
" laid down.

" My object in seeking an interview with the Lord
" Chamberlain was to state this to his lordship ; but
" as he did not wish such interview, I apologized to
" him for making the request.

" I shall therefore be obliged to you to apprise me
" if his lordship will be pleased to sanction the per-
" formance of a German opera, under the direction
" of the Chevalier Spontini, during the months of
" April, May, June, and July next ensuing.

" Yours very truly,
" ALFRED BUNN.

" As I must let the Chevalier know by the 28th
" instant, enable me to do so."

Which elicited this reply. These are numbered
on this occasion, that whoever takes sufficient interest
in such matters may mark a rich scene of humbug
and duplicity, in all its various bearings :

No. 3.

" Lord Chamberlain's Office,
" August 22, 1838.

" MY DEAR SIR,
" Lord Conyngham has read the last letter I re-

" ceived from you, and has only to observe that he
" has granted no license, nor promised a license, for
" the establishment of German operas anywhere.
" Very truly yours,
" WILLIAM MARTINS.
" A. Bunn, Esq. "

Mr. Martins' reply was followed by an explanatory
note, to which the short annexed answer speedily
made its appearance :

No. 4.

" Theatre Royal Drury Lane,
" August 22, 1838.

" MY DEAR SIR,

" Many thanks for your prompt reply. The
" Chevalier Spontini, on the evening preceding his
" departure, when I entered upon the subject of the
" German opera, gave me expressly to understand
" that Lord Conyingham had promised him the ex-
" clusive license, or its transfer to him he engaged
" with, and communicated to me the result of inter-
" views he alleged to have had with his lord-
" ship, and especially with her Royal Highness the
" Duchess of Kent. On the strength of this, having
" no previous time to wait on you, I signed a very
" serious engagement with the Chevalier, and the
" next day wrote to his lordship, with the view of
" laying all this before him. In a letter just re-
" ceived from Spontini at Paris, he hesitates to con-

" clude any other engagements until I have the
" Lord Chamberlain's license.

" This letter, if his lordship pleases, I will send
" you. In the mean time, as I cannot address him
" later than the 28th instant from London, I take
" leave to refer to the last part of my last letter, and
" to ask if his lordship will be pleased to grant me
" the license for German operas, at the period men-
" tioned, under the Chevalier Spontini's direction.

" Very truly yours,
" A. BUNN.

" W. Martins, Esq."

No. 5.

" Lord Chamberlain's Office, Aug. 23, 1838.

" My dear Sir,

" With reference to your letter, dated yesterday,
" which I have just received, I beg to inform you,
" that the proper course of application for a license
" from the Lord Chamberlain is to address him in
" writing, and to explain in full every particular
" relating to the subject, for his lordship's informa-
" tion.

" Very truly yours,
" WILLIAM MARTINS.

" A. Bunn, Esq."

Being thus called upon to make a formal application for a license, I did so, but seeing through, or
fancying I did, the speciousness of this request, it
became me to be extremely cautious. Being in pos-

session of a patent, which gave me, as generally understood, the power to play anything I pleased, it would not do for me to make any compromise of a property under lease to me ; but as I was at the time lessee of the English Opera House, circumstances might arise to render it advisable to have the German operas there instead of at Drury Lane Theatre. A general application was, therefore, made after this fashion :

No. 6.

" Theatre Royal Drury Lane, August 23, 1838.

" MY LORD,

" I beg leave, with much respect, to apply for " your Lordship's license for the performance of " German operas, in the months of April, May, June, " and July, ensuing.

" The operas will consist of the choicest works of " that school, be supported by the most eminent " vocal and instrumental talent, headed by Madame " Schroeder Devrient, which Germany can produce, " and under the sole direction of the great composer " Spontini, by whom the company of performers will " be engaged.

" I have the honour to be, my Lord,
" Your obedient humble servant,
" A. BUNN.
" To the Lord Chamberlain."

From the date of this application until the 10th of the next month, no notice whatever was taken of it,

which induced me to state, in a private note to Mr.
Martins, the necessity I was under of giving answers
to the various parties with whom negotiations were
pending, and my reminder led to this piece of official
foolery :

No. 7.

"Lord Chamberlain's Office, Sept. 10, 1838.
" SIR,

" I am directed by the Lord Chamberlain to ac-
" quaint you, that your application for a license for
" the performance of German operas, in the months
" of April, May, June, and July, ensuing, has been
" taken into consideration, with other earlier applica-
" tions to the same effect; and his lordship desires
" me to state to you, that it has been decided not to
" grant a license for the performance of German
" operas.
                    " I am, Sir,
                         " Your obedient servant,
                              " WILLIAM MARTINS.
" A. Bunn, Esq."

Another letter having reached me from the Chevalier Spontini, which laid the ground-work for re-opening the subject with the Lord Chamberlain, it
appeared to me important to come at once to a final
decision on two points, which were, whether his
lordship's determination to grant any license was
irrevocable, and whether he intended seriously to

suspend the powers of the Drury Lane patent. With that view, the first of the following letters was addressed to the Lord Chamberlain, and the second to his chief officer:

No. 8.

" Theatre Royal Drury Lane, Sept. 17, 1838.

" MY LORD,

" I have this instant received from the Chevalier " Spontini the enclosed letter, by which it would " seem that his letter to your lordship of the 7th of " last month has been so far misconstrued, that it " abandoned all idea of a lengthened license, and " only sought one, in conjunction with me, for " the next year. I have the honour, through the me- " dium (in your lordship's absence) of the Vice- " Chamberlain, to forward that letter, respectfully " trusting it may lead to a favourable reconsideration " of the subject. I venture to assure your lordship, " that no entertainment is at present in such demand " by the public—that it is proposed to produce it on " the same scale of grandeur as the Italian operas, " and yet, by being played on the intervening nights, it " cannot possibly interfere with the interests of that " or any other theatre. In the hope of your lord- " ship's protection,

" I have the honour to be, my Lord,
" Your obedient humble servant,
" A. BUNN.

" To the Lord Chamberlain, &c. &c."

No. 9.

" Theatre Royal Drury Lane, Sept. 17, 1838.

" SIR,

" On my return to town, I have been favoured with
" your letter of the 10th instant, apprising me of the
" Lord Chamberlain's decision not to grant a license
" for the performance of German operas. As no species
" of entertainment is at present in more demand by the
" public, and as it is one that does not at all interfere
" with the privileges or advantages of any other thea-
" tre, I shall be obliged to you to inform me if the
" supposed powers of the Drury Lane patent, by
" virtue of which German operas were given at this
" theatre, under the sanction of her Majesty, in the
" year 1833, will be questioned, and whether such
" performances under the said patent will be pro-
" hibited ?

" I am, Sir,

" Your obedient servant,

" A. BUNN.

" To William Martins, Esq."

—and with the annexed reply the business of the
German operas terminated :

No. 10.

" Lord Chamberlain's Office, Sept. 21, 1838.

" The Lord Chamberlain has received your letter
" of the 17th instant, enclosing one from the Chevalier
" Spontini ; and I am directed by his lordship to

" acquaint you, with reference to the Chevalier's
" letter of the 7th instant, that he was informed by a
" communication the next day, that only English
" entertainments of the stage were sanctioned at the
" Theatres Royal Drury Lane and Covent Garden.
" The other part of the letter of the 7th, to which
" you allude, was clearly understood and considered;
" and the Lord Chamberlain can only repeat what
" was stated on the 10th instant to all the applicants,
" that it is not intended to grant a license for the
" performance of German operas.

" I am, Sir,
" Your obedient servant,
" WILLIAM MARTINS.

" To A. Bunn, Esq."

What do you think of a PATENT THEATRE now,
good master reader? In the year 1833 we had a
German company, of the highest order of talent,
performing at Drury Lane Theatre, not merely un-
opposed by the Lord Chamberlain of that day, but
countenanced by the consort of our gracious monarch,
the exemplary QUEEN ADELAIDE, the promoter of
every useful institution, the patroness of all art and
science, the protectress of every wish, every want,
every necessity—who extended her support so far as
to allow her sanction to be publicly announced at the
head of the play-bills. In 1838 a license was refused
for such performances, and the authority under which
they *had* been given was disputed. Our benign

sovereign is too full of gentleness and consideration,
too anxious for the welfare of all places of public
amusement, too fond of the art and too fine a judge
of it, to have been, in my firm opinion, at all cognizant
of this transaction, which bore the impress of malice
and tortuosity on the very face of it. The loss of the
100l. annuity, and the sudden and unexpected
appearance of Killigrew's patent, having rendered the
prospect of any further emolument being derived
from Drury Lane Theatre somewhat apocryphal, all
desire to serve it had died away, and every inclination to oppress it became manifest.   The powers of
the Lord Chamberlain were given for the correction,
and not for the institution, of abuses, to purify all
matters submitted to the public taste, and not to
prevent any matter so purified from being submitted
to that taste ; and the present prohibition was a
profligate stretch of authority. Had parliament been
sitting, we could have found friends enough in either
house to have brought the matter under legislative
consideration ; but that not being the case, we were
compelled to submit. " There'll be a time " when all
that's " rotten in the state of Denmark " will be
cleansed and purged away !   O that I could at this
moment have said, as I felt,

> " When vice prevails, and impious men bear sway,
> " The post of honour is a private station :"

but I had to move onwards, and did so. It will naturally be asked, as it often has been, why any notice

was taken of such prohibition, and why the whole matter was not left to the public decision? The first step taken in such cases by the officers of the Lord Chamberlain is to intimidate the foreigners proposed to be brought over ; and however riotous they are in their own country, they are to a man remarkably nervous in entering into difficulties with the authorities of this. Madame Pasta would not cross the stage while the Chamberlain's *veto* was hanging over her head; and the Chevalier Spontini would not move an inch until the Chamberlain's sanction was obtained. Therefore, as long as any such officer enjoys the excellence of a giant's strength, and the tyranny of using it, so long will the patents (pretty little delusions!) be worth about a penny a piece, and be then *rather* dear at the price!

An eminent divine, whose name, if mentioned, would be a high authority on all matters connected with literature, dramatic or otherwise, favoured me, some time after the commencement of the season, with these valuable observations, so peculiarly applicable to the general disposition of the Lord Chamberlain, that it is important to give his note a place in furtherance of my own views. The principle exemplified in it furnishes a lesson which I very much doubt if the successors of Lord Halifax will like to study—certainly but few of them will be found to put in force :

" MY DEAR SIR,

" I have too long delayed thanking you for the
" admission to your theatre, for which I am much
" obliged. I am glad to see you make so vigorous
" a head against the common difficulties of manage-
" ment in our very dull time. I wish the great people
" would get over their propensities for the tinsel and
" trifling of the Italian Theatre. Something, I should
" think, might be done by a direct application to the
" Queen—a formal petition requesting her to patronize
" the English school of either (and both) tragedy and
" comedy. These high personages often require to
" have their attention turned on the things which
" they ought to see.

" Lord Halifax, when Lord Chamberlain, offered
" 500*l.* for the best comedy. If the present Lord
" Chamberlain would do the same, I am quite sure
" he would restore at least the dawn of a dramatic
" ray.

" Believe me truly
" Yours,
" &c. &c. &c.

" To A. Bunn, Esq."

An attempt was made at this time on the English
Opera House stage to palm off a young man, of the
name, I think, of Walton, as an actual descendant of
the bard of Avon. His countenance naturally bore

some resemblance to the best authenticated portraits
of the poet, and it was proposed to render his identity
still less doubtful by introducing him in the character of Shakspeare himself, in a piece concocted
for the occasion. From having witnessed his performance, I thought the young man had too much
talent to have resorted to any such quackery for the
mere purpose of making that talent known. It
required very little biographical information to believe
that the youth's lineal recommendations rested on a
very slight foundation, and his laying claim to them
was therefore only likely to impede rather than
advance his histrionic pretensions. What I felt, I
put in practice; for had I witnessed Mr. Walton's
performance, where it had not been ushered in with
such delusive proclamation, I should not have felt
justified in refusing him an engagement; as it was,
the assumption of so sacred a name might have
rendered all his exertions, as I fear they have done,
abortive. This was his application:

" I am induced to address you, from information
" that you are a gentleman not to be prejudiced by
" others, but always judging for yourself.

" I saw you at the Lyceum, when I lately made
" my début as the representative of my namesake
" of immortal memory, in a dramatic trifle which I
" had sketched merely for the purpose of my intro-
" duction to the London public. It may perhaps be
" called a bold, if not impudent attempt from a tyro;

" but as the audience expressed their approbation,
" (and Mr. Sheridan Knowles and yourself were
" amongst the number who did me that honour,*)
" I thought I had gained the point proposed, for I
" then knew nothing about newspaper reports. But
" the pot-house critics of the Sunday press (the gin-
" and-water co-mates of the actors, who felt indignant
" at having to perform indifferent parts to one whom
" they kindly termed an ill-clad, strolling vaga-
" bond) thought otherwise, and I have been abused
" by them with a rancour that has thrown me upon
" a sick-bed.

" You witnessed my performance—you have ex-
" perienced judgment, unwarped by prejudice—will
" you allow me an opportunity in the young Shak-
" spearian characters ? *Romeo, Orlando, Benedict,*

---

* People should be very cautious how they give an opinion. I was
t alking in the box-office of Drury Lane Theatre some years ago with
Charles Wright, when he had charge of it ; and happening in the
course of conversation to point out a passage in *Don Juan*, and to
express a doubt that any champagne in his store could come up to
this description, he sent me a dozen of superb wine in the course of
the day, begging me to give a candid opinion of its quality, and thanking me for such a puff ; and to my amazement, I read in all the next
morning's papers—

" LORD BYRON'S OPINION OF CHARLES WRIGHT'S CHAMPAGNE ! !

" And the small ripple spilt upon the beach
" Scarcely o'erpassed the CREAM OF *your* CHAMPAGNE,
" When²o'er the brim the sparkling bumpers reach,
" That spring-dew of the spirit ! the heart's rain !"

" or in others more melo-dramatic and operatic—
" *Gambia* in the *Slave*, *Daran* in the *Exile*, at the
" re-opening of Drury Lane ?
      " I am, with respect,
         " Sir, your humble servant,
            " W. WALTON SHAKSPEARE.
" 34, Bedford Street, Strand.
" To A. Bunn, Esq."

Madame Albertazzi having, during the recess,
made her *début* on the English stage by taking a
benefit on the 20th of August at Drury Lane Theatre,
was considered, as she proved, a valuable acquisition
to it ; and accordingly an engagement of a month,
previous to her return to the Italian Opera at Paris,
was proposed to and accepted by her ; and she opened
the theatre for the last season of my management.   An
adaptation of Rossini's *Gazza Ladra* was prepared
with the taste and judgment which distinguish Mr.
Bishop, and experienced a reception surpassing most
outbursts of enthusiasm that I remember.   Indeed it
was beautifully executed—the principal responsibility
resting with Mr. H. Phillips, Mr. Allen, Mr. Balfe,
Mr. Giubilei, Mr. Stretton, Miss Poole, and Madame
Albertazzi ; in whose hands anything short of complete success was not to be anticipated.   Here was a
chance for the worthy people of seeing an opera in
English, introduced in a manner I doubt me if it
will be soon produced in again.   The MAID OF
PALAISSEAU, thus represented, was performed ten

nights, the last time being supported by a spectacle entitled *Charlemagne*, in which my friend Ducrow again exercised all his wonted ingenuity, and displayed all the attractions of his establishment, and in which likewise appeared " the very head and front of ".my offending," *Mr. Van Amburgh and his lions!* The yell from the beauties, calling themselves Shakspe-rians, was as tremendous as it was ridiculous, and every shilling attracted to this medley was gall and wormwood to their conceit. In the blindness of their excitement they forgot that we had no Shak-spearian actors alive, and that an attempt at the re-presentation of any of the bard's immortalities would disgrace the theatre far more than any other per-formance. They forgot that *The Tempest*, perform-ing at the other house with the announced quotation of " the text of Shakspeare," owed all the attraction it possessed to the novelty of Miss P. Horton, " My gentle Ariel," singing while suspended in the air ; because it had been infinitely better acted, and infi-nitely better prepared in that very theatre, " many a time and oft." They forgot all that they ought to have remembered ; and contrasting the unconcealed cha-racter of the *mélange* at Drury Lane with that of the latent mummery at Covent Garden Theatre, they de-cried the one lessee, and hurraed the other, with all the frenzy which distinguishes fools and fanatics.   If the spectacle in question had been introduced as the staple commodity of the evening's entertainments, to the exclusion of more intellectual or refined per-

formances, it might have given reason for just re-
proach; but recollecting that the representation of
Shakspeare's noblest plays by Mr. Kemble, Mr.
Charles Kemble, and Mrs. Siddons, had been supported by *Blue Beard* and *Timour the Tartar*, with
Astley's whole stud of Horses at Covent Garden
Theatre, and that owing to the want of attraction of
some of our finest dramas in the hands of some of
our ablest performers at Drury Lane Theatre, the fortunes of that establishment had, in *the classic days
of* MR. SHERIDAN, been completely retrieved by a
dog, (which, though a Newfoundland one, would certainly, under such circumstances, be called by sportsmen, and with some justice, a *retriever*,) I could not
see that I was so very much to blame.

If it was found necessary by my predecessors, in
both theatres, to have horses clamber up the smoking ruins of a castle, and a dog to jump into a tank
of water, at the time that their respective establishments possessed the most celebrated performers our
stage has ever known, whose exertions in the best
pieces that were ever written proved abortive, how
much more necessary must it have been with me to
introduce a pageant* with these astonishing animals,
who had few other pieces and few other performers.
But this species of blockhead, who was now assailing

* Have these croakers forgotten that Garrick made more money by
a Shakspearian pageant than by all his Shakspearian acting ? Murphy
says, " Mr. Garrick, who always joined the strictest economy to the
" most liberal expenditure, brought Shakspeare's Jubilee from Stratford

us, invariably exercises prejudice at the expense of
reason, and in the absence of every kind of information. Let us only look at a slight result on the present occasion. Rossini's enchanting opera of *La
Gazza Ladra*, charmingly represented, was played
the first five nights to a net receipt of 530*l.*, making
a nightly average of 106*l.*, by which the theatre incurred a nightly loss of nearly 100*l.*! It was played
the *next* five nights, backed by *Charlemagne*, to a net
receipt of 1,371*l.*, being a nightly average of 274*l.*,
by which the theatre was a gainer of some 20*l.* a
night! What would your growlers do in such a case
as this? Why, they would advise you to persevere
in a course of legitimacy—but what they would *not*
do, is more easily disposed of—they would neither
pay you your losses, nor pity you for incurring them.

" to Drury Lane. The public was so charmed with this uncommon
" pageant, which was ingeniously contrived and judiciously managed,
" that the representation of it was repeated near one hundred times."

CHAPTER IV.

"War, war, no peace"—More "last works"—Difference between the salaries of horses and actors—Tria juncta in uno—Master Betty —Lord Mayor's day—Rossini's *Guillaume Tell*—Murphy alarmed at his own weather—A bad marksman—London Lions—Mr. Hill's prophetic "Pooh, pooh!"—Another reader of plays—More mems— C. Kean and Macready—Braham and Phillips—Mr. Durrant and the lion's mane—Her Majesty's patronage—Royal visit to the stage —A royal feed—State command, and its results—Farinelli—Bon mot of *the* Duke—Lenten entertainments again—Mr. Duncombe's humorous speech—Larks of the laity, and cautions of the clergy— The king's cock-crower—How the Lord Chamberlain passes Lent, and how the divines observe it—Lord John Russell's assertion, and Mr. Bunn's contradiction—Pleasant prospects for the British empire.

THE commencement of hostilities began this season, at the opposite house, after the usual fashion, both as respects the promises held out to the public, and the spirit entertained towards the lessee of Drury Lane Theatre, as this interesting *morceau* will bear witness :

" THEATRE ROYAL COVENT GARDEN.
" Mr. Macready begs most respectfully to an-

" nounce, that this theatre will be re-opened on
" Monday, September 24th, 1838.   In entering upon
" this second, and to him most serious experiment,
" he will only say, the same views with which he
" undertook the conduct of this establishment last
" season will be followed up, and his more specific
" pledges will continue to be strictly fulfilled.

" No exertion will be spared in presenting the
" national drama, whether as *a branch of litera-*
"*·ture,* or as a department of art, WITH EVERY AD-
" VANTAGE ! !

" The revival of the standard plays of Shakspeare,
" *in the genuine text of the poet,* will be persevered
" in with increased activity, and without regard to
" expense in attaining the utmost fidelity of historic
" illustration.

" New pieces will be brought out in quick succes-
" sion with the same attention to decoration, espe-
" cially pieces of such a character as to depend
" mainly upon extrinsic attractions ; and the system
" of abstaining from *all exaggerated and delusive*
" *announcements in the play-bills will be rigidly ad-*
" *hered to ! ! !*

We will dismiss these precious effusions with one
parting exemplification.   The reader has already
had under his observation the pledge which was
given, that " all exaggeration and delusive announcements in the play-bills would be abstained from ;"
he has also seen how the pledge was redeemed in

the announcement of Mr. Stanfield's " LAST WORK,"
last Christmas. He shall now see how the said
pledge was again redeemed in the subsequent instance of *another !* of Mr. Stanfield's " last works."

" KING HENRY THE FIFTH,

" FROM THE TEXT OF SHAKSPEARE !

" IN ANNOUNCING THIS

" LAST SHAKSPEARIAN REVIVAL,

" it may be advisable, if not necessary, to depart so far
" from the usual practice of this management, as to
" offer a few words in explanation, or apology, for
" what may seem an innovation ! !

" The play of *King Henry the Fifth* is a *dramatic*
" *history,* and the poet, to preserve the continuity of
" the action, and connect what would otherwise be
" detached scenes, has adopted, from the *Greek*
" *Drama,* the expedient of a Chorus to narrate and
" describe intervening incidents and events."

" To impress more strongly on the auditor, and
" render more palpable these portions of the story,
" which have not the advantage of action, and still
" are requisite to the drama's completeness, the
" narrative and descriptive poetry spoken by the
" Chorus is accompanied with

" PICTORIAL ILLUSTRATIONS,

" FROM THE PENCIL OF

" MR. STANFIELD ! ! !"

(Extract from the Covent Garden play-bill, June 10, 1839.)

In that very charming poem of *The House of Mourning* is a couplet, if I remember rightly, that must always be present to the mind of a metropolitan manager—it always has been to mine—and was so more particularly at the present moment. His season is just such a picture:

> " The foreground stormy, and the distance dark—
> " A covering deluge, but without an ark ! "

as a recurrence to my memorandum will fully testify.

October 22.—Produced the spectacle of *Charlemagne*, in which are displayed the genius of Ducrow, and the wondrous power of Van Amburgh over the beasts of the forest—it was quite successful. Now look ye at all these animals—horses, lions, tigers, leopards, &c. &c. Observe *their* docility, and *their* ability, and then look for those qualifications in the actors—the comparison nauseates one. There is more intellect and pliability in these extraordinary creatures, than in the present combined companies of Drury Lane and Covent Garden theatres. Yet I suppose " the great tragedian" gives himself at least what I used to give him, £30 a week—Phillips has £35 ; others have 25*l.*, 20*l.*, 15*l.*, 10*l.*, and so on: whereas a few pounds of meat, a few bushels of corn, and a few pails of water, and your horse and your lion will lick the dust before ye—" Quot homines, tot sententiæ ; " I only give *mine*.

October 24.—I have seen myself lustily abused to-day for wishing and trying to introduce the *Baya-*

dères at Drury Lane Theatre, and laughed at for being out-jockeyed by Yates. It does not follow that because, in one of his tomfoolery speeches, Yates chooses to say the patent theatres competed with him for the possession of these niggers, it is true. No one will suspect Macready of having made them an offer; and even the thought of doing so never once entered my head. That any one should credit Fred's jokes is odd enough, but that a varlet should discuss them as truths, to another man's prejudice, is unwarrantable.

October 27.—*Herminie Elssler*, by virtue of a pair of stout legs, and throwing them about in all directions, will please those who reside eastward of Temple Bar, though she disgusted the *habitués* of the Opera House. What a troublesome set of devils these foreigners are !

November 1.—I prevailed on Reynolds the dramatist to visit Drury Lane. His first appearance in a theatre for sixteen years—his age, seventy-four, (this is his birth-day, he being born the 1st of November, 1764,) does not hold out much hope of his making as many more as I could wish. I asked our ancient friend, Mr. Const, to meet him, and they sat it out, till within five minutes of " the chimes at midnight." Mr. Capel, the stock-broker, joined the party, and the ages of the three, if put together, would amount to at least 230 ! ! !

> " The psalmist numbered out the days of man—
> " They are enough —— "

But these old boys don't seem to think so. It was pleasant to see them; and to feel one was the cause of their evening's amusement was still pleasanter.

November 8.—Made an offer to the Master Betty's " Master Betty," who is now provincializing after the fashion his worthy father began upon : they tell me he has *materiel* in him—his name justifies my giving him an appearance, and the cockneys will soon find out what that *materiel* is made of—but he won't come yet—read his letter :—

" November 7, 1838,
" Sun Hotel, Southampton.

" Sir,

" I am commissioned by my father to acknowledge " your favour of the 5th inst.; and he desires me to " say that he is of opinion, as I am going on so pros- " perously in the provinces, and have so many en- " gagements in the country to fulfil this winter, that " it would not be advisable for me to accept any " London engagement, however tempting, at the pre- " sent moment. He takes leave to return you his best " thanks for your very polite and handsome reference " to his judgment; and

" I have the honour to be, Sir,

" With my father's most respectful

" Remembrances,

" Your obliged and very humble servant,

" HENRY J. BETTY.

" A. Bunn, Esq."

November 9.—Invited to the Annual Mansion House celebration by my hospitable friend the Lord Mayor (Wilson), harbinger of our worthy corps : an excellent man in all respects ; but I have too great a horror of these public festivities to enjoy even *his* excellencies on such an occasion. I do remember what was written, some many years rolled by, on the man who stood at my lord's back, in the armour worn by our fifth Harry at the battle of *Agincourt* :

" Our modern hero, clad in steel,
" With Henry's arms and martial port,*
" Proved at Guildhall, by many a reel,
" That he had been at *A-Gin-Court*?"

November 17.—The new ballet of " *The Spirit of Air*" came forth with great success. Wieland's *North Wind* " unique "—one great point to arrive at.

November 21.—Had a pleasant note from Thomas Moore, of poetical celebrity, expressive of a great anxiety to see " The Lions." All the world, especially the most intelligent part of it, wants to see them, yet a few in that world are abusing me like a pickpocket for engaging them. Had a still pleasanter treat, that of sitting in a box with the poet, nearly all the evening.

November 22.—A severe accident happened to Messrs. Gilbert and Wieland, in the new ballet, by the snapping in two of the swivel by which they were suspended, ten feet high in air—more managerial

* The printer's devil says this must mean the City Marshal-port.

pleasure—a successful ballet stopped in its career, and the two principal performers in it half killed, by the machination, perhaps, or, at all events, by the shameful neglect of some scoundrel of a carpenter.

November 22.—Issued the following manifesto for the edification of the cockneys :—

" ROSSINI'S CELEBRATED OPERA,
" GUILLAUME TELL.

" The lessee of Drury Lane Theatre begs leave to " announce to the patrons and professors of the mu- " sical art his intention of producing, for the first " time in this country, Rossini's acknowledged *chef-* " *d'œuvre, Guillaume Tell,* on Monday, December " 3rd, 1838.

" The obstacles which have hitherto prevented " the performance of the opera in England, viz. the " want of a sufficient number of principal singers, " and of choral strength—obstacles (which it might " have been reasonably expected would have been " overcome long since at the Italian Opera House, " a theatre supposed to be devoted to the cultivation " of the higher class of music) the lessee of Drury " Lane has made every effort to surmount.

" *Guillaume Tell* has been produced in almost " every country of Europe, England excepted. it " has consequently been the aim of the lessee of " Drury Lane to endeavour to efface an obloquy that " has attached to the musical character of the British " nation, which may be said to be nearly unac-

" quainted with the most perfect work of Ros-
" sini.

" The libretto will merely be a faithful translation
" of the lyrical drama of Messrs. Jouy and Hypolite
" Bis, to which Rossini composed his opera, in or-
" der that the character of the music may not, in any
" one instance, be departed from.

" It is therefore confidently hoped that the pro-
" duction of this distinguished work will meet with
" that liberal encouragement from the amateurs and
" professors of musical science in England, which will
" at once offer a deserved homage to the genius of
" Rossini, and redound to the honour of the
" country."

November 30.—Between last Tuesday and this
day (only three days in all) we have had severe frost,
and ice two inches thick; complete thaw; heavy
rains; a gale of wind; thunder as loud and lightning
as bright as you please; clattering hail, and brilliant
sunshine.   Such a variety in so short a space of time,
too, that

> " My young remembrance cannot parallel
> " A fellow to it."

Murphy is completely beaten; the elements are
too much for him, and yet, odd enough, this very day
I have received this very letter from him, accompany-
ing his prophecies for 1839—I can't help inclining
to him after all :

" No. 14, Trinity Terrace, Trinity Square, Borough.
November 30, 1838.

" DEAR SIR,

" As a slight return for your politeness at the com-
" mencement of the year, may I beg your accept-
" ance of the enclosed copy of my *Weather Almanac*
" *for* 1839? by which you will perceive that, not-
" withstanding the clamour raised against the work
" by certain parties, from the number of editions to
" which in the course of a few days it has reached, the
" public appear to take a different view of its merits—
" so that should the facts at the commencement of the
" year be in my favour, there is little reason to fear
" that the sale will fall short of that of the last.

" I cannot conclude without expressing my thanks
" for your letters of introduction when going to Paris,
" but more particularly for that to Mr. Goldsmith,
" whose attentions to me while there I shall not
" readily forget.

" With best wishes for your health and happiness,
" I have the honour to be,
" Dear Sir, your obliged and very
" Obedient humble servant,
" P. MURPHY.

" A. Bunn, Esq. &c. &c. &c."

December 3.—Never had a greater fag than the
adaptation of *Guillaume Tell ;* but out it came this
evening, and, as far as applause went, was most successful. But four hours and a half, even of Rossini,
are too much for your cockney, who pretends to a

great deal more than he either understands, or in reality likes. He and all that belong unto him are essentially undramatic.

The production of this noble opera was attempted to be forestalled and injured by another of those disgraceful efforts which had been made the preceding season at Covent Garden Theatre, in the instance of *Joan of Arc.* It is nonsense to call a proceeding of this kind, RIVALRY; it is quackery, and nothing else. In order to divert public attention from the elaborate attention paid at Drury Lane Theatre to insure a perfect representation of this opera, Mr. Macready announced for performance Knowles's melodrama of *William Tell,* WITH ADDITIONAL SCENES BY THE AUTHOR, aided by the introduction of chorusses. There could be but one motive in all this—for the gentleman was known to hate the performance of the principal character, and it has ever been proverbial that his affection for music is about tantamount to his knowledge of it. To unworthy attempts like this, is to be ascribed much of the mischief that has been done in those theatres, and much of the ruin hanging over the heads of the professors. Had the performances of each establishment been classified, this could not have happened; and with a dramatic public this would not have been tolerated. I can fearlessly assert, for hundreds upon hundreds will be found to back the assertion, that no piece was ever put upon the English stage in a more correct manner than this

opera was on the occasion in question :* but some
maintained (in " nameless print" to be sure) that a
few daubs and a few voices at Covent Garden were
more effective than some of the most characteristic
scenery ever designed by the Messrs. Grieve, and the
exertions of upwards of one hundred picked chorus
singers introduced at Drury Lane. But this was
called the " voice of the public press." It made me
savage at the time, as confirming the unfortunate conviction that a real theatrical feeling did not exist with
the community at large; but I laugh at it now, though
of the same conviction still. The position of these
two theatres will be defined sooner than is expected
by the rude hand of necessity; they will either both
be shut for want of a tenant, as they have been while
in possession of one, and the attention of government
be called to their condition; or the ploughshare
passing over the ruins of both, his grace the Duke of
Bedford will turn one into a brewery, and extend
Covent Garden market into the body of the other.
This latter case is the one to back, for all the atten-

* A humorous circumstance, connected with its *mise en scène*, was
somewhat calculated to nullify this eulogium. Mr. Braham proved
so indifferent a toxopholite in the celebrated trial to which *Tell* was
subject, during the rehearsals, that the arrow was discharged by a skil-
ful hand behind the scenes, Braham covering the party, and receiving
the approbation due to another. On one occasion the arrow acci-
dentally missed the apple, and Braham finding the audience disposed
to a titter, threw them in a loud roar by advancing to the footlights
and saying, "Ladies and gentlemen, it wasn't *I* who shot at the apple !"

tion that government will ever pay to the subject, will be to regret the loss, and its inability to make it up.

The outcry of the Shakspearian clique, by which are meant Mr. Macready and his toadies, was renewed with increased violence at this time, by its becoming known that the highest personage in the realm, who was about to return from the dull routine of the Pavilion enjoyments to the more animated ones of Buckingham Palace, had expressed a strong desire to witness the wonders enacted by Mr. Van Amburgh; a tolerably strong proof that the humbug preached up about the legitimate drama was exposed, in the most refined circles, to the ridicule conveyed by that cutting truism, " Maintenant rien n'est plus légitime " que tout ce qui ne l'est pas du tout." There is no demand now-a-days for tragedy, for one very good reason, that there are no actors to act it; and for another, that people have plenty of it at home ! ! It is to be hoped that a time will come when the little gang (the pressgang if you will) who have fooled their idol into a belief that he is a fine performer, will leave off their luminous larkings. They may assert, and vow, and fume, and fret, and entertain whatever notions they please; but the people, almost to a man, will at last adopt a favourite and comprehensive saying of mine excellent and kind-hearted friend Thomas Hill, and exclaim, " Pooh, pooh, I happen to know " to the contrary."

The introduction of the last Christmas novelty

placed by me before the London public, and the last I hope that ever *will* be placed by me, (that is to say —if I have to pay for the pleasure of so doing,) terminated the labours of the year 1838, consisting of the usual harlequinade of the season. The Lord Chamberlain's license for this pantomime was sent to Drury Lane Theatre enclosed in the blank cover of a letter that had already done duty by having been the envelope of a letter from Mr. Martins, of the Lord Chamberlain's office, to Mr. Lowndes of Lincoln's Inn; and conceiving it to be as extraordinary a mode of sending an official document as could well be adopted, I enclosed it to Mr. Martins, with these few words :—

" My dear Sir,

" The license of the pantomime has been sent to
" this theatre in the enclosed unceremonious manner,
" the said license being countersigned ' *Wm. Loftus*
" *Lowndes.*' Will you allow me to inquire of you,
" before I make any other application, what alteration
" has taken place in the readership of plays ?
" I am, my dear Sir,
" Yours truly,
" A. Bunn.

" W. Martins, Esq.
" Theatre Royal Drury Lane,
" Dec. 27, 1838."

I have already discussed the peculiar and singular circumstance of the novelties of Drury Lane being submitted to the perusal of a performer at Covent Garden Theatre. That was a droll affair undoubtedly ; but the fact of their being submitted to the examination of a lawyer, as ignorant of *my* trade as I am of *his*, merely because he happened to be the legal adviser of the examiner himself, out-heroded Herod. That such, however, was the case, the subjoined reply to my letter will testify:

"St. James's Palace,
" Saturday.

" MY DEAR SIR,

" Mr. Lowndes officiates for Mr. Kemble, who is " absent on leave.

" I have asked for an explanation as to the cir-" cumstance of the license coming to you in the " manner it did ; but I am quite sure that no disre-" spect could have been intended.

" Very truly yours,
" WILLIAM MARTINS."

But the province of the manager of a theatre is a curious one indeed : for inasmuch as his situation must provide him with a sufficient number of enemies, so must he either submit to unheard-of discourtesies, informalities, injustice, and oppression, if he wishes to preserve a comparative degree of peace ; or if he does, what every other man would, resent such indignities, he at once increases to a frightful extent the number of his antagonists. I

find the close of the year—which was a forerunner of
a close of the season—thus summed up amongst my
memorandums, and it is therefore respectfully submitted to my readers :

MEMS.

There's Phillips deeming he'll sing better
In *Tell* than Braham,—sends a letter
Vowing, enough to rouse one's laughter,
He'll rather go, than sing it *after*.
Mem.—As we starve, and may be closed too,
To let him go, if he's disposed to.
Then Charley Kean, engaged to come up,
The *pros* and *cons* contrives to sum up,
Thinking his fame is getting seedy,
Or that the " Press" is for Macready,
Or the receipts will never pay him
The usual figure, when we play him,
Or that some accident will mar gain,
Has written to be off his bargain!
Mem. —He forgets they may forget him—
And other things—however, let him !
My famed St. Alban's correspondence
Might put the Duke in deep despondence,
And, as the lot before of Zany,
Might prove that " *one* fool maketh MANY."
Mem.—In whatever light I view it,
'Tis wiser therefore not to do it.
Were one sharp weapons prone to handle,
I might just now indulge in scandal ;
But wish her well, and won't believe it—
Mem.—So it's best alone to leave it.
A joke, by Hook, is very current,
" The lion turned his *mane* on Durrant."
Mem.—As he made a very wry face,
I'm rather glad 'twas not in *my* face.

So as with managerial bother,
With one disaster and another,
The year to no one good has tended,
Mem.—I'm d——d glad the year is ended!

It is impossible to conceive a greater degree of excitement and interest than that which had attended
Mr. Van Amburgh's exhibition up to the close of the
year 1838, unless it be that which followed it through
the earlier part of 1839, while he remained with me.
A natural curiosity to witness *such* a natural curiosity
pervaded all ranks of society ; and it is an indisputa-
ble fact, that while a few discontented and conceited
scribblers were arraying themselves against this performance, with the latent view of upholding, by contrast, " Shakspeare and Shakspeare's representative,"
the most illustrious families in the kingdom were
nightly and daily to be found in Drury Lane Theatre,
to see such an extraordinary representation, and
everything in connexion with it. The deep interest taken by her most gracious Majesty, and all the
circumstances thereto relating, having been matter
of public notoriety, I may be pardoned for entering upon a subject which otherwise would be delicate ground to touch upon. The high honour con-
ferred by our illustrious sovereign on Drury Lane
Theatre, in the first month of the past year, will form
a memorable epoch in the annals of that establishment. Having been apprised at Christmas that it
was her Majesty's pleasure to witness the extraordinary performance of Mr. Van Amburgh, I did not

hesitate one moment in concluding a re-engagement
with the proprietors of the animals. Immediately
on the Queen's return from Brighton, her Majesty
honoured Drury Lane Theatre with her presence—
this was on January 10. On the following Thursday, January 17, a similar mark of honour was con-
ferred on this establishment, and on the ensuing
Thursday, January 24, the same flattering distinction
was shown. On this latter evening, pursuant to arrangements which had been made for the purpose,
our gracious Mistress condescended to cross the stage
of the theatre for the purpose of seeing the animals,
in their more excited and savage state, during the
operation of feeding them. It is almost unnecessary to observe, that this gratifying scene took place
after the departure of the audience, and that every
possible caution was adopted for the comparative
comfort and seclusion of the Royal Visitor, which
the resources of the theatre permitted, such as enclosing the entrances with crimson draperies, and
carpeting the stairs; not merely to shut out the
draught of the night air, but to exclude the prying
gaze of the many stragglers who remained behind,
in hopes of bearing testimony to so unprecedented a
compliment paid to the theatre. The animals had been
kept purposely without food for six-and-thirty hours,
strong symptoms of which had become manifest during Mr. Van Amburgh's performance, by the lion and
the panther having simultaneously attacked the
lamb on its being placed in their den; and they

would have evidently made but a mouthful apiece of it, had not their almost superhuman master literally lashed them into the most abject and crouching submission. The first portion of food thrown amongst them, seized by the lion as a matter of priority, was enough to convince any sceptic of the fearful savageness of their nature, when out of the control of the one hand whose authority they acknowledged. The rolling of the tiger's eye, while he was devouring the massive lump of meat and bone, clutched between his fore paws, seemed to possess the brilliancy as well as the rapidity of lightning; and was only diverted by a tremendous and sudden spring of the lion, who, having demolished his own portion, seized upon what was left of his ferocious neighbour's fare. The dash against the sides of the den sounded like the felling of huge trees, and was enough by its force and fury to shake the strongest nerves; but it was a positive fact, that while the boldest of the hearts in the royal suite speedily retreated at this unexpected plunge of the forest-monarch, the youthful Queen never moved either face or foot, but with look undiverted, and still more deeply riveted, continued to gaze on the novel and moving spectacle.

Her Majesty's inquiries were not those of a youthful mind, merely intent upon ordinary and unmeaning questions, but bespoke a scrutiny of mind little to be expected in one of such tender years. It was not to be expected that a circumstance, so altogether without precedent, as the ruler of this vast

realm condescending to pay a personal visit to the
stage itself, could escape the observations of those
malicious partisans the sole object whose of life is
to carp and cavil at the actions of their equals,
and who naturally lie in ambush for an opportunity of attacking their superiors ; and the more exalted in rank, the better for the purposes of such people. This visit of their sovereign, this unbending
from the cares of state, and indulging in the recrea-
tions most suitable to the earlier years of life, when
the mind is thirsting for every kind of information,
and naturally preferring to mingle the *utile et dulce*,
this harmless entertainment was to be questioned,
because the Queen was in the case, while every one
of her subjects was at full liberty to enjoy it. Pretty
sophistry this ! because destiny has placed a crown
upon your brow, that you are to be debarred from
every pursuit of pleasure in which people with not a
crown in their pockets are bent upon participating !
It is a wonder such logicians admit the propriety of
their sovereign even walking or talking, or, except
as a mark of especial favour, partaking of any repast
beyond " the cameleon's dish ;" and, deeming royalty
to be a mere state cipher, that they do not require
its members to be kept under glass globes, or wrapped
up in silver paper.

To my way of thinking and feeling, a more beautiful or truly interesting sight could not be devised,
than to behold this young and lovely creature
emerging from the trammels of state which must of

necessity confine her so much, and seeking relief
in those diversions which instruct and amuse at the
same time ; and none but a fool will withhold the
award of both these qualifications from Mr. Van
Amburgh's surpassing exhibition. Her Majesty's
patronage of this particular class of entertainment
did not end with the bestowal of such a high mark of
favour, for on the Tuesday following, January 29,
her Majesty honoured the theatre with a STATE COM-
MAND, and Mr. Van Amburgh's exercises were especially included in the entertainments ordered for the
occasion, which consisted, in addition, of the *Maid
of Artois*, and the ballet of *The Spirit of Air*. Exclusive of this great distinction, Landseer's celebrated picture, exhibited last year in Trafalgar Square,
was expressly ordered to be painted, and every facility that could be afforded to this gigantic genius,
this prince of painters, this wonder amongst the wonders of art and artists, it is needless to observe, was
cheerfully rendered. Her Majesty, moreover, honoured Mr. Van Amburgh with a conversation of
some minutes on retiring from the Royal Box ; and
her inquiries during their conference, while they bespoke a mind already richly stored with the knowledge of natural history, betrayed the utmost desire
for increasing that store.

The malcontents who could discern so crying a
sin in these harmless pursuits of their Sovereign,
were not backward in circulating all sorts of reports
antecedent to this state visit; and foremost amongst

them all, was the alleged assurance that, through the decline of the Queen's popularity, the house on this occasion would be nothing to boast of. It would reconcile me to all the horrors of management for the rest of my natural life, if I could boast of a few such receipts throughout a season, as the attraction of her Majesty's visit produced on this occasion; and acting upon the principle I have adopted throughout, of supporting my assertions by documents, I subjoin an abstract of the returns to the treasury; and, by comparing it with that of her Majesty's first visit, the reader will be enabled to judge of the dreadful falling off in his Queen's popularity ! !

Amount of the receipts on the occasion of her Majesty Queen Victoria's second state visit to the Theatre Royal Drury Lane, Tuesday January 29, 1839.

	FIRST PRICE.				SECOND PRICE.		
	£	s.	d.		£	s	d.
Box, P.S. - -	35	7	0	-	8	1	0
O.S. -	51	16	0	- -	12	5	0
Pit, P.S. - -	64	19	6	- -	2	12	9
O.P. - -	78	4	6	- -	1	2	0
Gallery - - -	53	3	0	- -	2	2	0
Upper - - -	16	14	0	- -	0	11	0
	300	4	0	- -	26	13	0
Box Tickets - -	243	10	0				
Private Boxes (exclusive of annual ones)	100	16	0				
Passes - - -	4	0	6	- -	0	9	0
Stalls - - -	36	15	0				
Total - -	685	5	6	- -	27	2	0

£712 7 6

Twice in the fortnight following this command
night was her Majesty pleased again to honour
Drury Lane Theatre with her gracious presence;
being the sixth visit, in the short space of as many
weeks, which she had condescended to pay that establishment.

Nor was the enthusiasm or curiosity felt for Mr.
Van Amburgh confined to the illustrious personage
whose favours we have been recording, nor to that
of the distinguished individuals forming the royal
cortège. His Grace the Duke of Wellington came
twice to see the exhibition, and held a conference of
full half an hour each time with our modern *Lysi-*
machus. The Marquis of Anglesea, Lord Brougham,
and a long list of remarkable and fashionable characters, poured into the theatre, day after day, even as
early as nine o'clock in the morning, to witness the process of feeding the animals, and to see (more anxiously than anything else) the extraordinary individual
who held such control over them, to the surprise*
as well as admiration of all beholders. It was, in

---

* I have heard a *bon-mot* of his Grace the Duke of Wellington,
very applicable to his visit on this occasion to Drury Lane, although
upon a very different subject; and while I cannot vouch for its authenticity, I may be allowed to believe in it. A nobleman ventured, in a
moment of conviviality at his Grace's table, to put this question to
him : " Allow me to ask, as we are all here tiled, if you were not
" SURPRISED at Waterloo?" To which the Duke responded, " No—
but I am now !"

very truth, a wonderful performance, and merited all
the eulogy and countenance it received.

Barnett's new opera of *Farinelli* was the immediate novelty of any consequence which succeeded the
Christmas revels, and was received with the favour
that, under any circumstances, must attend the compositions of this gifted master, in the production of
whose works I have never felt but one regret, arising
out of the unequal libretto with which he has wedded
his delightful music. A very interesting circumstance
relative to this opera having transpired at the time, is
entitled to particular mention ; and as it can be best
explained by the letter of the party who introduced
it to my notice, that letter is subjoined :

" 39, Essex-street, Strand, 22d February, 1839.

    " SIR,

    " You have probably heard of a curious fact con-
" nected with the residence of Farinelli at the court of
" Spain, and with the subject of Mr. Barnett's new
" opera, (a fact recorded in the life of Farinelli,)
" namely, that during ten years of his residence at
" Madrid, he sang the same song every evening to
" King Philip the Fifth.

    " This identical song is now in the possession of a
" lady, at whose request I take the liberty of address-
" ing you. It is preserved in a manuscript of the
" late Mr. William Walker, of Hayes, the astrono-
" mer, who was personally acquainted with Farinelli.

" Mr. Walker possessed refined curiosity in matters
" of musical taste. He attached great value to this
" composition, which, he often said, no other person
" in England possessed. It is a song of acknow-
" ledged beauty and power, as indeed may be inferred
" from its almost magic influence on the Spanish
" monarch ; and these recommendations to public
" favour are obviously enhanced by the association
" with the two leading characters and the subject of
" the new opera.

" It therefore seems evident, that the song (which
" is called ' Pallido il sole,') is an essential feature of
" the opera of ' *Farinelli* ;' and I may submit to
" your experienced judgment, whether the restora-
" tion of this song would not at the present moment
" be peculiarly attractive and interesting, and whe-
" ther the public would not listen with curiosity to
" the identical melody which had such touching in-
" fluence on the Spanish monarch.

" No copy of the MS. has ever been given, and
" but for these considerations its possessor would not
" agree to make it public now.

" I have corresponded with Mr. Barnett on the
" subject, who states that he should have been glad
" to avail himself of the opportunity, had not his
" opera already appeared ; and he suggests that
" Messrs. Cramer and Co. would like to publish the
" song in question.

" The lady at whose desire I address you, thinks,
" however, that it should first be submitted to your-

" self; and I therefore hasten to address you on the
" subject, and to request the favour of an answer at
" your earliest convenience.

"I have the honour to be, Sir, respectfully,
" Your very obedient humble servant,
" WM. SIDNEY GIBSON.
" To A. Bunn, Esq."

If this communication had made its appearance
previous to the first performance of *Farinelli*, the
introduction of the song in question would have been
quite a feature ; but the opera having been before the
town nearly three weeks when the first intimation
was made to us upon the subject, its subsequent production could have answered no earthly purpose, nor
could it possibly have repaid the sum which would
naturally have been demanded for it. The document,
however, contains a valuable theatrical anecdote, and
as such it is gratifying to me to be enabled to give it
place amongst the many others herein introduced.

The success which had attended the performance
of Mr. Van Amburgh, and the peculiar patronage
extended to it by the court, induced me to speak to
the Marquis Conyngham, (my darling friend, who
still stuck to me like a leech,) and to solicit his lordship's permission to introduce it on the nights in Lent,
when dramatic performances were prohibited ; and I
was the more induced to make this request, and to
believe it would be granted, from my knowledge of
the miserable mélange of absolute trash hitherto

sanctioned on those nights at the Adelphi and other theatres in his lordship's jurisdiction. The Marquis appeared to admit the reason of my argument, and begged me to commit it to paper. I did so, after this fashion:

" MY LORD,
" I take the liberty very respectfully of inquiring " if there will be any objection to the exhibition " of the lions on those ensuing evenings, when " ordinary theatrical performances are prohibited ?

" The case is one of such peculiar circumstance, " and so different from any other of parties who may " seek a similar indulgence, that I venture to submit " it to your lordship's consideration. If I am unable " to exhibit them on the nights in question, the pro- " prietor of them will thus lose one-third of the in- " come he can receive at unrestricted theatres; and I " shall consequently be obliged to relinquish the " future engagement of them altogether, from my in- " ability to use and pay them more than four nights " a week.

" I therefore respectfully ask if there will be any " objection to an evening exhibition on those days, " introduced either in a promenade, or with a mis- " cellaneous concert ?
" I have the honour to be
" Your lordship's obedient humble servant,
" A. BUNN.

" The Most Noble the Marquis Conyngham."

Those who know Lord Conyingham's manner, and have watched the progress of his lordship's persecution of this theatre, will not be surprised to learn that he refused my petition. The disgusting scene of humbug that had been so long practised, and which I had so long combated, respecting the lenten performances, was therefore again called in question by his lordship's refusal, and was made matter of more serious discussion than it had hitherto experienced, or than was anticipated by his lordship's allies and subalterns. Mr. Duncombe, who had distinguished himself in a previous session of Parliament by his able exposure of this heterogeneous scene of folly and misrule, notwithstanding the rejection of his bill by the House of Lords, again undertook the advocacy of the business; and not obtaining from Lord John Russell any satisfactory information on his first mention of the subject, he made a direct motion on the 28th of February, in a speech of so much genuine humour, containing so much excellent argument, and so irresistible in all its conclusions, that I should consider the case but very partially placed before the reader if it did not, as it deserves, cut a very prominent figure amongst other documents :

Mr. T. Duncombe said, "As the noble lord opposite " had stated that it was not expedient to bring on, at " that late hour of the night, his motion of the block- " ade of Mexico, perhaps it might be thought that he " (Mr. Duncombe) was not justified in bringing for-

" ward the motion, of which he had given notice,
" as to the blockade of the city of Westminster
" by her Majesty's Lord Chamberlain. *(A laugh.)*
" But he hardly thought it necessary to apologize
" for a motion which was founded in common justice
" and common sense. If there was any fault in
" bringing it on, it rested with the noble lord, the
" Secretary of State for the Home Department, who,
" when he brought the matter forward the other
" night, would not give the house the slightest infor-
" mation about it: if, therefore, any apology was
" necessary, he left the noble lord to make it. He
" was aware that the noble lord had a very large
" majority who supported him on that occasion,
" because they thought that he (Mr. Duncombe) was
" irregular both in point of time and in point of
" form ; because he wished to make a motion on a
" petition without notice ; and in point of form, be-
" cause, as the Lord Chamberlain must have acted
" under the advice of her Majesty's ministers, it
" seemed ungracious to make her Majesty a party
" in the dispute. But he (Mr. Duncombe) had been
" told by many of these members, that if he brought
" forward the matter as a substantive motion, he
" should have their support ; and if the noble
" lord laid the city of Westminster under a proscrip-
" tion, merely because he said ' it shall be so,' the
" house, he hoped, would require a reason from him,
" be the religious or political opinions of members
" what they may. The grievance which was inflicted

" on the city of Westminster was, the being restricted
" from theatrical entertainments on Wednesdays and
" Fridays in Lent, when, on the other side of Oxford-
" street, and on the other side of the river, there
" were no such restrictions : and when parties, and
" balls, and levées (*Hear, hear !*) were going on, why
" should the inhabitants of the city of Westminster
" alone be precluded from rational amusements?
" And the evil not only fell on the inhabitants of
" Westminster, but on those unfortunate persons, the
" players and operatives (*A laugh*) of that city, (*Hear !*)
" one-third of whose pay was stopped every week. An
" hon. member had said that these individuals had
" entered into engagements with a full knowledge of
" what was to be expected; but they had no engage-
" ments ; they were paid by the night, and by this un-
" just prohibition one-third of their income was stop-
" ped. He should like to ask her Majesty's ministers,
" the chief actors in the great political drama, how
" they would like to have one-third of their salaries
" stopped, (*Laughter,*) merely because there happen-
" ed to be no house? (*Laughter.*) He did not think
" that his friend Mr. Rice, of Downing Street, would
" like it any more than Mr. Rice of the Adelphi.
" (*Hear, hear, and laughter.*) On looking into the
" *Morning Post,* he found that yesterday, Wednes-
" day, one of the days when nobody ought to give
" entertainments of any kind, when everybody ought
" to be devout and pious, and never think of eating
" and drinking, or listening to music, he found, on

" looking into the *Morning Post,* that this very
" Wednesday in Lent several grand entertainments
" had been given. In the first place, there was a
" grand dinner given in support of Drury Lane Thea-
" trical Fund, (*hear, hear !*) which was a sort of broad
" farce, with musical entertainments added, to which
" those who subscribed three guineas were admitted.
" A very illustrious individual (the Duke of Cam-
" bridge) presided at the dinner, and the whole went
" off with what the papers called the extreme of convi-
" viality. (*Loud laughter.*) In the course of the even-
" ing some songs were sung by several distinguished
" vocalists who were present; among others, a parody
" on Rory O'More," (*Hear! hear and a laugh,*) and
" after that Mr. Rice—(*A laugh*)—he did not know
" which Mr. Rice, but he was described as the ' real
" Jim Crow'—(*Shouts of laughter from all parts of
" the house,*)—sang, ' Sich a getting up stairs,' with
" three encores—(*Roars of laughter,*)—and then ' Jim
" Crow,' with some new verses, which, as the *Post*
" said, ' we obtained, but for which we have no
" space.' Rice was warmly received, (*laughter,*)
" and, after the departure of the Duke of Cambridge,
" was voted into the chair to sustain the convivi-
" ality of the ' after evening.' (*Hear, hear !*) Now
" this took place the day before, on a Wednesday in
" Lent. Well, then, he looked a little further, to see
" what was going on in the Palace, (*a laugh,*) and he
" found that on that day her Majesty had a very large
" dinner-party, and that in the evening the band of

" the Life-guards entertained the party with music.
" (*Cheers and laughter.*)   At this meeting there was
" a great number of distinguished individuals, and
" the very first name among them was, that of the
" Marquis Conyngham, the *arbiter elegantiarum,*
" the *custos morum* of the city of Westminster.—
" (*Laughter and cheers.*)   Far be it from him
" (Mr. Duncombe) to suggest that the Lord Cham-
" berlain did not point out the inconsistency to her
" Majesty, and he was therefore warranted in assum-
" ing that the Lord Chamberlain did suggest to her
" Majesty that the royal party was doing exactly the
" very thing which he had forbidden in the city of
" Westminster. Well, then, he looked a little further
" to see what was going on in what was called high
" society, and he found it stated in the *Morning Post,*
" the organ of fashionable life, that the Marquis of
" Lansdowne had a grand dinner-party on Wednes-
" day. (*Hear, hear! and laughter.*)   Still he went a
" little further, for he wanted to see how the church
" was occupied, and he found it stated that yester-
" day, Wednesday in Lent, the Bishop of Landaff
" gave an elegant dinner (*loud laughter*) at the
" deanery, St. Paul's, to a large circle of gentlemen
" connected with his lordship's diocese.   (*Renewed*
" *laughter.*)   Now, when the people of the city of
" Westminster saw how others occupied themselves
" on the Wednesdays in Lent, he wanted to know
" whether they had not a just reason to complain
" if they were not able to enjoy the rational amuse-

" ment they saw others enjoying ? They did not
" grudge her Majesty the band of the Life-guards.
" All they asked for was to be allowed to pay for
" their own band, and to listen to it in the boxes
" of Drury Lane Theatre. He could not understand
" what ground there was for refusing his motion, but
" he understood that it was to be refused. There was
" no law in favour of the Lord Chamberlain's con-
" duct; it had only custom to support it.'' After referring to an opinion to this effect given by Sir J.
Scarlett, and to the 10th George II., the hon. member went on to say, " that if the Lord Chamberlain
" had a right to shut up the theatres in the city of
" Westminster on the Wednesdays and Fridays dur-
" ing Lent, they ought to be shut up throughout the
" town. As to the plea of custom, that was not
" valid. How many old customs were there, which
" day after day were abandoned ? He could give the
" house instances of many old Lenten customs, which
" had now very properly been abolished. For in-
" stance, what was the Lenten custom in the time of
" George II., at the time when the bill to which he
" had referred was passed ? At that time there was
" one of the officers of the royal household who was
" denominated the King's cock-crower. (*Loud*
" *laughter.*) It was the duty of this exalted indivi-
" dual, during Lent, to crow the hours of the night,
" which at other times were proclaimed by the
" watchman. It however happened, that one night
" the Prince of Wales had a supper-party, when the

" King's cock-crower passed under his window, and,
" according to custom, crowed the hour. The Prince,
" not aware of the custom, and not understanding the
" language, (*a laugh*,) took these sounds as a personal
" insult, attacked the unfortunate officer, and nearly
" strangled him ; and it was some time before he re-
" covered. This accident called forth the grave con-
" sideration of the court and the court circle, and
" the result was, that this very absurd custom was
" abolished. (*Hear, hear !*) But if old customs were
" always to be kept up, he did not see why the
" Lord Chamberlain should not revive the King's
" cock-crower. He believed he had stated what were
" the grievances of which the people of Westminster
" had to complain. In France a large sum of money
" was voted from the public purse for the support of
" the theatres, and they had the theatres rent-free.
" His clients did not ask for money from the public
" purse, nor to live rent-free ; all they asked was,
" to be put upon an equality with the other parts of
" the metropolis. (*Hear, hear !*) The-only ground
" on which the restriction was defended was, that the
" custom was an old vestige of Popery, and that it
" afforded the Lord Chamberlain an opportunity of
" displaying a petty tyranny, to the great inconve-
" nience of her Majesty's subjects in the city of
" Westminster. He would therefore move, ' That it
" is the opinion of this house that during Lent no
" greater restrictions should be placed upon thea-
" trical entertainments within the city of Westmin-

" ster than are placed upon the like amusements at
" the same period in every other part of the metro-
" polis."—(*Loud cheers.*)

After the introduction of a variety of nonsensical
arguments by Lord John Russell, Lord Teign-
mouth, Sir James Graham, (out of charity to Lord
John,) and Mr. Spring Rice, Mr. Duncombe returned
to the attack in the same amusing strain, with the
natural result from a display of such downright fun,
and better still, such striking truths :

" Mr. T. Duncombe, in reply, denied that he had
" made the comparison imputed to him by the noble
" lord, the member for Marylebone, between a theatre
" full of prostitutes and a dinner-party at a bishop's
" house. He had not pretended to say what sort of
" company might be at such a dinner-party.—
" (*Laughter.*) As to the observance of Wednesdays
" and Fridays, he would ask, did the noble lord
" happen to know that the illustrious consort of the
" Duke of Cambridge was at the Queen's Theatre on
" Friday last ? (*Hear, hear.*) The hon. baronet, the
" member for Pembroke, was mistaken in supposing
" that it was in the city of Westminster only that
" the Lord Chamberlain had jurisdiction. There
" were the theatres-royal York, Manchester, Brighton,
" and other towns throughout England ; and over all
" these the Lord Chamberlain had jurisdiction, if he
" thought proper to exercise it. But, to show the
" caprice with which this jurisdiction was exercised,

" he would just mention one fact. The year before
" last, in the theatre at Brighton, which is right
" opposite the Pavilion, DURING THE TIME THE LORD
" CHAMBERLAIN WAS THERE, the following pieces
" were performed on *Ash Wednesday!!* 'Charles XII.,'
" 'The Maid of Switzerland,' and 'The Vampire!'
" (*Hear, and laughter.*) The noble lord, the member
" for Marylebone, had shifted the question from his
" own shoulders, and had gone to the Bishop of
" London, and asked him what he thought of allow-
" ing theatrical performances on Wednesdays and
" Fridays during Lent, and the bishop very naturally
" replied, that it would be a heavy blow to the Pro-
" testant church. (*Laughter.*) The noble lord, the
" Secretary for the Home Department, had said he
" would not care if the resolution had passed. Did
" the noble lord not care? Only let the house give him
" (Mr. T. Duncombe) that resolution, and he would
" then try whether he could not make the noble lord
" attend to it.—(*Laughter and cheers.*) The noble
" lord should not attempt to set the house, or the re-
" presentatives of the people in that house, at defi-
" ance. He might imagine that he was taking time
" by the forelock in assuming such a tone; but he
" (Mr. T. Duncombe) was not sure of that. Perhaps
" the opinion of the house would not only be found
" against the noble lord on this occasion, but it might
" soon tend to remove the noble lord and his col-
" leagues from the benches they now occupied.—
" (*Cheers.*) To continue the present system of
" things, would, as the noble viscount, the member for

" Durham, had observed, only be downright hypo-
" crisy, and a gross absurdity.—(*Cheers, and cries of*
" ' *Question.*')

The house then divided, when the numbers
appeared—

For the previous question - - - 72
Against it - - - - - - - 92
Majority - - - - - —20

The announcement of the numbers was received
with tumultuous cheers.

In consequence of this unexpected manifestation
of the opinion of the House of Commons, the following correspondence passed between Mr. Duncombe
and myself:

" Theatre Royal Drury Lane, March 1, 1839.
" SIR,

" I take the liberty of inquiring whether the result
" of your motion last evening in the House of Com-
" mons (to remove the restriction on this theatre in
" Lent) be correctly reported in the morning papers ?

" While I ask this question for the regulation of
" my next week's entertainments, I avail myself of
" the opportunity afforded me of saying, that the
" theatrical community owe you a heavy debt of
" gratitude.

" I have the honour to be, Sir,
" Your obedient humble servant,
" A. BUNN.

" To T. Duncombe, Esq., M.P."

"The Albany, March 2, 1839.

" SIR,

" The report to which you allude is, I believe, per-
" fectly correct.

" I enclose a copy of the resolution agreed to by the
" House of Commons :

' That it is the opinion of this house, that during
' Lent no greater restrictions should be placed on
' theatrical establishments within the city of West-
' minster, than are placed upon the like amusements
' at the same period, in every other part of the
' metropolis.'

" It seems to me impossible, after this deliberate
" proceeding of the House of Commons, that the
" Lord Chamberlain should any longer interpose his
" *veto* to the further injury of those who have
" already suffered so much by the course which the
" House of Commons has condemned. The words
" of the Act show that the subject is wholly in the
" discretion of the Lord Chamberlain : he may, *if he*
" *pleases*, and without any appeal from this decision,
" put a stop to all theatrical amusements in West-
" minster, AT ALL TIMES. The Act does not specify
" the Wednesdays and Fridays in Lent, nor any
" other days or day in the year, but places absolute
" powers of prohibition in the hands of the Lord
" Chamberlain.

" It is, therefore, I repeat, a mere question of dis-
" cretion, and I cannot for a moment imagine that
" this officer of the court will exercise his discretion

" in positive defiance of the recorded opinion of the
" House of Commons.

" In allusion to the latter paragraph of your letter,
" I must be allowed to say, that the theatrical com-
" munity who have been cruelly deprived of their
" bread, and the people of Westminster who have
" been absurdly deprived of a rational amusement,
" are not indebted to any individual, but to the com-
" mon sense of the majority who voted on this ques-
" tion.

" I have the honour to be, Sir,
" Your obedient and faithful servant,
" T. S. DUNCOMBE.
" Alfred Bunn, Esq.,
" Theatre Royal Drury Lane."

My object in addressing Mr. Duncombe was to
elicit the exact position of the case from him, rather
than to trust to newspaper report, because upon the
truth of that report depended my own position. Con-
curring with that part of Mr. Duncombe's letter on
which he deems it impossible that the Lord Chamberlain should any longer oppose his *veto to* our performing on Wednesdays and Fridays in Lent, I made
arrangements for opening Drury Lane Theatre on
those evenings, and began by engaging the whole
band, which had rendered the Musard concerts so
popular at the English Opera House. Though announced merely to give a concert, its performance was
interdicted ; and I therefore took the bull by the horns,

and advertised the full opera of *Farinelli* for Friday March 8th. The interdiction which closed the theatre on the previous Wednesday, March 6th, was conveyed from the Lord Chamberlain's office " by direction of her Majesty's ministers ;" but by what Act of Parliament, or by what authority, they thought proper to interfere with the business, I have not the remotest conception. However, to bring the matter altogether to issue, for the satisfaction of the many noble advisers who favoured me with their opinions upon that subject, and for my own guidance in the matter, I made official inquiry of the Lord Chamberlain, from whose office this despatch was received :

" Lord Chamberlain's Office, March 6, 1839.

" SIR,

"With reference to your letter to me of yesterday,
" I am directed by the Lord Chamberlain to state,
" that the communication made to you was intended
" distinctly to convey a prohibition against any other
" than the usual performance of oratorios on the Wed-
" nesdays and Fridays in Lent.
                    " I am, Sir,
                        " Your obedient servant,
                            " WILLIAM MARTINS.
    " A. Bunn, Esq.,
 " Theatre Royal Drury Lane."

Upon the receipt of this, my announcement was finally withdrawn, and we sneaked out of the affair in the most unbecoming humility; but the honourable member for Finsbury did not naturally choose to let it sneak out of the House of Commons in the same manner; and therefore, on the 11th of March, he brought forward the business again. In the mean time, the feelings and opinions of the community at large became considerably agitated; and being conveyed through the medium of the metropolitan and provincial press, gained ground every hour. I have not space for the insertion of all their doctrines, largely as I subscribe to them, and convinced as I am that every reader I may be fortunate enough to find would do the same: but as a sample, I cannot resist inserting the subjoined animadversion from the pages of the *Morning Chronicle,* written with admirable spirit, taste, and truth:

" Morning Chronicle, Feb. 27, 1839.

" It is singular that at the present season the most
" religious people in Westminster, and *à fortiori* in
" all England, should be the poor players. They
" alone keep Lent, and fast on Wednesdays and Fri
" days. They alone abstain from their usual occu
" pations on those days, and forfeit their usual gains.
" They neither work nor play. Where shall we find
" the like piety? The clubs are all open in the west;
" the city is upon 'Change in the east; parliament
" sits, both Lords and Commons, and not a lie the
" less is told in even a court of law; bishops dine,
" though we deny not that their chaplains say grace

" over salt fish ; and the band of the Coldstream
" guards is redolent of musical profanity in the pur-
" lieus of the palace. The players are at the sum-
" mit of sanctity. In primitive times, long gone by,
" Christians gave to the poor the meals from which
" they themselves abstained ; but the poor actors
" leave the unpaid price of their uneaten meals in
" the pockets of their wealthier patrons.

    " The worst of it is, that this ascetic pre-eminence
" is enforced. Roscius does not desire the pillar of
" *Simeon Stylites* for his pedestal. All through
" Lent he is lusting for the flesh-pots of Egypt.
" The corps dramatique is forced into the front rank
" of the fasting host, to cover the bishops and their
" clergy in the rear. It is a forlorn hope by con-
" scription, and not by volunteering—a very forlorn
" hope, and not ' misnamed.' Surely we should
" have thought that the church of England had will-
" ing piety enough amongst its members to make
" Lent a holy season, and needed not the seasoning
" of persecution to its salt fish, by thus enforcing
" the pains of penance where they are alleviated by
" the merit of obedience.

    " The question is not so much ecclesiastical as
" topographical. Why is there toleration at Tottenham
" for what would be desecration at Drury ? Why is
" the performance not sinful at the Surrey, that would
" be deadly at the Adelphi ?—and why may Shak-
" speare be disfigured all over the country, so that
" he is not illustrated at Covent Garden ? The Lord

" Chamberlain seems to confound the boundaries of
" parishes with the boundaries of virtue, and to take
" Temple Bar as a barricade against profanity.
" Westminster is his Holy Land. But Palestine was
" enriched by Providence for the piety of its posses-
" sors, while the Lord Chamberlain impoverishes the
" Westminster theatres by the abstinence he enforces
" on their tenants. If Lord John Russell does not
" feel it his duty to advise the Chamberlain to lower
" his piety, he should feel it his duty to advise the
" Duke of Bedford to lower his rent.

" There is an old story of a footman applying for
" a place, who had no objection to family prayer, pro-
" vided his master remembered it in his wages.
" Let ' her Majesty's servants' be treated with similar
" liberality. Neither Church nor Chamberlain ought
" to refuse to make up their curtailed emoluments
" from fees or tithes. It is a public disgrace to al-
" low our piety to be paid for by the players ; to
" borrow their shoulders for the burden of our Lent ;
" and render our sanctity a public saving out of the
" earnings of actors and the salaries of scene shif-
" ters.

" This very trumpery affair ought to have been set
" right the moment it was mentioned. The prohibi-
" tion is as absurd, and almost as cruel, as the old
" law for the drawing all the teeth of any one who
" should be convicted of eating flesh in Lent. That
" dramatic exhibition is any greater offence against
" the sacredness of the season than ten thousand

" things that are daily done in every street, is an
" argument which it is strange that any man should
" hold with a grave face. Theatres, properly managed,
" and amply patronised, are amongst the most power-
" ful agencies of civilisation. We respect, never-
" theless, the religious prejudice that denounces them
" altogether. But no such respect is due to the in-
" consistency that, according to mere locality, allows
" them to be open, or commands them to be closed :
" to the hypocrisy that, from whatever motives or in-
" fluences, upholds an arbitrary custom under the
" pretence of piety ; or to the injustice that subjects
" any class of persons to peculiar needless and un-
" merited privation.

" The Church of England received the Lent fast,
" with many other observances, from the Church
" of Rome, by which it had been extended from
" forty hours to forty days before Easter. But, in
" general, the Church of England has interpreted
" this observance, as it has the rest, with consi-
" derable latitude and liberality. All serious inter-
" ference with health, or business, or any rational
" enjoyment (except that of a theatre within a certain
" district) has been judiciously avoided. Why, then,
" continue this injurious exception ? We have
" called it a trumpery affair, as only relating to the
" amusements of some six or eight thousands per
" night, and the receipts of some two thousand or
" thereabouts. But no affair is trumpery which in-
" volves hypocrisy on the one part, and injury on the

" other.   We like not the maxim *de minimis non*
" *curat lex*, especially if it be construed ' players are
" below the protecting care of parliament.'   Our
" theatrical system needs revision, especially as to the
" privileges of the patent theatres, and the anomalous
" authority exercised by the Lord Chamberlain.
" If there be any truth. and we believe there is deep
" and important truth, in the importance assigned to
" the fine arts as purifying the manners of a people,
" this subject deserves more attention than it has
" hitherto received from legislators and reformers."

This article was sent forth to the public on Wednesday the 27th of February, one of the lenten evenings of prohibition, on which the memorable princely fête at Goodwood was given to celebrate the attain-
ment of his majority by the Earl of March.   Without
the slightest disparagement to the hospitality or
morality of his grace the Duke of Richmond, whose
noble and expanded views laugh to scorn the narrow
ribaldry, for it is nothing else, put forth and maintained in this prohibition, the opportunity was too
tempting to be passed by, and accordingly a few
days after, the following notice, coupling the two
circumstances, appeared in the same newspaper:

" THE MODE IN WHICH THE CLERGY OBSERVE LENT.*

" The *Brighton Herald* of Saturday last contains
" an account of the more than princely fête at Good-
" wood, on Wednesday last, the 27th of February,

* Morning Chronicle, March 6th, 1839.

" the day the Earl of March attained his majority.
" The ball seems to have been attended by half the
" aristocracy of the kingdom. The dancing, we
" are told, commenced shortly after ten o'clock, and
" the last carriage did not leave till a quarter past
" seven o'clock. The names are all given, and we
" should recommend it as an excellent clerical guide ;
" for we question if a single beneficed clergyman
" of the county was not present with his family.

" The Bishop of Chichester could not attend the
" ball, being at his post in London; but his family
" were there, including Mrs., Miss, and Mr. Otter.

" The following names of clergymen, which we
" have culled from the account, is peculiarly instruc-
" tive as to the opinion of the Church of England,
" that the abstinence from all secular amusements is
" due to the established religion of the country on
" Wednesdays and Fridays in Lent :

" Rev. Henry Atkins.
" Rev. Mr., Mrs., and the two Misses Bradford.
" Rev. Mr. and Mrs. Buckner.
" Rev. J. Blackeston.
5 " Rev. Mr. and Mrs. Batson.
" Rev. Mr., Mrs., and the Misses Bayton.
" Rev. S. and Mrs. Brown.
" Rev. Mr. Broadwood.
" Rev. Mr. Bethuen.
10 " Rev. Mr. and Mrs. Cooper.
" Rev. Mr. and Mrs. Collins.

" Rev. Mr. Caunter.

" Rev. Dr. and Mrs. Clark.

" Rev. Mr. Calhoun.

15 " The Rev. Mr. and Mrs. S. Douglas.

" Rev. Mr. and Mrs Deacon, the Misses Deacon,

" Mrs. J. Deacon, and Mr. Henry Deacon.

" Rev. Mr., Mrs., and the Misses Elmes.

" Rev. Mr., Mrs., and Miss Eedle.

" Rev. Mr. Fairless.

20 " Rev. Mr. and Mrs. Green, Rogate.

" Rev. Mr. and the Misses Green, Ruslington.

" Rev. Mr. Green, Oving.

" Rev. Mr. Howe.

" Rev. Dr. and Mrs. Holland.

25 " Rev. W. and Mrs. Holland.

" Rev. Mr. and Mrs. Johnson.

" Rev. Mr. and Mrs. Kinleside.

" Rev. C. Klanert.

" Rev. Mr. and Mrs. Lyne.

30 " Rev. Mr. and Mrs. Luxford.

" Rev. Henry Legge.

" Rev. Mr. and Mrs. Langdon.

" Rev. Mr. and Mrs. Malthus.

" Rev. Mr. and Mrs. Murray.

35 " Rev. Mr. Munsor.

" Rev. W. and Mrs. Miller.

" Rev. Mr. Mackie.

" Rev. Mr. Miller.

" Rev. Mr. Newland.

40 " Rev. G. and Mrs. Porcher.

" Rev R. Powell.

" Rev. J., Mrs., and Miss Pannell.

" Rev. Mr. Rasinghill.

' Rev. Mr. and Mrs. Roberts.

45 " Rev. G. Smith.

" Rev. Mr. and Mrs. Schomberg.

" Rev. Mr. and Mrs. Tredcroft.

" Rev. Dr. and Mrs. Thornton.

" Rev. Wiliiam Turner.

50 " Rev. Mr. and Mrs. Twyford.

" Rev. J. Tuffnell.

" Rev. Mr. Thompson.

" Rev. Mr. and Mrs Witherly.

" Rev. Henry and Mrs. Wood.

55 " Rev. G. Woods.

" Rev. Mr. and Mrs. Watkins.

" Archdeacon and Mrs. Webber.

" Rev. C. Webber.

59 " Rev. Mr. and Miss Wells.

Mr, Duncombe's motion, on the 11th of March, was to the following effect:—

" This House learns with regret and surprise that
" her Majesty's ministers have thought fit to inter-
" fere with the wholly unfettered discretion which
" the legislature has been pleased to vest in the Lord
" Chamberlain, with respect to theatrical entertain-
" ments in Westminster, by directing that officer of
" her Majesty's household so to exercise his discre-
" tionary authority as to defeat the manifest object of

" a resolution of the Commons House of Parlia-
" ment."

But the motion was withdrawn after a short debate,
on the understanding that the question would be considered, as regards the hereafter. As Lent is coming
on, we shall see. What a scene of ridicule if they give
in, and what a scene of deceit if they do not ! In the
course of the debate, Lord John Russell thought
proper to make these observations upon me :—

" In the present instance Mr. Bunn, according
" to one of the letters that had been called for,
" thought proper to incur considerable expense,
" upon that resolution being adopted by the house.
" He would say, with all due regard to resolutions
" of that house, that they were not to be allowed to
" set aside either the law of the land, or the preroga-
" tives of the crown ! (*Hear !*) Therefore when one of
" the lessees, namely, of Drury Lane, chose to adver-
" tise that there would be performances on future
" Wednesdays and Fridays, the Lord Chamberlain
" (acting under the sanction of her Majesty's minis-
" ters) informed Mr. Bunn that such performances
" could not be countenanced or allowed—he would
" repeat that he thought they were perfectly justi-
" fied in acting as they had (*hear, hear !*) and he
" certainly conceived, that if they had proceeded
" otherwise, if they had recognised a resolution of
" that house as so sufficient upon a trifling case of
" this kind, they would but have established a pre-
" cedent most injurious to the proceedings of Parlia-

" ment, and the prerogative of the crown. Mr.
" Bunn, it appeared, held in contempt, and set at
" nought, the prerogative of the crown."

One is obliged sometimes to remember what " the
" insolence of office" forgets : and as a very little
man, armed with a great deal of authority, can
do a great deal of mischief, I did not think proper
to indulge as freely in reply as I could have wished ;
and contented myself therefore with issuing this
rejoinder :

" *To the Editor of the Morning Herald, Wednesday,*
March 13, 1839.

" SIR,

" This morning's papers reporting Lord John
" Russell to have asserted last evening, in the House
" of Commons, that ' Mr. Bunn had set at nought the
" prerogative of the crown,' I request the indulgence
" of your journal to detail the simple facts of the case.
" I had the pleasure of seeing Mr. Duncombe the
" day after the correspondence which had passed
" between us upon the success of his motion in the
" House of Commons, when he stated his belief,
" that if Drury Lane Theatre were opened on the
" following Wednesday, no interference would take
" place on behalf of the Chamberlain's office ; and he
" gave me as his reason for such belief, that he had
" understood persons connected with the government
" (I think he named Mr. Fox Maule) had publicly

" stated as much. In consequence of this communi-
" cation, my announcement was made ; when to my
" astonishment I received the next day the letter from
" the Lord Chamberlain's office, already published.
" I did not refuse to comply with the pleasure of her
" Majesty's ministers therein contained, (though it
" was the first time their names had been used in
" any communication from that office to this theatre ;)
" I merely stated that I could not comply without great
" loss ; and on the receipt of a distinct prohibition,
" I submitted to that loss.

" I therefore beg to say, that if the report in ques-
" tion be correct, Lord John Russell has taken an
" unjustifiable liberty with my name, in asserting that
" ' I have set at nought the prerogative of the crown,
" for her Majesty has not a more loyal or devoted
" subject in all her dominions, than

" Your obedient humble servant,

" A. BUNN, *Lessee.*

" Theatre Royal Drury Lane,
" March 12, 1839."

After all this tomfoolery, what would the reader
like ? A good laugh would be too great a compliment—a sneeze would be too troublesome : in sober
truth, a lament—a lament is nearer the mark ; for as
sure as fate,

" This royal throne of kings, this sceptered isle,
" This earth of majesty, this seat of Mars,
" This other Eden, demi-paradise,

" This fortress, built by nature for herself,
  Against infection and the hand of war,
" This happy breed of men, this little world,
" This precious stone set in the silver sea,
" Which serves it in the office of a wall,
" Or as a moat defensive to a house
" Against the envy of less happier lands;
" This blessed spot, this earth, this realm, this ENGLAND,"

will assuredly go to the devil, if the persons permitted to sway its destiny do not occupy themselves about something better than such an immense
quantity of rubbish as is contained in the foregoing
compendium of some of their proceedings.

CHAPTER V.

Posthumous opera by Sheridan — How to pay a coal-merchant's account—Poole in a pucker, and Reynolds unable to get him out of it—Judgment upon manuscripts—Gratitude of performers— To what account it was turned—Fashionable booksellers and one of their fashionable dinners, reported in verse—Death of Boaden— Death of Nourrit—Dupronchel and Duprez—Neither emphasis nor discretion in the generality of singers—A sure way to make up one's losses—A good dinner, and the good effects of one—Deer-stalking—Monsieur Scrope and Monsieur Bunn, Monsieur Auber and Monsieur Balfe—Rehearsals on the French stage—How a prima donna renews her engagement—An author's vanity and interest at variance—The small of your back.

A SLIGHT reference has already been made to the entanglement in which the manager of the winter theatres too frequently finds himself with authors. At this time an offer, previously made, was renewed, of two posthumous dramatic works by Sheridan, for which, as it may reasonably be supposed, a considerable, but not too large, a sum of money was required. The former stipulation of not giving up the MSS. until the money was paid (on the prudent plan laid

down by Sir E. L. Bulwer) was subsequently abandoned ; and I had therefore an opportunity of con-
sulting a gentleman on the subject, quite capable of
decyphering one of the charms which it was stated
the said MSS. contained, viz. Sheridan's handwrit-
ing. Mr. Dunn knew as much of Sheridan as any man
in existence—living at one time under the same roof
with him, and being always in his fullest confidence.
Pretty pickings from that said confidence, if one could
only extract them ! Billy drops an instalment* now

* Mr. Robert Mitchell, who supplied Sheridan with coals, had a
heavy demand against him, long outstanding, and for which he was
bent upon waiting no longer. Mr. Dunn, therefore, finding remonstrance useless, undertook to pilot the coal-merchant to Sheridan's
residence in Hertford-street, and to usher him into the manager's presence. Mitchell attacked Sheridan mercilessly, accused him of having treated him shamefully, and swore he would not leave the house
without the whole of his money. As the amount was several hundred
pounds, and Sheridan had not as many shillings, compliance was more
easily demanded than obtained, and it was consequently necessary to
resort to stratagem—with what success this dialogue will determine.

Sheridan.—" True, my dear Bob, true all you say—I'm really very
" sorry, but I say, Bob, you don't want it ALL to-day, hey ? won't
" a part do ?"

Mitchell.—" No, sir, it won't—*I will* have it all—*I must*—I darn't
" go home without every farthing of it. My wife is distracted, my
" house is beset with creditors, ruin is staring me in the face, and by
" G— I will not leave this room without my money."

Sheridan.—" Come, come, Bob, you're rather too hard upon me—
" to be sure you have drawn a distressing picture, and I am much con-
" cerned by it—wouldn't half do to-day, and a bill for the remainder—
" hey, Bob?"

Mitchell.—" Not a farthing less than my whole bill, Mr. Sheridan ;
" as I said before—I dare not show my face at home without it."

and then, and there are plenty of people ready to pick it up. It was Mr. Dunn's opinion that a part of one of the pieces was in Sheridan's writing, but that the rest decidedly was not. He moreover had never heard either work named, or even remotely hinted at; and wound up his observations by one of his usually shrewd remarks, which settled my enthusiasm in a minute. He stated that, to the best of his belief, not only had Sheridan raised every farthing he possibly could upon every line he had ever written, but that there were wags to be found capable of asserting that he had raised a great deal upon what he had never written. This may be all erroneous, and God forbid that I should underrate any composition, particularly one supposed to emanate from such an inspired source; and as the dramatic productions in question are still, I presume, in existence, and if so, still of course to be purchased, I should be sorry to undervalue them.

Sheridan (*pausing and then apparently much moved*). " Then " would to heaven I could assist you ! I cannot—but (*and here he took* " *a deep dip into his pocket,*) one thing I can, I will, I ought to do— " there," (*taking Mitchell's hand, shaking it, and putting something in* " *it,*) " there—never let it be said, that while Sheridan had a guinea in his " pocket, he refused it to his friend *Bob Mitchell.*" Sheridan seemed agitated, Mitchell stood aghast for a minute or two, then carefully tucked up the guinea in a corner of his leather breeches pocket, forgot his wrongs, and with the familiar expression of " *Bob*" ringing in his ears, he bolted out of the house, and to the latest hour of his life was, in an occasional moment of enthusiasm, fond of displaying " the last " guinea his friend Sheridan had in the world ! !" This is perhaps the greatest feat Sheridan ever did, except when he softened an attorney.

It is a hard task to deal with quacks of the quill—
still harder to deal with writers of acknowledged
powers and merit. My worthy friend Poole once
sent me a piece which, on perusal, I felt assured
would fail. It is a ticklish thing to reject the work
of so able an author as Mr. Poole; for not only do
you call in question *his* capabilities of composition,
but *your own* capabilities of judgment. In apprising
Poole of my misgivings, he was not only naturally
disappointed, but unnaturally indignant, and sent a
mutual friend, (and a d—d good judge by the way,)
John Hamilton Reynolds, to expostulate with me.
He could not have pitched upon a better man, one
who has, to use a familiar saying, more stuff in his
little finger than is to be found in the heads, put together, of one half of those he is compelled to associ-
ate with, and who by such association should rise
up wiser and wittier than they sat down. I put the
piece in Reynolds's hands, with this observation,
" Read it yourself, and if you say I OUGHT to act it,
I " *will*." As Reynolds could not say so, I could not
act it; and it subsequently came out at the Haymarket,
where it " died and made no sign."

But a slight summary of pieces sent to the management of a London theatre for examination, and in
the hopes of approval, during a very short period, will
give my present reader some rough idea of what a
past reader of mine had to wade through. I do not
refer to mine excellent and dearly beloved friend
Frederick Reynolds, who is " alive," and though

through infirmity not "kicking," in comparatively good health, but to poor Morton, now "gathered round the hearthstone of his ancestors," and whose further drolleries, therefore, I may be pardoned for introducing, in addition to a very amusing one given in an earlier part of this book. Mr. Morton returned me, after a careful examination of their pretensions, a packet of manuscripts with his remarks attached to the name of each. The list ran thus :—

Paired Off.—The plan, characters, and dialogue of this piece are by no means objectionable, but I fear it is not up to the mark, for the breadth necessary for a one act piece. The part intended for Mrs. Glover is tame, and what she *could* or *would* do nothing with.

Nicolas Pedrossa.—Sad stuff—to be returned.

The Adventurers.—Not worth adventuring—sure to be damned.

Saucy Alceste.—This piece must belong to my worthy friend *Thompson.* I have unhappily wrecked so many of his pieces, that my spirit is grieved when I am compelled to say, I do not think this up to the mark. Do a good-natured action, by doing an ill-natured one—take the burthen of the refusal on your own sufficient shoulders—for poor as I am, I would give five guineas, if I could honestly say the *Saucy Alceste* would be wafted into Port Drury, by the *aura popularis* of public favour.

Perversion.—Cannot be acted.

Theory and Practice.—The subject of this play is

paper money—but the author's MSS. can never be changed into cash.

The Chimney-piece.—Is a fair farce, and smartly written; the only danger in the piece is the FAR TOO FREQUENT mention of Mrs. Horn. A certain author says, " Push the duke as far as he'll go ;" Mrs. Horn, is pushed too far, and verifies Sheridan's words, " when these fellows get hold of a good thing, " they never know when they've enough of it." I have pencilled at the end a finishing speech, which, if the author pleases, is at his service. (N. B. This was by Rodwell, and was played with much success.— A. B.)

The Way to get Mad.—May be returned to Mr. Heaven-knows-who, for I can't even make out the author's name, but his address is ————.

Woman.—An elegant bit of French comedy—the intrigue clever, the dialogue smart and nimble. In the hands of Gautier, Lafont, and Leontine Fay, it could not fail of being effective—but (d—n it, there's always a " but") Sir Harry Hauton would be far too gay for Farren, and Cooper could not be feathery enough for *Sir George,* nor would the blandishments of *Lady Emily* be ably sustained by Miss Phillips. Its merits (could it be well played,) I think, entitle it to a hearing; but whether that hearing would reward the theatre, you as manager must determine.

Everybody's Relation.—I cannot be in love with the piece, whatever I might be with the lady writer.

Whitefeet.—This piece is quite unfitted for representation.

Oratory Tablet.—This I had read, but the contents had escaped my recollection—a bad sign. It is another sad instance of the misapplication of powers to an ungrateful subject. In my opinion, its acceptance could answer no good purpose to either manager or author.

The Iron Shroud.—Avoid it.

Radulph.—An old acquaintance, but he does not improve upon it.

Panthea.—Read the last page! (I did so, and found that six people stabbed themselves in less than six minutes, and four of them were eunuchs! A. B.)

The Ballot.—Written by O'Keefe, in 1809, when nothing was left of his genius but its irregularities and its vulgarities.

The Baron.—Written by his daughter; contains many snatches of talent, but overlaid by mystery and quantity.

Edelbert.—Respectably written—but of what use to Drury Lane would a *respectable Saxon* TRAGEDY be? Certainly none.

The Assassin.—Is unskilful and unavailable.

The Day of Mishaps.—A farce in one act. Should this piece be started, it could only live by its activity. It is a stage coach, and though without a drag, it would not be overturned—but I could not warrant it a run—perhaps *I've lost my place* might be a smarter title to it.

Imbio, or the *Requital.*—Nonsense.

The Refusal.—No better.

The Nervous Man.—A farce rewritten, introducing
a new first act, with a new character, for Power. I
think it improved by the alteration; if you think
with me, I suppose the Dons Farren and Power
must be consulted.   (Written by Bernard, and acted
with much success.—A. B.)

Prince of Naples.—Won't do—any one but you!

The Two Catherines.—The perusal took me more
time to understand than half-a-dozen better ones;
and after all, the riddle was not worth finding out.
It cannot be used.

Pyramus and Thisbe.—This I have seen or read
somewhere—it is whimsical and fairly farcical; but
this *dissection* of the stage I have never seen answer.

The Post Obit of Fame.

" DEAR BUNN,

" This sad evidence of the wreck of genius made
me melancholy; you may say, when the age is in
the wit is out.   I deny it, and am proving it, by
achieving what no existing author dare attempt—
namely, a five act comedy.

" T. M."

One fool makes Many.—The author, I am sorry to
say is, one of " the many."

The Dead Alive.—Quite hopeless.

Murtoch M'Griffin and O'Dogharty in Spain.—
The merit this piece has consists in an intimate

knowledge of the manners, localities, and habits of the Spaniards—warlike and domestic—but the essentials of passion and dramatic interest are not in sufficient force. I think the author overrates his Irish hero. He has called on me, telling me Power has reduced the piece from five to two acts, " at one fell swoop;" it might not be condemned, but could not be attractive.

Matilda de Shabran.—If an opinion (supported by experience) be true, viz. that no music will succeed unless bottomed by a good drama, then this piece is hopeless—next, in reply to the convertability of the music into *Roxalana*, I should say it could not effectively be done, for the Sultan is purely comic. The music of this piece must be, from the nature of the piece, heroic, warlike; for there are dungeons, battlements, and the other clamorous accompaniments which could not fit what is positively comedy. As for *my* piece on the subject, I (as you may guess) converted the *Comedy* into *Farce*, which removes to a greater distance the character of the two pieces. Mine was all *breadth* and *breeches* for Madame Vestris.

Swamp Hall.—This piece I have either read or seen, as all the circumstances are familiar to me. Won't do at all.

The Baby.—Hasty and trivial—the inviting thing is the title, which I think a good one ; but the business is commonplace.

Podesta.—This play could not be advantageously

acted. The plot is complicated—to an audience inex-
plicable; it has all the confusion of an Italian feud:
but none of the grandeur of a *Fiesco,* or a Foscari.
There is some poetry, some dramatic power, and
some dramatic situations, but not enough to balance
the defects.

By the King's Order.—A bustling affair, but very
dangerous : as when there is *any* hope, however
small, I never wish to exclude it, it may be worth
while for you to run it over. (N. B. I *did* run it
over, and found *none.*—A. B.)

Marriage à-la-Mode.—As far as embodying the
pictures of Hogarth, the piece is well contrived, but
the agency of dialogue is very dull, and unrelieved by
the least gleam of gaiety. A recollection of the
paintings will convince you that coarseness and the
tragic effects of adultery and murder are dangerous
tools to handle dramatically. As a drama (independ-
ently of pictorial reference) it is very humble.

Women as they are.—Are very bad.

This list comprises but a small batch of the many
I was favoured with from my facetious and yet dis-
cerning officer. Having passed away from the stage
of life,* to the infinite regret of all lovers of the
other stage his writings had so long adorned and
upheld, the publication of these his comments " can-

* Another respectable, though uninspired, writer for the stage, at
the period when Morton so amused the town, died this season. Mr·
Boaden was a man of excellent taste, a scholar, and a passable dramatist—but pompous and prosy.

not touch him further;" and to prevent the possibility of annoying the living, I have studiously avoided mentioning the names of the authors. The declaration of the titles of their pieces will serve two purposes; it will enable the authors of them to improve upon what was imperfect, and managers to avoid their many imperfections. It may, therefore, readily be believed that where some hundreds of pieces of the quality herein described are submitted to the decision of the manager of a theatre, the task of deciding, to say nothing of reading, is quite harassing enough.

On the day of my last benefit in Drury Lane Theatre, (March 7, 1839,) the subjoined letter was addressed to me, signed by every member of the company; and as the devil is invariably painted blacker than he is, it is here introduced in testimony of such an ancient and respectable adage:

TO ALFRED BUNN, ESQ.

" Theatre Royal Drury Lane,
" March 7th, 1839.

" DEAR SIR,

" We, the undersigned performers, &c. of Drury " Lane Theatre, take this opportunity of expressing " the great satisfaction we have derived in witnessing " the spirit, enterprise, and unremitting industry " evinced by you during a season replete with diffi- " culties—difficulties which your activity, talent, and " manly perseverance, could have alone overcome. " As a very small and inadequate testimonial of the " feeling by which we are all animated, we request

" of you to accept our best services *gratuitously*
" on the night of your benefit, with the warmest
" wishes that the receipts of the house may exceed
" your most sanguine expectations.
                " We remain,
                    " Dear Sir,
                        " Your faithful Servants."
        (Here follow the signatures of the entire company.)

As a matter of course I subjoin my reply, and
very much regret that the necessities of the treasury
were such, that I returned into it the handsome sum
this suspension of a night's salary came to, to enable
me to pay the salaries of its subscribers, instead of
expending it, as I wished to do, on some memorial of
their good feeling.

                        " Theatre Royal Drury Lane,
                            " March 7th, 1839.
    " LADIES AND GENTLEMEN,
    " I have received your letter of this day's date,
" more complimentary to me from the spirit of its
" contents than from any pecuniary value that could
" possibly be attached to them. The approbation
" of so many professors, (most of whom have toiled
" so many years with me,) imparts a feeling of more
" real gratification than any event of my life.
    " Great as have been, and are, the difficulties to
" contend with, and useful as your handsome contri-
" bution might be, I prefer expending it on some

" token whereon may be engraved, as the memory of
" it is on my heart, the names of those who have
" done me so much honour.
" Believe me,
" Ladies and gentlemen,
" Your obliged and faithful friend,
" A. BUNN."

On the same day a curious and equally agreeable
circumstance happened—(indeed on this day only
one *dis*agreeable circumstance occurred, which to a
bénéficier is particularly so, *viz.* that it snowed
without cessation both day and night.) It is not
unknown to the public generally, but especially
to persons of *ton*, that several fashionable librarians
at the west end of the metropolis are extensive spe-
culators in theatres. The principal parties are
Messrs. Andrews, Sams, Mitchell, Ebers, and Hook-
ham. The three first are large dealers, the two first
the largest, and considered to be the wealthiest and
most important. This may appear very strange to
the uninitiated, who may not be able to understand
what one man can have to do with another man's
business, and above all, with such an exclusive kind
of business as all theatrical business must be: but
they may depend upon it there is barely one of the
gentlemen herein named, who would not rather give
up the proceeds of his own calling, than resign all
connexion with mine.

There is a class of people in this town (as elicited

in the recited conversation of a lady of rank with
Charles Kean) who affect not to know where a theatre
is, unless they obtain their information " at the library; and having obtained it, would not even drive,
much less walk, there, although it should be considerably nearer their own houses than the said library. There are more reasons than one for this
assumed affectation; but the principal reason after
all is, that if they take their boxes at the office of
the theatres, they must exhibit their purses; but
if they go to Bond Street, or to the corner of St.
James's Street, their names get into the books of the
manager and the librarian at the same time. CREDIT,
credit is the great consideration with this part of the
community. Putting your hand in your own " till"
is with them a serious matter; but putting it in the
till of other people is not of the slightest consequence; and there are few of this *genus* who would
not much rather promise to pay a librarian five or
six guineas for a box, than actually pay a manager
half that sum for one. With some of them the said
amount—whole or half, no matter—is vital during the
season, for all the necessary amusements of town;
and at the end of the season they make a point of
bolting out of it—with others, fashion, carelessness,
habitude, convenience, all combine to make it more
agreeable to put their hands in their pockets but
once a year, and then they do not at all object to
pay pretty good interest for so doing. There is a
particular set, (pretty well known to the librarians

by this time, or they ought to be,) who, not at all objecting to a *lee*tle bit of fleecing, think it may be as well done occasionally with an opera-box as with a dice-box, there being plenty of "play" in both. To supply, therefore, the wants and wishes, to consult the laziness and the lounging, and now and then the depravity of the *beau monde*, these gentlemen have become the principal managers of the principal London Theatres. Nor is it by the accommodation they render to the world of fashion alone that their state has become so important; it is by the assistance they have rendered, and at all times do render, the manager, as well as his patrons, that they have "grown so great." Their vast speculations in the Opera House are almost as well known as the Opera House itself, and they are, comparatively speaking, as extensive dealers in the property of minor establishments. The immense sums vested by them annually in her Majesty's Theatre have become so public, through the notoriety of Messrs. Chambers' affairs, that no indelicacy whatever could be charged against me were I to enter upon the subject, and to allege that the funds and securities of some two or three of the librarians herein cited have been the sole means of there being latterly an Italian Opera in London. Laying aside that view of the case, and not unnecessarily mixing myself up in other people's business, let me apply myself more immediately to mine own.

I have for several years past had dealings to a

large amount with Messrs. Andrews, Sams, and
Mitchell, and for the satisfactory result of those
dealings I cannot do better than refer any sceptic to
the parties themselves, by whose decision I shall be
perfectly content to abide. They generally speculate
on the character of the management—they did so
upon mine, and I should wish no better bit of fun
than to compare the extent of their dealings with
my predecessors and successors (including " Shakspeare and Shakspeare's representative") and those
they had with me. It would furnish another valuable leaf to the memorandum book of " my learned
friend," Mr. Serjeant Talfourd. It is a source of un-
speakable satisfaction to know that gentlemen who
have placed confidence in your exertions for many
years, by risking, during that period, thousands upon
thousands of pounds, have never had that confidence
abused, have not regretted its application, and not
only have not lost by their enterprise, but " put
money in their purse."

The reader will be inquiring probably what all
this has to do with the 7th March, 1839: he shall
know. Messrs. Andrews and Sams having been some
time at variance upon points of business, upon which
1 have nothing and wish to have nothing to advance,
perceived at last, like very prudent men, that their hostility was prejudicial to their respective interests, and
extremely beneficial to the interests of other people.
It was, therefore, suggested by many well wishers
of both, that a reconciliation should be effected

between them, which was accordingly done; and, with the view of completing a matter so auspiciously begun, Mr. Sams invited the principal librarians, and the principal managers they dealt with, (Laporte and myself,) to a dinner on the day in question. I have long been intimate with both these gentlemen—with Mr. Andrews probably most so; and while in Mr. Sams I have invariably found good faith in dealing, and good fellowship out of it, I need scarcely add that the name of Mr. Andrews is a passport wherever liberality in business, and all the distinguishing qualities of human nature, are to be found. It was gratifying to me, therefore, to assist at so agreeable a ceremony as the re-union of (what Mr. Lover has written so delightfully, and Michael Blood warbles so delightfully)—

> " Hearts that had been long estranged,
> " And friends that had grown cold!"

We sat down to the dinner-table, at one end of which was Mr. Sams, and at the other Mr. Andrews; and between them were to be found what the *Morning Post* calls " all the delicacies of the season;" and while it was pleasant to see the attention paid by each to those they were surrounded by, it was still pleasanter to see the marked attentions they paid each other. *Mister* Andrews and *Mister* Sams, emphasised with an extra degree of " French polish," resounded through the room with the demolition of every mouthful; but while all this denoted the display and the acceptance of hospitality, it seemed to me to be mixed up with a prodigious quantity of reserve, to which the following exquisite passage may be well applied :

> *Bru.*—" How he received you, let me be resolved.
> *Luc.*—" With courtesy, and with respect enough ;
> " But not with such familiar instances
> " As he hath used of old !
> *Bru.*   " Thou hast described
> " A hot friend cooling : ever note, Lucilius,
> " When love begins to sicken and decay,
> " It useth an enforced ceremony !"

—such seemed to me to be the case on the present occasion, and however one might regret any difference, or rejoice at any arrangement of it, one could not help an inward titter at the *modus operandi*. At a moment when it was palpable that outward form and inward feeling were still a little at variance, the following view of the case was taken in shorthand by a party present on the occasion :

RECONCILIATION DINNER

GIVEN BY MR. SAMS TO MR. ANDREWS, MARCH 7, 1839.

MR. SAMS.—*Mister* Andrews, I can strongly
          Recommend this carrot soup !
MR. ANDREWS.—" Pins " of late have gone so wrongly,
          I fear appetite will droop.
MR. ANDREWS.—But, *Mister* Sams, permit me—
          These smelts, sir, are not bad !
MR. SAMS.—To a tittle you have hit me,
          If some turbot you will add.

Mr. Sams.—*Mister* Andrews, try the mutton,
Why, to kill it was a grief!
Mr. Andrews.—I *for once* would turn a glutton,
Had it been a round of beef!
Mr. Andrews.—But *Mister* Sams, allow me,
Do try this nice *ra-goût!*
Mr. Sams.—(*Aside.*) The fellow thinks to cow me—
Well, I don't care if I do!
Mr. Sams.—*Mister* Andrews, now suppose we
Mar no more each other's wealth!
Mr. Andrews.—And, *Mister* Sams, propose we
Each other's better health!
Mr. Sams.—*Mister* Andrews, here's to you, sir!
(*Then aside.*) It has gone off pretty well :
Mr. Andrews.—*Mister* Sams, let none abuse, sir—
(*Then aside.*) *Mister* Sams may go to h—ll.

The day following my benefit, and the little
amusements herein detailed that were incidental to
it, was marked by a fearful event in the dramatic
world, although not immediately affecting the interests of the British stage—the frightful suicide, by
Monsieur Nourrit, (one of the most accomplished
singers that ever lived,) by throwing himself from a
window of the hotel in which he was living at
Naples, and dashing himself to pieces. The non-
renewal of his engagement at the *Académie Royale,*
Paris, produced in his mind a considerable degree of
despondency, which was heightened into frenzy by
the singular and sudden popularity of his successor,
Monsieur Duprez ; and these combined effects ope-
rating upon a mind of no very peculiar strength,
drove it beyond the confines of reason. It has been

said of a dancing-master that he has no occasion
whatever for a head, unless it be to enable him to
look like other people, and to have a peg to hang his
hat upon. Pretty much the same may be said of the
greater part of vocalists, modern or ancient;* but
Nourrit was a partial exception to so general a rule,
and threw into the exquisite powers of his art the
resources of a refined taste and a fervid imagination.
I have not heard Monsieur Duprez, though I have
heard great things *of* him; but in common with
thousands of his enthusiastic admirers, I have listened
with more delight, than I suspect I am likely to feel
again, to the enchanting tones of *Adolphe Nourrit*.
Monsieur Duponchel, the present director of the
Académie, whose brains would make but a very slight
addition to the contents of the dancing-master's hat,
was severely commented upon for allowing Nourrit to
leave a theatre where he was so beloved, and with
the business of which he was so mixed up; but if,
as I have heard, the separation arose from the in-

---

* I had a principal male and female singer once playing in *Rob
Roy*, under my management, who on the same evening thus acquitted
themselves. The lady wishing to introduce *The Soldier Tired*, and
being in some doubt as to an appropriate place for its introduction,
chose the scene of the interview and separation of *Diana Vernon* and
Francis Osbaldiston in the first act, and as she left the stage, she simply said, " There he goes, putting me in mind of a *Soldier Tired!*"
    The gentleman who represented *Francis* has to say, "Rashleigh is
" my cousin ; but, wherefore I cannot divine, he is my bitterest
" enemy." But he preferred his own punctuation, which ran thus:—
" Rashleigh is my cousin, but wherefore I cannot divine : he is my
" bitterest enemy."

creased expectations of the warbler, a manager,
however great a fool he may be in other respects,
cannot well be considered one in this, where he
protects the treasury and the reputation of the theatre
at the same time :—I say reputation, because there
were plenty of people to be found in Paris who
thought Nourrit's *se*cession amply compensated for
by Duprez's *ac*cession.

We have been enumerating (nothing like a WE in all
scriptory cases, as sounding more important, although
not in reality less egotistical than *I*, albeit it may seem
so,) some curious circumstances that *have* occurred
to managers of London Theatres, and I will now mention one more that occurred, as curious as any that
have been, or can be, recited. On reaching the theatre
on Tuesday evening, March 12, 1839, I found on my
desk a very small brown paper parcel addressed " To
A. Bun, Sqr.," looking very dirty and very suspicious,
and weighing wherewithal sufficiently heavy as to
increase such suspicion.   The town had at that
moment been partly astonished and partly amused by
" Madame Vestris's infernal machine," and the
narrow escape the party had who first opened it.
Having no desire for any similar experiment, I hesi-
tated in unfolding this mysterious packet, more
particularly when my messenger described the dingy
looking fellow that left it at the stage-door, with an
injunction that it was " to be delivered into Mr.
Bunn's *own* hands."   However, overcoming any apprehensions of gunpowder, and setting whatever of the

combustible it might contain to the amount of a mere squib, I sent for my under-treasurer, and in his presence opened some half dozen pieces of paper, each tightly bound by some half dozen pieces of string, and inside the last I found,

					£	s.	d.
32 Sovereigns	-	-	-	-	32	0	0
10 Half Sovereigns		-	-		5	0	0
13 Half Crowns -			-		1	12.	6
27 Shillings	-		-		1	7	0
1 Sixpence	-		-		0	0	6
					40	0	0

I began to think that this was the contribution of some eccentric supporter of Drury Lane, anxious to reward its manager's exertions, yet, with a rooted modesty, anxious to conceal his name : but such an occurrence was so totally without precedent, that I gave up that conjecture in utter hopelessness. Then I bethought me of more than one performer who had literally robbed me to such an extent; and pondered over the probability of this being a return thereof, arising out of a touch of conscience; but as what little consciences most of them *have* got are very seldom touched, I abandoned that surmise with even a greater degree of despair than I first of all entertained it. *By* whom it was sent, or *for* whom it was sent, I am totally unable to tell : it was added to the general receipt of the exchequer for the benefit of all those having any claim on it, though the chances are it was forwarded for my own individual advantage. The donor is hereby thanked, be he or she whoever he or she may ; and I can only say, if many more such had made their appearance, the disasters of Drury Lane Theatre would have been obviated or provided against. Now, is not a manager's life an odd life, and are not the people he has to deal with a very odd set of people ? and if he should do odd things, can no excuse be found for him by your pickers and stealers, and evil speakers, and liars and slanderers ? I can only say, if there is none, there should be.

The great patronage which had been extended to Mr. Van Amburgh personally, added to the reputation which his performance had obtained, inspired that gentleman with a very grateful feeling towards his patrons, and with the natural wish of manifesting it. He consulted me upon the subject, and seemed to labour under one difficulty, and that was the mode of evincing it. In selecting the obvious one, he was only fearful of appearing ostentatious, where he but wanted to appear thankful ; and his scruples having been over-come, a DINNER was determined upon. What a salve for every sore is that said commodity, a dinner ! especially in a country where more are given, and more devoured at them, than in most parts of the habitable globe. Exclusive of all the considerations enumerated in the famous song upon the subject, there are few disagreeables in this life so rooted, that you may not " drown them in the bowl." I do not deliver this opinion from any particular propensity of mine own that way inclining, having neither the disposition nor the constitution essential to the qualifications of a thorough imbiber; but from observation, which convinces me that few things can impede the progress of, or dispute the virtue to be found in, a set dinner. Animosities of the bitterest kind have been reconciled, affections cold and blighted have been rekindled, dealings doubted have had their doubts removed, estrangements have warmed into regards, the tide of the eye has ebbed, the sigh of the heart has been allayed, and the sunniest smile has become brighter, over the sociableness of the festive board. There are those to be met with, who would even "consort with their eternal enemy" for the purpose of partaking of it. It is one of those vast contributions to individual comfort in which there is no hypocrisy; where, in the midst of self-indulgence, so little of selfishness is to be traced, one half of its pleasure being derived from seeing that your neighbour is faring as well as yourself. It is remarkable what effect the good things of this life have over the sternest souls, and how soon an introduction of them into the corporeal system oils and unfastens the rustiest recesses of the heart. But as we are preaching a doctrine none will be found to dispute, let us proceed from the theory to the practice.

Mr. Van Amburgh gave a splendid dinner on Wednesday, March 13, in the spacious saloon of Drury Lane Theatre, a day in Lent especially selected, because though Lord John Russell could make our doors fast, he had not the power to make US fast. The invitations were extended, with respectful application, to the many noblemen and gentlemen who had admired his performances, and to the whole *dramatis personæ* of Drury Lane Theatre who had assisted in them ; and as, in addition to the recited advantages of a dinner, amusements of another kind came in with the dessert, it may easily be believed that the room was crowded to suffocation. Few persons having the power, object to pay for a good " spread," but I should presume there is not a mortal on earth to be found, who would not partake of one if it be given to him. The amusements on the present occasion consisted of some of the finest music sung in the finest style that the ear of revelry need listen to ; for it is marvellous how fertile is the fancy, how exuberant the taste, and how incessant the desire to please, of a performer in the halls of festivity, when compared to his exertions on the public stage. Here comes out the practical part of my argument, for, while a performer often goes through the duties of his profession, on their immediate scene of action, doggedly and without inclination, his better nature is sure to prevail with his transfer from the scenic to the festal board, where, though his hunger be easily appeased, his thirst for distinction beyond his brethren is only assuaged by using his utmost efforts to effect it.

Our party could lay claim to high rank and high

talent amongst many of its number, and but one
opinion prevailed—that Mr. Van Amburgh's manli-
ness of character and undaunted nerve were accompanied with so mnch modest reserve, unmixed with
the slightest alloy of vanity, as to make it a matter of
great regret that the dinner was not given TO him
instead of BY him. It was certainly proposed by one,
seconded by another, and maintained by all, that, on
the common score of reciprocity, the compliment
should be returned; and in a still more substantial
way than by dirtying a plate—viz. by the presentation of a piece of clean plate; but lovers' vows and
dicers' oaths are not less to be depended upon, than
are the good resolves entered into at a dinner-table.
We demolished my friend's luxuries, and felt that we
ought to give him an opportunity of demolishing ours.
We considered his pre-eminent courage entitled to
some solid acknowledgment of our estimation of
that noble quality, and we promised to allot him the
task of receiving, and ourselves the pleasure of giving
it—but all that we felt and promised died away with
the occasion that gave rise to such excitement.
The recoil from entertainments of this description is
as remarkable as the inkling to the enjoyment of
them, in the first instance: hit the iron while it is
hot, and you may fuse it into what shape you please,
but suffer it once to cool, and there is an end of its
pliancy. When a man is filling his mouth, he has
not the slightest objection to your emptying his
pocket; but only once suffer " digestion to wait on

appetite," and his system undergoes a most extraordinary change. A man duly gorged is in a state
of inaction, his soul has sunk into his stomach, and
all his notions of the *ideal* are absorbed in his con-
victions of the *real*.

It had been slightly hinted to me at this time, that
a good melo-drama might be put together from the
admirable publication, by Mr. Scrope, on DEER-
STALKING. How the notion only crudely mentioned,
and never seriously entertained, could have reached
the ears of the author, I have no idea ; that it did so,
the courteous offer contained in the subjoined letter
will testify :

" SIR,

" Having been informed that it is your intention
" to dramatise some part of my publication on *Deer-*
" *Stalking*, I beg to say that I will readily afford
" you any information or assistance you may require,
" should you persist in your design.

" I think some of the poaching incidents, such as
" the burning of the sheeting in the lake &c., the
" stalking the deer at bay in the cataract, the
" witch of Ben-y-gloe, contain in themselves mate-
" rials for dramatic effect, if skilfully and scienti-
" fically treated. Your writer might begin with
" Lord Reay's breakfast at the poacher's.

" But *deer-stalking* is now so well understood by
" the higher orders of society, and indeed theoretically,
" if not practically, by all sportsmen, that some in-

" structions from an experienced sportsman would
" be absolutely necessary for the complete success
" of your undertaking; and these I shall have great
" pleasure in supplying you with.

　　　　　　　" I am Sir,
　　　　　" Your most obedient Servant,
　　　　　　　　　" WILLIAM SCROPE.
" 13, Belgrave Square,
" March 15, 1839."

I was not dissuaded from the attempt by any nonsensical apprehensions of abuse for such production,
having long since passed through ordeals of that
nature—scathed or unscathed is not a matter of
the slightest consequence. The popularity of Mr.
Scrope's book, and the able way in which he has
treated the subject, were inducements to the undertaking; but the preparation would have occupied
much time, and incurred great expense, without em-
ploying that portion of the company whose talents
it was advisable to bring before the public, and on
which our main reliance was placed.

I had been occupied for three months past on the
composition of an opera, in conjunction with Mr. Balfe,
a great portion of which was already in the hands of
the copyist, as had been the *répertoire de la scène*
in the various departments for some time past. As
respects my own share in the transaction, it may not
perhaps behove me to say that I never felt more
sanguine upon the result of a composition, and was
convinced that whatever favour had been extended to

"*The Maid of Artois*" would, at least, be entertained for this. Making every allowance for the
vast distinction between Madame Malibran and
Madame Albertazzi, I yet felt as assured of my
libretto as if it had run fifty nights. Of Mr. Balfe's
music in it I fearlessly assert, that, whenever it may
be heard, it will be admitted to be his *chef d'œuvre*,
and firmly fix his reputation amongst the best of our
native composers.

With such means at my disposal as the great extent of the subject enabled me to resort to, I had
every reason to calculate on more than ordinary success; and having entered into an engagement with
Perrot and Carlotta Grisi, to give animation to the incidental matter, there seemed to me a prospect,
with the combination of so much material and novelty,
of realising what had now become unusual good fortune, and which the triumphs of *Gustave* and *The
Jewess* had lulled us into the belief of being ordinary
matters. In spite of all the losses and disasters to
which this season had been subject, I was sanguine
enough (mine ancient failing) to believe that they might
to a great extent be relieved by the result of the present undertaking. Having elsewhere been dilating
on the vanity of authors, it would not be altogether
unnatural for the reader to dilate upon mine; but
should he feel disposed to do it ever so much, I have
unfortunately argument in store to silence him. We
are all a vain set of varlets, beyond a doubt—vanity
is the main ingredient of our nature; and in a theatre

every author thinks he writes best, every actor that he acts best, and every manager that he manages best. When a man, however, has to combine in his own person any two of these qualifications, the contention between interest and *amour propre* is a very peculiar one ; and standing, therefore, in the double capacity of author and manager, I was compelled to draw a delicate line of distinction. During the progress of this new speculation, Auber's opera of *Le Lac des Fées*, which had been long in preparation at the *Académie Royale*, Paris, was announced for production, the night of which was eventually fixed for Easter Monday. In the middle of the preceding month, February, I had met at D'Almaine's table the Parisian proprietor, by purchase, of Auber's score, who had come over to possess D'Almaine's house of a similar advantage in this country ; and though unable to name any day when its first representation might be safely looked forward to, we made arrangements for an early transmission of a copy of the music, with a view to its introduction at Drury Lane. Those who are acquainted with the slow coach progression of theatrical novelties, during their stages of preparation, in the larger theatres of Paris, will admit that I could not suffer the resources of Drury Lane to be paralysed, and all its operations to lie dormant, while matters were only being agitated in Paris. Those who are not acquainted with their movements shall be told them.

From about a year to a year and a half, before

one of their great works makes its appearance,
the author and composer having made all the necessary arrangements with the manager, an initiatory rehearsal is called. Some of the principals, who have
nothing else to do that morning, attend; and after a
few questions about the weather, the purchase of
gloves, the cut of a coat, and some favoured *rendez-
vous*, the interview with each other ends in the grand
consideration with all Frenchmen, *où dinez-vous au-
jourd'hui?*—and just as they have settled that important point, and are about to leave the theatre,
they casually inquire of each other, *Eh bien, comment va le nouvel opera?*—FIRST REHEARSAL. At the
next they all meet again,.and after many very similar discussions, they all turn into the *Café de l'Opera*
for gossip—SECOND REHEARSAL. Subsequently the
chiefs of departments assemble with the mechanical
people, and after disposing of a cup of coffee or a
basin of *bouillon*, owing to the intensity of the cold
on so large a stage, they get rid of a THIRD REHEARSAL.
After many such meetings with such results, matters
are a little more seriously entered upon. One act
begins to make its appearance, and, having drawn
" its slow length along," is relieved by the second.
Then comes the introduction of the grand lever upon
which all its movements turn—the pleasure of a
prima donna, and the pleasure of her *amant*. She
has certain stipulations to make, before she can consent to be ready by any particular time ; and, while
naturally fearful of offending against law, she sticks

pretty close to custom. She can be ill whenever she pleases, and can get fifty doctors to give her fifty certificates that she is not expected to live the night out. The manager, therefore, is entirely at her mercy; and by coquetting and coying with him, she may defeat all his arrangements, without possessing the shadow of right to mar a single one of them. If her dress does not please her, she will contrive to have half a dozen made until some particular one *does:* but if her perquisites are not enough, or if her engagement be near its termination, the Lord have mercy on the director! He may fix twenty different nights for the performance of his opera, but she will provide twenty different excuses for its delay; and as in some instances such delay may be ruinous, he finds it far better to yield to any stipulations, than by procrastination to incur a greater loss than those stipulations would amount to. The case simply stands thus. The *entrepreneur* fixes a given day for the production of a novelty, when the principal singer is taken suddenly ill, and sends a medical certificate of her indisposition. The manager is disposed to look upon this, what it really is, as a trick, but he has only his own conjectures to assist him; he considers very justly that her time with him being nearly expired, she is careless as to her remaining performances, and with this impression on his mind he confers with her lover. If he escape having a sword run through him, he at least meets with a full justification of the lady's conduct, and plenty of abuse, for

expecting any one to sing in such a state of health ;
and as soon as wrath has given way to reason, a respectful and insinuating inquiry is made, whether
any inducement can be held out to prevail upon her,
the lady, to MAKE AN EFFORT. Though plumply negatived at first, the matter is reconsidered ; and while
she is still too unwell to be spoken to on business,
he will endeavour to persuade her ; and after a visit
or two more, an additional tender inquiry, a few
hints, and eventual demands, the business is settled.
I could name a French singer, whose article of engagement was on the eve of expiration, and who obtained a renewal of it for three years, solely by this
pretty process.

In the midst, therefore, of all these rehearsals, and
the scenes they lead to, the public is regaled week
after week, and day after day, with the promise
of the new opera on a certain night. On that night
they are promised it another, without the show of
apology, or the assignment of any cause : and between
the real perplexities, the opposed difficulties, and the
many absurdities incidental to the French stage, it is
no uncommon thing for a grand opera to be twelve and
fifteen months in preparation. But all this matters
little to its excheqner, where no rent is paid, where a
large Government allowance is accorded, and where
the spirit of the people is purely dramatic.

With a knowledge of all these probabilities, I may
almost say certainties, it was impossible for me to
delay or to impede the preparations entered upon for
the production of my own opera ; and, leaving myself

totally out of the question, it was neither delicate nor just to Mr. Balfe to do so. In the midst, therefore, of the utmost exertions for its speedy performance, we were astounded by receiving the unalterable determination and arrangement of the Paris director to bring forth *Le Lac des Fées* on Easter Monday. Its success was such, that, with the usual want of faith in anything national, I was beset by all, begging me to lay aside my own work, to make way for that of Monsieur Scribe. *Personally* speaking, there could not be a question as to the line of conduct I ought to pursue—*professionally* there were many. It is pretty clear that if I had attempted to stuff my own work down the throats of the people, in preference to one by so renowned an author, I should have received, whatever else I might have merited, unmeasured abuse, and, by giving way to him, I should probably receive but little credit.* I had, however, to consult Balfe, to whose reputation and pocket the production

* My darling old friend Reynolds, to whom I had read my opera, and who was pleased to express himself in high terms of it, sent me these few lines on my withdrawing it, which made amends for all my disappointment :

" My dear Bunn,

" Wonders will never cease ! ! for at last I have discovered an au-
" thor without *vanity* ; and his name is Alfred Bunn. Who else
" would have consented to the putting aside his own opera, and bring-
" ing out another, with all grand appurtenance, &c. ? Certainly
" *none* of the dramatic witlings that used to meet in conclave against
" him.

" Ever, ever yours,

" F. R."

of his opera was important; and finding that, with
extreme good taste, he instantly gave preference to
Monsieur Auber, I could do no less than follow his
example by giving way to Monsieur Scribe. This
sudden derangement of all my plans, owing to the
outcry made by other people, and in violation of my
own judgment, led to its being made known to the
public after the following fashion, enough in itself to
satisfy the veriest theatrical cormorant that ever
existed :

" In rehearsal, and will speedily be produced, with
" every possible advantage of scenery, machinery,
" dresses, and decorations,
" AUBER'S LAST GRAND OPERA OF
" THE FAIRY LAKE,
" (*Performed for the first time at the Académie
Royale on Monday last.*)
" An arrangement having been made with Messrs.
" D'Almaine and Co., proprietors of the music, by
" which its exclusive performance is confined to this
" theatre, its adaptation has been undertaken by
" Mr. H. R. Bishop, and will be supported by
" Madame Albertazzi,
" M. M. W. Balfe, Mr. Giubilei,
" Mr. Allen, Mr. Stretton, Mr. S. Jones,
" And Miss Romer :
" supported by the entire choral and orchestral
" strength of the establishment, and numerous auxi-
" liaries. It will be followed by

" A NEW BALLET,
" *In which the most celebrated dancers of Europe,*
" MONSIEUR PERROT AND MDLLE CARLOTTA GRISI,
" will have the honour of making their first appear-
" ance upon the English stage."

There are but few of my readers, presuming them
to be of a theatrical turn of mind, who have not
heard Liston's delicious exclamation, " Between two
" stools you *may* happen to hurt the small of your
" back." And as there was never an instance in which
that respectable adage was more completely verified,
they shall be told how the fall hurt MINE !

189

CHAPTER VI.

Various opinions of various people—The invariable result of a London
season—Madame Albertazzi's style of correspondence—The exact
nature of a commonwealth—The loss of one week multiplied by three
—Singing small—Turning the tables on Mr. Balfe—Difference between singing *with* acting and *without* it—Glory—Strawberry Hill
—Horace Walpole and other great men—Shakspeare's birth-day
—A screw loose—Musical fools—Value of an oration—A man ignorant of his wife's situation—*Lapsus linguæ*—An invitation accepted—Lucubrations of a literary friend—The last lay of the
Minstrel—Its benefits, and its acknowledgment—Letter to the
Guardsman—Landseer and the lions—Men making beasts of themselves—Garcia and De Beriot—A tiger—Royal marriage *in pros-
pectu*—Penny postage—England going to the devil.

IT is singular (and it would be diverting to a manager
if it were not done at his expense) to hear the various
opinions which various people deliver on the probable chances of a London season, in either of the
patent theatres. I have seldom met with a professional man, who, in delivering his judgment on the
subject, did not regulate it by passing events, without looking into their causes, or examining their

consequences. If, at the moment of conversation, the theatre happens to be doing well, the concluding sentence of his remarks is, " Come, now you " can afford to lose a little ;" if things happen to be looking extremely black, the only consolation held out to you is, " Well, you must expect to lose just now." The universal impression on minds that *won't* reflect, and minds that *can't* reflect, is thus summed up. Every soul you meet after your season has begun badly, attempts to comfort you with this observation, " You must always expect to lose *before* Christmas." When this period has passed by, and you have had a good four or five weeks' business, and with the return of the children to school the returns of the theatre drop off in proportion, you are retorted upon, " Oh! you must always expect to lose *after* Christ-" mas." Then, as you progress through Lent, you are compelled to hear, " No money is ever made at this " time of the year :" and finally, when Passion-week has flown over, you are regaled with the last bit of managerial alleviation that can be extended, " It has " always been so; nothing is ever done *after* EASTER !" Thus, according to the general impression, the only glimpse of BLUE SKY in the atmosphere of nine months is the single month of the Christmas holidays ! One month's gain to eight months' loss is very easily summed up, but not easily disposed of.

In a general point of view, this calculation is correct, and I have struggled hard in the hopes of falsifying it. I have always tried to make my grand effort at the beginning of the season, and in some cases have greatly succeeded; for if nothing be done by Christmas, one-third of the season has set in with a loss that the other two-thirds cannot possibly make up. But people, supposed to be most acquainted with the matter, and others quite ignorant of it, *will* discuss the subject, and will err in their discussions; and having been once asked by a distinguished nobleman, then attached to the court, "*who wrote Twelfth Night?*" I can account almost for anything I hear and see.

Albertazzi, who had been engaged for two months from Easter, did not arrive at the stipulated time, and, when she *did* arrive, was not equal to her duty* (more managerial delights!) and when she *did* appear,

---

* The following is a transcript of Madame Albertazzi's communication on the subject, not introduced to disparage her, for I always found her an obliging, pleasant creature; and, without any desire to be Monsieur Albertazzi, I join my own admiration with that of her thousands of admirers. The style of the letter is what tickled my fancy.

"April 4, 1839.

" DEAR BUNN,

" Is it not possible to defer my appearance until Monday? I can " assure you I am not in a fit state to sing. I should not be able to do " myself justice. On Monday I promise you to be in fine voice, and " in good condition for all you may require! Grant me this favour, " and I will sing anything that in any time you may require *year* " *after?*

" Believe me to be, dear Bunn,

" Your devo :

" EMMA ALBERTAZZI."

all interest in her individual performance had died away. It will hardly be believed, that, in such a building as Drury Lane Theatre, some of the finest musical compositions, supported by the best talent the English stage could lay claim to, (including Madame Albertazzi,) and backed by a new and successful Easter piece and a popular ballet, could possibly have only produced on each night's performance such receipts as these :

Monday April 8.—Maid of Palaiseau and Devil on Two Sticks. —(*Madame Albertazzi's night of re-appearance*) - - - - - - • - - £70   19   6
Tuesday, April 9.—Farinelli, the Brigand, and the Little Hunchback - • - - - - -   42   13   0
Wednesday, April 10.—Don Juan and the King of the Mist - - - - - - - -   62   13   6
Thursday, April 11.—Maid of Palaiseau and Daughter of the Danube - - - - - - -   61   8   6
Friday, April 12.—La Sonnambula, Little Hunchback, and King of the Mist - - - - -   51   5   0

The expenses of the theatre all this time were not a farthing less than £200 a night, Albertazzi's salary alone being £50 for every four nights' performance. It will, therefore, be very easily credited, that in the fortnight bearing date from Easter Monday, the losses exceeded £1500. It was impossible, in the midst of this disaster, to produce the only one thing that would relieve it—Auber's *Fairy Lake*—in less time than three weeks ; and if the last two had produced such a frightful damage as that just recorded, the ensuing three must more than double it. A more desperate or dangerous position could not well be conceived; for, to go on with the regular performances would be to incur responsibilities which there were no funds to meet, and to form a republic was even to incur greater difficulties. Some clever fellow (Tom Cooke, I think,) has wisely and wittily remarked that a commonwealth is " COMMON *without* the WEALTH ;" and the truth of this observation cannot be too forcibly impressed upon the minds of all persons aiming at the establishment of one. Then to close the theatre, was to put an extinguisher at once upon management, actor, author, composer, and every soul concerned. I took the advice of several distinguished theatrical men, and I acted upon their advice ; mind me, I do not mean to say that I entirely agreed with them—I only mean to state that I was solely and wholly, and most lustily abused for carrying into effect the thoughts of other people, by announcing a series of *Valentino concerts*, to give me time, without shutting up the theatre, to produce a novelty altogether worthy of it.

The first party who assailed me were the performers, to whose more immediate benefit the result was to be applied. Those who could not sing were apprehensive that the receipts would be swallowed up by those who could ;—those who *could* sing, *wouldn't ;* while the mere dependents were obliged to sing—small.*

* That all singers *don't* " sing small,'' may be gathered from the

The head rebel on the occasion was the gentleman whose fortune I had been the means of making; who without my assistance would have been to this day very likely an unknown man; and who, therefore, on the mere score of reciprocity—gratitude too, if there *be* such a word—to say nothing of prudence, should have been the first to aid the theatre in its dilemma. But Monsieur Balfe thought otherwise, or at all events acted otherwise, declined to cross the stage until some trifling arrear had been paid up,*

perusal of a note I received at this time, which convulsed me with laughter. I never saw the gentleman, but I hear he has musical talents. His former letter I answered verbally through my musical director, but his present letter was so unanswerably cool, that a hearty roar was all it required :

> " 52, Poland Street, Oxford Street,
> " London, April 4, 1839.
>
> " Sir,
>
> " I have written to you frequently for an engagement, and you " have never given me an answer. Well, let that pass !
>
> " I now write to you for an order to see ' *Farinelli*,' for which I " shall feel obliged ; but if you will not give me that, I'm damned " if I shall trouble you any more.
>
> > " I am, Sir,
> > " Your obedient Servant,
> > " CLEMENT WHITE.
>
> " To Alfred Bunn, Esq.
> " Theatre Royal Drury."

* Without wishing my friend Balfe otherwise than well, I could not help smiling when I heard of a similar infliction being visited upon him a month or two afterwards, during his management of the English Opera House. On the night of his own benefit the curtain was unusually late in its ascent ; and when Balfe came forward and told the au-

and then only consented to assist at these concerts, on condition of a new and exclusive engagement being entered into.   Mr. Balfe's example was followed by others; and as that would have been the case in whatever view he had taken of the matter, the view he *did* take was the more reprehensible.

Amongst the many horrors under which a London manager has to groan, pretty freely mentioned and commented upon herein, has yet to be included the character of musical people, who, though bound to sing in the theatre at all times and on all occasions, have the effrontery to stipulate for other terms than their engagement warrants, if required to SING in a concert, though given under the same roof in which they are bound to PERFORM.   Singers who may be in the receipt of two, three, four, or five pounds per night, by virtue of which they are compelled to act *and* sing for three or four hours, to the utmost extent of which their energies are capable, will, if required to sing only a couple of songs in an orchestra, the singing of which will not occupy a quarter of an hour, and the exertion require no excitement, coolly demand ten guineas: they might with equal justice stop you on the highway, and take as much from your purse.

The receipts to the commencement of the *Valen-*

dience that some malicious person had taken away the handle that was to wind up the said curtain, he might more truly have said, that the carpenters were making a handle of him, by refusing to take it up until he did to *them* what Balfe required me to do to *him.*

tino concerts nearly trebled those which had been
produced by a representation of the regular drama—
but they grew " fine by degrees," until the glory of
them, if they ever had any, shared the fate of all
other glory :

> " Glory is like a circle in the waters,
>   Which never ceaseth to enlarge itself,
>   Till by broad spreading it disperse to nought !"

There is an inward satisfaction in the heaviest
visitation that can be inflicted upon one, which
is derived from the consciousness of having done
the best that circumstances would admit of. In
addition to this, is the gratification of finding that
half the world agrees in making such allowance, even
though the other half denies it altogether. I had
plenty of friends to support my movements, though I
had plenty of enemies to ridicule them : but the one
main thing which has always been wanting, and
always will be, was absent on the present occasion—
the *animus* of the people ; but as that has not been
changed, and has been already commented upon, we
had better leave it for pleasanter matter, if any is to
be found. The humiliation entertained by the necessity of resorting to such an expedient to keep open
the doors of a national theatre, was compensated
for, the day after it took place, by a morning's revel
among the wonders and delights of Strawberry Hill,
to the enjoyment of which I was privileged by the
kindness of the kindest of owners, the Earl of Walde-
grave. Oh, the exquisite taste, (finical, though it

has sometimes been dubbed,) the minute research, the nice discrimination, the lavish expenditure, wherever taste demanded it, the rich display, and admirable arrangement (the vast labour of a long life!) manifest in this domain of Horace Walpole. Though some Goth has converted the celebrated Press-room (the Strawberry Hill Press, reader!) into a laundry, and the chapel in the garden has been suffered to go partially into decay, yet, with these exceptions, the place is precisely in the condition in which Walpole left it at his death in 1797. To witness the disposition of a place of so much celebrity, preserved in the very same order it was left in by its gifted owner, who quitted this world exactly a year after one happened to come into it—NOW FORTY-THREE YEARS AGO—is a sight which creates strange feelings and strange thoughts; and when one thinks that Walpole left the world that same year together with Burke, Dodsley,(Burke's respected publisher,) Addison's only surviving daughter, Mason, Mary Wollstonecraft, Wilkes, Mrs. Pope, Macklin, &c., as if with the departure of so much greatness, there was nothing more worth living for,—a notion flits across you that you made your appearance on earth just as all its noblest spirits were going away from it. Then the very room where the *Mysterious Mother* was composed, the author's own copy, printed on the spot, now *in* that room, and the illustrations of it hanging on the walls, to which a reference is made in his own hand writing;—oh, but these be true delights to gaze and to reflect on! Then the famous painting that gave birth to the *Castle of Otranto*, and the study where that romance was engendered! and the Gothic apartments, and the faces of those who owned the gifted author, hanging out from the walls in all the verisimilitude of genius, of rank, of power, of riches, and renown! Of a verity, the contemplation of all this is too absorbing and too ennobling for the miserable manager of such a miserable place as a theatre, and the mention of it only pardonable, perhaps, as involving an occasional reference to the works and the personages of the stage, which is his more immediate province.

On the 17th of the month now under discussion, (April,) I was favoured with the following invitation—a testimony that the honest admission of a man's inability to do justice to the works of the immortal bard did not deprive him of the disposition to pay becoming homage to his natal day, and that it was fully as acceptable as the quackery of others who profess to do what is not in their power:

" The Shakspeare Club present compliments to
" Mr. Bunn, and would feel happy if Mr. Bunn will
" favour the members of the Club by dining with
" them at the Albion Tavern, on Tuesday evening
" next, at half-past seven o'clock, to commemorate
" the natal day of Shakspeare.

    " Albion Hotel,
  " Wednesday, 17 April."

The discussion of theatrical matters, on an anniversary such as this, naturally furnished me with an opportunity of explaining the difficulties I had so often laboured under in repeated attempts to do any degree of justice, in the present state of the stage, to the matchless plays of the great Bard. It enabled me moreover to state a fact, which may be disputed by a set of monkeys, but cannot be controverted by men of sense, that Shakspeare's genius had never before been in such alarming jeopardy at the two national theatres as it was at the present moment, when it was hemmed in by *Valentino Concerts* at Drury Lane, and d——d bad acting at Covent Garden. To such a position of affairs, it may be repeated again and again, has the assumption, the presumption, and the cupidity of many, ay most, of our principal performers, reduced the splendid temples in which the Bard was wont to be so worshipped.

Though matters were now as bad at Drury Lane as they could possibly be, the parties at Covent Garden were by no means lying in clover. Ill blood* had arisen amongst many of the performers, and eventually between the lessee and the proprietors, with whom negotiations were now pending for the

* In evidence of this assertion may be mentioned the fact of Mr. Haines, author of the libretto of Mr. Rooke's Opera of *Henrique*, having waited upon me and conveyed to me an offer of the services of Mr. Harrison, the newly-introduced tenor singer, and the use of the book and music on a reasonable understanding, *owing to the ill-treatment which he alleged all parties had received at the hands of the Covent Garden management ! ! !*

continuation, or rather for the fresh preparation, of a lease. But the stipulations of the said lessee were too preposterous, it should seem, to be listened to. Impressed with the belief that he had elevated the character of the theatre to an unusual degree of reputation and prosperity, and that he could much easier do without a theatre than they could without a manager, his expectations were commensurate with his vanity: while they, conceiving that he had done more for himself than he had for them, preferred losing him altogether rather than conceding to him too much. The negotiation was therefore broken off, and an immediate announcement made of that heart-rending and distressing national event,

THE LAST NIGHTS OF THE PRESENT MANAGEMENT!

It was a wonder the whole country did not go into deep mourning: as it was, they went into fits, but they happened to be fits of laughter—and so the matter speedily died a natural death. The proprietors of the theatre, however, conceiving that some explanation of the business, if only of their own conduct in it, was due to the performers, summoned them together, and gave *such* an explanation as only added to the previous dissatisfaction of that body. A curious circumstance came out at this meeting, not tending in the least degree to allay any excitement of feeling, from its developement not being particularly complimentary to one important branch of the profession. Some communications that had passed between the lessee and the proprietors were read at this meeting; and as it forms no part of my business to question the delicacy of such a proceeding, I shall deal merely with the fact, and that is, the postscript of one of the letters, descriptive of the difficulties of management, contained this fatal truth,—" I can make nothing of your MUSICAL FOOLS."

As the affairs of one house were no secret, I was strongly advised not to let those of the other remain one; and by calling *my* company together, frankly to impart it to them. I might, in justification of all measures that had been taken, allege the fact of my having come into re-possession of the theatre in the beginning of August, by which time the principal performers were engaged elsewhere, the plans of my antagonist *were* nearly completed, and mine *ought* to have been. I might truly have said that, by such engagements, the production of the more expensive commodities of opera, ballet, and spectacle were forced upon me, — that all parties engaged in the establishment had received full pay for more than one hundred and thirty nights; and that when proprietors and performers used more regularly to be paid in full, it was before the King had granted licenses for new theatres, and extended the term of those already in existence, and before the Lord Chamberlain had passed by the King's patents granted to Drury Lane and Covent Garden theatres, by rescinding the most valuable part of their pri-

vileges. Supposing, as I could truly and consci-
entiously have done, that I had advanced all this
argument, what possible end could it have answered ?
Performers are the least reflective of created beings ;
and all the protestations they might have made in
reply to my statements, the breath of the first
person they happened to meet after leaving the scene
of my oration, would have turned the whole current
of their dispositions. No ; the best thing to do was
to act, not preach ; and as any prolongation of the
concert exhibitions could only increase the impending
ruin, it was far better to stop them—and I did so.
I made a conditional arrangement with the parties
involved in the performance of *The Fairy Lake*,
upon the production of which we instantly set to
work. The pledge which had been given to the
public in respect to that opera was on the point of
being redeemed, when intimation reached me of
Madame Albertazzi having apprised her husband of
her intended departure for Paris on a given day, she
being *enceinte*. This was a settler for us all. The
opera could not have been played above a night or two
before the principal performer in it was bent upon
bolting ; and then, had she remained longer, the part
of a *fairy* must have been played by that principal
performer, when she was " in the way that ladies
wish to be who love their lords." I sent, in a
devil of a fury, for the husband, and accused him of
having wantonly and shamefully deceived me, and
of being the cause of my deceiving the public ; but

if it had been the death of me, I must have burst
into a fit of laughter, when the poor fellow assured
me, on his sacred honour, *he had not the remotest
idea his wife was in such a situation !* Thus terminated my managerial career at Drury Lane theatre,
victimized from the first, and unto the last, by the
caprices, the impertinences, the avarice, the conceit,
and the injustice of most with whom I had any
dealings, and wantonly assailed by many a dog with
a slanderous tongue in his mouth.* While these

* By way of returning from grave to gay, I may mention a humorous application of the major part of this expression. Poor Wynne, a
fiddler once in my company, on whose eccentricities Mathews based
many of his most amusing studies of character, having gone to
market to lay in provision for the week, purchased, amongst other
" articles, a *bullock's tongue*, and brought it home dangling on the
edge of his basket, to astonish and delight the partner of his table.
But the tongue had met in the way, it would seem, with a *lapsus
linguæ*, for it was nowhere to be found. Off the poor scraper
started, and, being nearly blind, ran against every person and thing
he met. His first sally was against a huge cart-horse, the stump of
whose docked tail nearly blinded what little sight Wynne had left ;
he stood bowing and apologising, and obtaining no answer, he con-
soled himself by moving on and exclaiming, *sotto voce*, " No gentleman, that's pretty clear, or you would have said something."
Rushing on then into the market, he learned from a little boy that
he had seen a dog run away with the unfortunate tongue. The
poor man became half frantic, and, in the wildness of his wanderings,
nearly upset every person whom he chanced to encounter, till
coming in full contact with a colossal gamekeeper, poor Wynne
spun back a yard or two, and, under the rebound from his body, he
recovered himself by respectfully saying, " I beg you ten thousand
pardons, I'm sure sir,—but do you happen to have seen a dog with

operations connected with the performers and the public were progressing, or being retarded, I had to enter upon discussions connected with the internal arrangements of the establishment, quite as vital as the rest. With every desire to conduct Drury Lane theatre as it had been customary *to* conduct it, (for it was stipulated in my lease that I *should* thus conduct it,) it was impossible so to do,—and the sub-committee who regulate the affairs of that concern viewed with as much indulgence as they could command, and with more concern than they liked to express, the disastrous state of affairs. Unfortunately for the welfare of this theatre—not in the particular instance in question, but generally speaking—this *sub*-committee has over it the occasional control of a *general* committee, which, assembling only on great emergencies, has the power of deranging the plans of the smaller body, which have been matured by stated attendances throughout the season. An assembly of this description was held on Saturday, April 20, at which it was resolved that the theatre should be thrown again into the market at the end of the season, but announced for letting at once ; and that I should be *invited* to do *this* year what I *volunteered* to do *last*—surrender my lease.

a tongue in his mouth ?" The unfeeling fellow, not knowing the cause of the inquiry, and supposing the querist to be joking, coolly answered, " You d—d old fool, did you ever see a dog *without* a tongue in his mouth ! "

I cheerfully assented to the part of their resolutions dependent upon *my* own pleasure, but strongly objected to that part of them dependent upon *theirs ;* and when, pursuant upon my willingness to meet their views, their solicitor brought me the necessary document for signature, I thought it but just to all parties concerned, to address this remonstrance to the sub-committee :

> " Theatre Royal Drury Lane,
> " April 26, 1839.

" GENTLEMEN,

" Mr. Burgess having submitted to me, for signa-
" ture, the document by which it is proposed that I
" should surrender the lease of the theatre ; and per-
" ceiving in it a clause giving you immediate power
" to advertise the property, I inquired of that gentle-
" man if it were probable that you would act at once
" upon that power, and he has stated his belief
" you would.

" Before, therefore, I sign it, I beg to ask whether,
" (without any inquiry as to how such a step may
" affect my future situation—in the midst of my pre-
" paration for the production of an expensive work,
" which may thereby be rendered useless—in the vor-
" tex of struggles brought about in an attempt to keep
" open your theatre) it is your intention to make a
" hasty announcement, which will paralyze all my
" exertions, and put any advantages to yourselves and

" others, arising therefrom, totally of the question,
" but which might be calculated upon by a slight
" and reasonable delay?
    " I am, gentlemen,
        " Your obedient, humble servant,
                        " A. BUNN.
    " To the Sub-committee, &c. &c."

The sub-committee adopted my view of the case,
by sanctioning a short delay in the meditated announcement, and I occupied as much of the intervening time as I could abstract from the duties of
management and authorship, (having, on the completion of my opera with Balfe, and on its withdrawal to give place to *Le Lac des Fées*, undertaken the translation and adaptation of that work,)
to a consideration of my future plans. Having
taken as clear a survey as I was capable of taking,
not only of my own situation, but of the general
situation of the profession itself, I submitted my
observations to the consideration of an officer of
my cabinet, a dear and undeviating friend, to the
coolness of whose deliberation, and to the acuteness of
whose judgment, experience had told me I could always
confidently apply. Mr. Reynolds' answer, if I mistake not, will amuse and instruct others, as it amused
and instructed me; and, proceeding from such an
excellent theatrical authority, it claims an especial
corner among the many valuable documents with
which, I trust, my pages are stored:

" May 5, 1839.

" MY DEAR BUNN,

" Yes,—like you, I literally cannot solve the enigma
" —for ' true it is, 'tis pity; and pity it is 'tis true,' that
" the same actors and actresses, who some twelve or
" fourteen years ago were moderately applauded, are
" now received amidst waving of hats and handker-
" chiefs, by the house rising *en masse*. Nor is that
" all—for, on the fall of the curtain, my Lord John
" Bull, my Lady John and common John, all rise again,
" and the said actors and actresses return to the
" charge, amidst a volley of huzzas, laurels, and
" bouquets!

" ' Now, there is surely more in this than is dreamt
" of in our philosophy, Horatio!'—for here are the
" identical ladies and gentlemen with the same
" voices, the same action, the same faces, the same
" comic trip, the same tragic strut, in short the same
" everything, except the same salaries! which na-
" turally *rise* with the audience—and if you ask me
" who is answerable for all these unaccountable whirli-
" gig proceedings, I reply—' decidedly not the per-
" formers '—no ; and, fully aware of the *certain un-*
" *certainty* of their profession, I hail their success !
" and sincerely hope they'll continue to make the
" most of this new *rising generation*, who know *no*
" more of acting than those in the two grand Palace-
" yard theatres know of ——. However, as I do
" not exactly understand what is or what is not a
" breach of privilege, I believe I had better confine

" myself to the case more particularly before the
" court, namely, *that* of stars, star-gazers, and ' *The*
" STAR-*chamber*.' (You remember when a late
" facetious manager was in the " *King's Bench*, he
" *thus* dated his letter.)

" I am old enough (unluckily) to recollect when
" Lord Camden, Burke, Dr. Johnson, Fox, Sheridan,
" Wyndham, Erskine, and Sir Joshua Reynolds, were
" frequently seen among the audience, and (at dif-
" ferent periods) when Garrick, Barry, Henderson,
" Lewis, Mrs. Abington, Mrs. Jordan, John Kemble,
" and Mrs. Siddons, were seen amongst the per-
" formers !

" When manly sense, when nature mix'd with art—
" When thorough knowledge of the human heart—
" When pow'rs of acting, vast and unconfin'd,
" And fewest faults with greatest beauties joined—
" When strong expression and strange charms that lie
" Within the magic circle of the eye—

" Oh ! such was the histrionic talent of those days !
" but alas ! could any one of them be ' called from
" the peaceful grave '—ay, if even Garrick himself
" were now to appear before one of our modern non-
" descript audiences, what would be the result?—why,
" his school having been *totally* different from the
" present approved and established style, he would
" probably be deemed old-fashioned and obsolete !
" yes, and on a similar principle to that of the Spar-
" tan auditory, who violently applauded the squeak-
" ing of a *sham* pig, and as violently hissed the same

" facetious expression from a *real* pig ; so Roscius
" himself might be glad to escape from the honour
" of being greeted with more compact and marking
" offerings than those of harmless bouquets and
" laurel wreaths.

" Of course this opinion being in direct opposition
" to *that* of our present unfledged race of playgoers,
" they will retort, and contemptuously exclaim, 'Who
" made you a judge, old Squaretoes ;' or, 'Who asked
" your opinion, old twaddling Don Snapshorto de
" Teste ?' Well ! granted I *am* a twattle ;—but are
" there not young twattles as well as old ones ? at
" least I hope there are, if solely that they may still
" go on—not only biting at modern acting, but also at
" modern dinners, (mind, though, I don't mean those
" which performers *give*, but those which are *given*
" to performers,) where the *semper instabile vulgus*
" actually ' makes the meat it feeds on ;' for owing to
" the well got-up reiterated shouts for ' one cheer
" more !' and the usual prepared laudatory speeches
" from good-natured peers and M. P.'s, and the usual
" applicable toasts and songs.—Oh ! it's rare fun alto-
" gether ! and but for bothering old age and gout,
" be assured, my good fellow, I would not miss one of
" these ecstatic exhibitions, and, after all, would
" heartily join in proving that John Bull *collectively*
" was never right but once in his life ; and that was
" (as I have elsewhere said) when he d—d a comedy
" of mine ; yet *individually* he is such a thoroughly
" good-natured fellow, that I should be the very worst

" of 'old squaretoes,' if I endeavoured to lessen his
" joy, or deaden his admiration !

" But, notwithstanding all this, I admit there is no
" fun in a lessee's case—at least not in yours—for
" to manage sub-committees, general committees,
" lawyers, &c., as well as performers, authors, editors,
" &c., seems to me impossible ; and *ergo* (under ex-
" isting or rather *expiring* circumstances,) why not
" turn your mind to Covent Garden ? where, having
" punctually paid rent for the whole of your term,
" (above 17,000*l*.) the proprietors must listen to your
" proposals ; and then wishing success to Drury, and
" hoping it may find another tenant that will keep it
" open for another five years, (though *entre nous*
" where is he to be found ?) why ' cross the gutter,'
" and cry ' hurrah for old Covent Garden and the
" house of Harris !'

" Believe me, dear Bunn,
" Always yours,
" FREDK. REYNOLDS."

The two patent theatres may now be said to have
been tenantless, for those in occupation were bringing their respective seasons to a close, and both their
domains were publicly announced to be in want of a
lessee for the future. If my finances had been in a
flourishing condition, I should have paused before
I took up my friend Reynolds' hint, by entering
seriously into a new speculation with an uncertain
property and arbitrary landlords ; but as they were

in a state of utter derangement, any contemplation of it was totally out of the question.

The last act of my management afforded me more true pleasure and satisfaction, though exercised on a very melancholy occasion, than most occurrences that took place during my long connexion with the theatres royal. I look back upon it with pride ; but if it should be the reader's opinion that there is nothing particularly to be proud of in performing a simple act of duty, I will make him a present of that term, and select another—delight. One of the most distinguished of modern poets, Mr. Haynes Bayley, departed from a scene of sorrow and sickness, without being enabled to make a sufficient provision for the survivors of his misfortunes. His last and most admired compositions will be found exquisitely portrayed in that undying verse by Montgomery (JAMES, for fear of mistakes) :

> " The bard, to dark despair consigned,
> " With his expiring art
> " Sings, 'mid the tempest of his mind,
> " The shipwreck of his heart ! "

Some admirers and friends of the deceased minstrel being anxious to make up as far as possible the deficiency in his widow's resources that had become manifest, applied to me with a view of taking a benefit in Drury Lane Theatre, where, by public sympathy and private contribution, so laudable and so desirable an object might be attained. It would be

an absurd display of vanity to talk of the readiness
with which their praiseworthy plans were entered
into : it will be much better to place amongst my other
memoranda their own announcement, which winds
up a continuous chain of interesting events in the
order in which they occurred :

" THEATRE ROYAL DRURY LANE.

" The late THOMAS HAYNES BAYLEY, Esq.
" The nobility and gentry are respectfully informed,
that it is proposed to give, *under high and distinguished patronage,*

A GRAND DRAMATIC AND MUSICAL PERFORMANCE
AT THIS THEATRE,
" *On Friday, June* 7, 1839,
" FOR THE BENEFIT OF
"THE WIDOW AND CHILDREN OF THE ABOVE-NAMED
" POET AND DRAMATIC AUTHOR,
" whose long illness, terminating in his lamented
" death, has thrown his pecuniary affairs into a state
" of embarrassment, from which it is the object and
" hope of the promoters of the present undertaking to
" relieve them. The most handsome offers of pro-
" fessional support and assistance are already coming
" rapidly in, and the general esteem in which Mr.
" Haynes Bayley's poetical works were held, toge-
" ther with the great popularity of his dramatic
" writings, afford the strongest grounds for believing
" that this appeal to the best sympathies of the pub-
" lic will be one of the most successful that has been
" made for many years.

" THE ENTERTAINMENTS WILL CONSIST OF
" TWO OF MR. BAYLEY'S DRAMAS,
" ONE TO BE PERFORMED BY THE
HAYMARKET COMPANY, AND ONE BY THE OLYMPIC
COMPANY.
AND BETWEEN THE DRAMAS
A CONCERT
" will be given, in which some of *the first talent*
" *in the country,* vocal and instrumental, English and
" foreign, will assist. A host of professors have
" kindly volunteered to form a committee for the
" management of the concert, and all requisite atten-
" tion will be given to the dramatic portion by the
" members of the *Dramatic Authors' Society.*
" MR. BUNN
" has most handsomely given the gratuitous use of
" Drury Lane Theatre, and *Madame Vestris and Mr.*
" *Webster* have, with the like liberality, offered every
" facility with reference to the assistance of
" THE OLYMPIC AND HAYMARKET COMPANIES.
" Any communication tending to forward the object
" in view will be thankfully received, addressed to
" ' Mr. R. B. Peake, at the stage-door of the theatre."

The benefit took place on the day announced, viz.
June 7th, and the amount it was the cause of realiz-
ing has been so far the means of increasing the slender store that remained to his family, as to place
them above the humiliation of any further public
appeal. I had the pleasure of Mr. Bayley's acquaintance, and was, with the rest of my fellow-creatures

who have eyes and ears, an enthusiastic admirer of his delightful writings. The pleasure they have often afforded me, was feebly but full-heartedly returned on the occasion, by the assistance I was enabled to lend ; and if my purse had been as loaded as my feelings, I would more substantially have marked my admiration. It is a mournful consolation to subjoin this acknowledgment, on the part of the committee appointed to regulate the arrangements of the evening :

"BENEFIT FOR THE WIDOW AND CHILDREN
"OF THE LATE
" *Mr. Thomas Haynes Bayley.*

"June 8, 1839.
" SIR,
" I am directed by the committee to return you " their most heartfelt thanks for the very kind assist-" ance afforded to them on the above occasion.
" And have the honour to be, Sir,
" Your obedient servant,
" R. B. PEAKE.
" To Alfred Bunn, Esq."

And, with a record of this sad memento, I wish repose to the ashes of a gifted son of song, of whom his bereaved partner may well exclaim, " Je regrette ta mort et ma vie."

It would be difficult to find a corner for the various trifling occurrences which took place during this season, some of very little moment; still, as being for the most part mixed up with theatrical life, a general record was kept of them. An officer of the Guards with whom I have long been intimate, being on the point of embarking for Canada (after it was uncertain whether Mr. Mackenzie had made away with it or not!) and having had all his life the visitation of a theatrical mania upon him, extracted from me a promise to give him from time to time, as my leisure would admit, a full, true, and particular account of what was going on amongst that select part of the community to be found in theatres. I fulfilled that promise, and finding a copy of the epistle despatched to him, I have ventured, at the risk of incurring a charge of absurdity, to give it a corner here :

My Johnny,
 As something has, I trust, conveyed you
  By this time to that precious climate,
 I keep the promise which I made you
  Of sending word of all that *I'm* at !
 Imprimis, your old friend, the marquis,*
  Is sticking like a leech unto us,
 And if one might a statesman dare quiz,
  He's trying all he can to " do" us !

Then, although London's full of lions,
  Yet none of them one-half the rage are
 (Especially amongst your high 'uns)
  As those which in Van Amburgh's cage are.
 Your royal mistress, Heaven bless her !
  Considers all their tricks so sightly,
 And hoping they'll at last caress her,
  Doth pay a visit to them nightly.

    * Conyngham.

And Landseer hath a *billet* written,
    Of finest scent and finest breeding,
To say he's with their charms so smitten,
    He'd give the world to see 'em ʋeeding.
Between ourselves, if I mistake not,
    His easel's booked Van Amburgh's phiz for ;
And if your sense your soul forsake not,
    You'll guess *the party* whom it *is* for ! !

WE had a feed too, vastly pleasant,
    So crammed one scarcely could get *in* there,
And as some " pals" of yours were present,
    I only wish that *you* had been there.
Poor Malibran ! whose name undying
    Though dead herself, so have we missed her,
I've been with Sieur de Beriot trying
    " Tarnation" hard to get her sister.

He says she for the stage not ripe is,*
    But as I know these nice rapscallions
And also what a precious gripe, his,
    You'll find she'll go to the Italians !
We've brought an opera out by Barnett,
    With Romer's most enchanting singing—
Of merit, but they won't disarn it,
    For not a shilling is it bringing !

---

* The following is Monsieur de Beriot's reply, which bore out my
suspicion ; for though he states that Mademoiselle Pauline was " trop
jeune" to come out last year, she appeared a month or two afterwards at the opera ! The first part of the letter refers to his promised
bust of Malibran :

'· Paris, Hôtel de Paris, rue de Richelieu,
" Le 22 Janvier, 1839.

" MON CHER MONSIEUR,

" Excusez le retard de ma réponse. Une absence que je viens de faire
" est la cause.

Then you who love all matters manly,
Must know we're looking for a tiger
As black as h—ll, which Captain Stanley
Has brought home from the banks of Niger ;*

" Je vous ai en effet promis un buste, et je tiens à remplir ma pro-
" messe ; mais il me faudra probablement un mois, pour vous le faire
" parvenir, car je craindrais en vous expedient une copie trop fraiche
" qu'elle n'arrivât à Londres tout endommagée.

" J'ai communiquée votre proposition à Madame Garcia, mais je re-
" grette de n'avoir pas une réponse affirmative à vous donner. Elle pense
" avec raison que sa fille est trop jeune encore pour prendre un engage-
" ment avant l'année prochaine—d'ici-là vous aurez le temps de vous
" voir et de vous entendre.

" Recevez, cher Monsieur, mille complimens empressés,
" C. De Beriot."

* An animal of a very rare species, which Mr. Van Amburgh was
most anxious to possess ; and with the view of purchasing it, an application was made to the Earl of Derby, whose property it was supposed
to be. His lordship's reply settled the question :

" Knowsley, March 12, 1839.
" Sir,
" In reply to the letter I have this day received from you, I have to
" inform you that I have nothing to do with the animals you speak of.
" They were brought over to this country by a relation of mine, who
" kindly offered them to me, but they would not at all answer my
" wishes ; and in consequence of my declining this kindness, he has, I
" am told, consented to their being disposed of, and I believe they have
" been purchased by Mr. C. Wombwell. Captain Stanley is now with
" his vessel, the Wolf, at Plymouth.
" I remain, Sir,
" Your humble servant,
" Derby."

Poor Harris, sadly circumvented,
  Strong-minded, and, what's more, good-hearted,
Beloved as he will be lamented,
  This " vale of tears" has just departed ! *

Then—such a " Derby"—only fancy
  That on this day we all so dote on,
You could not o'er the course a man see
  Who had not got a thick greatcoat on.
Then—jockeys in a snow storm riding,
  And horses on the greensward skating
And all in booths or stables hiding,
  Wherever they could stuff their pate in.

While those who brought champagne for icing,
  Found plenty there, already made too ;
But brandy being more enticing,
  They longed for what they so well paid, too ;
And then—the darling women, bless em !
  In silks and muslins were so quiv'ring,
We were compelled to closer press 'em,
  In order to prevent their shivering !

* I was seldom more shocked, and never more surprised, than on the
receipt of this afflicting letter:

  " MY DEAR BUNN,

  " As I know, that notwithstanding all your present troubles and
" difficulties, you are anxious about poor Harry Harris, I am sorry to
" say, my fears were too true : he left this transitory world yester-
" day at half-past one o'clock, and died so easily, that all round his bed-
" side thought he was asleep. Thus, perhaps, I have lost the nearest
" and the dearest friend that ever man was blessed with. You, who
" know that for so many years he formed a part of my fireside, and that
" during the whole period he never uttered an unkind word, must, I
" am confident, sympathise in my loss—personally also you must feel
" it, for you were always on very good terms with him, and, like my-
" self, will acknowledge, ' We shall not look upon his like again.'

      " God bless you, and believe me
          " Ever, ever yours,
"Monday May 13, 1839."   " F. REYNOLDS."

I thought of you, where now you're tied up—
—That land of which such things are written—
Where half the year by heat you're dried up,
And t'other half by frost are bitten!
Then—one at Court who rather high is—
And whose reports do not miscarry,
Tells me the universal cry is,
  Her Majesty intends to marry!

And as few ladies living, therefore,
  Who, if they had their own way, wouldn't ;
I cannot see good reason wherefore
  A lady who *can* have it, shouldn't!
Then—as we found the stage decaying,
  We gave them concerts A LA MUSARD ;
And had you heard some varlets playing,
  You would have ventured to abuse hard!

Of Parliament I know but little,
  Which little 's in a " blest condition ;"
Its work, which suits it to a tittle,
  Lies in a " Penny Post petition ;"
But when the state's estate is *minus*,
  'Tis not the aptest time to dock it,
So, for some other tax they'll fine us,
  And put the change in Rowland's pocket.*

Thus, while you, reckless what befell you,
  In foreign fun and frolic revel—
Permit me, Johnny, just to tell you,
  That England's going to the devil!
At least some learned men, who quiz not,
  Assert most roundly that it true is,
And all I promise you, if *'tis* not,
  At all events I know one *who* is!

          " And he is yours,
              " While this machine is to him,"
                    " A. BUNN."

* Mr. Rowland Hill, the well-paid projector of this precious plan.

CHAPTER VII.

The Steward's reckoning—Contrast between a paid and a paying
manager—The three *h's*—Drury Lane committee—Recapitulation
of difficulties—Parliamentary definition of the legitimate drama—
Shakspeare and other authors—Six years' good work, and five
hundred and sixty-eight good performances—The Road to Ruin—
A perfect company detailed, both foreign and native—Eighty new
pieces, and five damnations to boot—Music *versus* language
—A manager's authorship—Virtues of comparison—How to "cast"
plays, without talking about it—The advancement of the drama—
Vestris and Macready, and Augustus Cæsar—A practical display of
the result of metropolitan management.

A STEWARD entrusted with the management of weighty
and extensive affairs should, at the end of his term, if
he be honest, give some account of his stewardship. I had long resolved upon this ; but to do it correctly was a work of time, and to do it incorrectly was
worse than not doing it at all. Without a particle of
knowledge to assist them in framing their animadver-
sions, a set of scribes have amused themselves with
abusing me, with no other reason than what malice
could furnish them, for a long waste of time—betray-
ing in their lucubrations ignorance alike of *their* pro-

fession and of *mine*. There is not one among them
who, had he been placed in the same situation, and
always under the same trying circumstances as I have
been, would not have betrayed at least as much stu-
pidity; but if it be not easier, at all events it is pleasanter, to point out the beam in your neighbour's
eye, than to acknowledge you have a mote in your
own. The fact is, that many people of discretion,
but fools invariably, are led away by the latest impression on their minds; without examining into
causes, they pounce at once upon effects, and come
to the conclusion that because the exertions of a
person may for the moment be paralysed, he has
NEVER made *any* exertions.

Without taking into consideration the efforts which
had been made through so long a connexion with
the London stage as mine, it would appear to a
stranger, from the merciless attacks of the parties
who assailed my final retirement from it, that some
ignorant experimentalist, some novice in a profession
requiring the utmost experience, some theorist who
had never before crossed a stage, had attempted to
dive into its profound arcana, without being able to
solve any portion of its mysteries or its secrets. I
am as willing as any other person to be " written
down an ass" by wiser men than myself, of which
thousands upon thousands are to be found; but I
cannot consent to be so classified by those who are
more *assi*fied than I am, and who indulge in their
spleen at the expense of even what little intellect

they possess. To vindicate myself from false charges
entertained by feelings of malice, and not by the
scrutiny of judgment, has been the principal aim of
these pages ; but that would, alone, be but an egotistical and uninteresting piece of business. I have
therefore added a collection of valuable theatrical
documents, useful to all who care for the welfare of
our drama, and those who seek to cultivate it; and
which, but for such circumstance, would most likely
never have seen the light. I have, however, a much
greater task to accomplish, before I can satisfy myself, and even when I have done that, it remains to
be proved whether I shall satisfy my reader. With
the same good feeling (always supposing such to be
the case) in which he has thus far gone on with me,
I must hope he will go back with me, to enable me
to complete my argument.

The mere question of SELF is very easily disposed
of—if it depended merely *upon* self; for my ambition
would have been just as well satisfied, and my pocket
much *more* satisfied, had I remained, as I intend
pro futuro to remain, a PAID and not a PAYING manager. I should then have avoided all the cares, all the
obloquy, all the indignities, all the privations, all
the misrepresentations, and all the mortifications,
which wait upon power, be it wielded never so consi-
derately. I should have avoided the inevitable
consequence to any manager of the patent theatres,
— who has neither ingots nor acres to melt, —

of being dragged, however full of honesty and good
intention, before a legal tribunal for public examination, where, however flattering and triumphant may
be the scrutiny into character, the feelings of humiliation and degradation, (temporary though they be,)
are barely durable, and only become so by the consciousness ofrectitude, and a determination of purpose
to appear that you *are* what you would *seém*. Being
one of moderate desires, I should have amassed by this
time as much as would have gone a considerable way
towards the comforts of advancing years, which so
many by MY exertions have, during the period of their
being made, actually done—and thus have had, what
every man is entitled to, the emoluments arising from
his own labour. The duties of management came upon
me by desire, by advantage, by study, by travel, by
fate if you will—but the *responsibilities* of it by CIR-
CUMSTANCE.   To fulfil the promise made to my predecessor, and to maintain the position in which I
then stood before the public, *was* THAT CIRCUM-
STANCE : and when those responsibilities were once
upon my shoulders, I had to make every exertion
which industry, ingenuity, or expediency, could de-
vise, where I had no other backers but them to assist
me.   When once involved in an enterprise of this
nature, there is a prospect, always believed to be
within your reach, which induces you to persevere ;
and the excitements of a theatrical life, while they
are the most delusive, are at the same time the most
alluring imaginable. Had I possessed those beneficial

means which should be at the disposal of a manager of such enormous buildings, that prospect might yet have been realized; but the first grand consideration, without which all others are unavailing, was wanting— CAPITAL! *My* " capital" was in my head, my heels, and my hands,* instead of being in my pocket. At times when that overwhelming difficulty has been temporarily got over, I have found myself repeatedly discussing the terms of my future tenancy of the theatre, at a period of the year when all my plans ought to have been matured. The arrangements of an ensuing season should be nearly all complete before the preceding season has expired, trusting for their total completion to the casualties which every season naturally brings along with it: but when a man does not definitively know until August that he has to open a national theatre in September, he may be looked upon as a lucky fellow if he can open it at all.

It must not be set down that I seek to impute to my landlords, the committee of Drury Lane Theatre, the blame that, under other circumstances, would naturally attach to persons apparently so subject to the

* These three *h's* remind me of three others, by which the three popular comedians of their day, Elliston, C. Kemble, and Richard Jones, used to be distinguished. They were called the three H's, because Elliston's comedy was to be found in his *h*eart, Charles Kemble's in his *h*ead, and Jones's in his *h*eels; and whoever has examined the joyousness of the one, the studied and artificial manner of the other, and the invariably bustling *entrée* of the latter, will admit the truth of their nomenclature.

charge of procrastination; for I have already explained the situation in which they are placed, and
must continue to be placed, by their constituency,
until relieved by the repeal of a most absurd Act of
Parliament. They are men of too much practical
sense, and too alive to the interests of the great charge
committed to their care, to receive or to continue in
their confidence any person who experience had not
told them was to be depended upon. That experience
had convinced them, as I feel assured it *will* convince,
if it has not done so already, others they have to deal
with, of the utter hopelessness of obtaining a tenant
practical and responsible at the same time; and
where they have been unable to obtain the latter,
they have invariably endeavoured to make the best
bargain they could with the former. Those blatant
boobies, who assail without reason, and always in
ignorance, have visited this committee with a degree
of abuse correspondent with that which they have
lavished upon me, presuming that the *ipse dixit* of an
uninformed person, merely because it appears in a
newspaper, is to be preferred to the knowledge,
gained by practice, of men of information, ability,
and station.

To the other difficulties just cited, must never be
lost sight of the proceedings of a liberal Lord Chamberlain having thrown open so many more places of
public entertainment than ever before had been in
existence; and that when, by his so doing, the principal performers were lured away to those theatres, and

the patent houses had to resort to every species of mixed entertainment, the said Lord Chamberlain questioned the privilege of those patents by which such entertainments had, for years previously, been given, and altogether forbade them. To this wanton obstacle, and in a measure to be attributed to it, must be added the yearly increasing demands of the performers, already so fully entered upon, which in their progress have done most, but not all, of the mischief they *will* do. Add to this, again, the transportation to America, which had been sufficiently injurious without the aid of steam, but which has now become absolutely ruinous to the London stage. There is but one hope for this latter part of the business, which is, that scarcely a performer, possessing any pretensions to a refined taste, but returns from the land of Columbus so thoroughly disgusted, (and by no means so richly rewarded as he expected to be,) that no inducement will prevail on him to go back again.

These are the principal matters discussed in the preceding pages, upon which I anxiously desire that my reader should cast a retrospective glance, that he may be the better able to examine the issue, as I shall place it before him. Without the slightest wish to exalt myself, it is at all events my duty to prevent, if possible, other people from debasing me. I must state the difficulties I had to contend against, and I must state the way in which I *did* contend against them, leaving the reader to determine whether the combat was maintained creditably or otherwise. It is needless to go into details with the numberless friends and supporters whom for so many years I have found, and still possess—my object is to undeceive those who have mistaken the spleen of private calumny for the result of public opinion.

My attention had been directed, after I had made up my mind to the necessity of adopting this line of conduct, to some very clever strictures in a public print upon the subject, purporting to be a brief view of the English drama, with suggestions for ameliorating its condition. With some portion of that laudable treatise I fully agree; and while I differ *toto cœlo* with a great part of it, as demonstrated in many instances throughout these volumes, I respect the ability displayed in it, notwithstanding that I believe its tenets to be mistaken.

The gravest charge, indeed the grand one upon the pivot of which all minor charges turn, that has been preferred against me, consists of my having neglected the legitimate drama, and in its stead presented gewgaw and pageantry, wherein SENSE has been compelled to give way to SHOW: and that, in so doing, I have debased performers of eminence, whose genius was capable and worthy of better employment. I suppose the reader to have made up his mind as to what the legitimate drama really *is;* if he has not, perhaps the following dialogue between Mr. T. S. Duncombe, M.P. and Mr. Douglas Jerrold, dramatic author, extracted from the " Minutes of Evidence before a Select Committee of the House of Commons

on Dramatic Literature," may enable him to do
so :

"*Mr. Duncombe.*—Was not *Midas* first produced
" at the Royalty Theatre?

" *Mr. D. Jerrold.* — Mr. Garrick was produced
there, and played the legitimate drama.

" *Mr. Duncombe.*—How do you describe the le-
" gitimate drama?

" *Mr. D. Jerrold.*—I describe the legitimate drama
" to be where the interest of the piece is mental;
" where the situation of the piece is rather mental than
" physical. A melo-drama is a piece with what are
" called a great many telling situations—I would call
" that a melo-drama. I would not call a piece like
" *The Hunchback* a melo-drama, because the interest
" of the piece is of a mental order.

"*Mr. Duncombe.*—A piece rather addressed to the
" eye than to the ear?

" *Mr. D. Jerrold.*—Certainly.

" *Mr. Duncombe.* — Is Tom Thumb a legitimate
" drama?

" *Mr. D. Jerrold.*—Tom Thumb is a burlesque.

"*Mr. Duncombe.*—That goes *under the head* of
" THE LEGITIMATE DRAMA now?

" *Mr. D. Jerrold.*—Yes."

Supposing, which is not at all unlikely to be the
case, that, upon a perusal of this interrogatory, the
reader is still unenlightened, it may not be very far
from the mark to say, that under the head of the LE-
GITIMATE DRAMA may be classed, amongst others, all

the works of Shakspeare, Ben Johson, Massinger, Beaumont and Fletcher, Rowe, Otway, Lee, Southern, Addison, Garrick, Cibber, Goldsmith, Vanburgh, Steele, Colman, Colman the younger, Sheridan, Cumberland, Murphy, Young, Centlivre, Cowley, Lord Byron, Joanna Baillie, Knowles, &c.; most of whose writings are of a high mental order, and most of them appealing rather to the ear than to the eye. A manager who, during a long connexion with the London stage, has attempted to do justice to the works of such ornaments to the dramatic literature of their country as the above recited men, cannot consistently be accused of neglecting the legitimate drama; and when it is taken into consideration with what a set of performers he had to go through so difficult a task, I think he will be acknowledged to be a bolder legitimatist than he has left behind him.

That a correct opinion may be formed by the reader of the justice or the injustice of the damnatory attacks that have been made upon me, not so much to knock me down (though having that effect) as to uphold another, (also having that effect,) I will " show his eyes, and grieve his heart," with a catalogue of my legitimate crimes. Between the beginning of the season 1832-33, and the end of the season 1838-39, (consisting of my recent uninterrupted management of the London theatres, and having no reference to my former stage management of Drury Lane Theatre,) ALL the acting plays, with but one or two exceptions, of the immortal Shakspeare have been represented together *two hundred and sixty-two nights*, while the works of our other less gifted but noble writers enumerated above, have in the same space of time been performed *three hundred and six times.* In this period no account must be taken of my last season 1838-39, because the arrangements of it were of necessity made to the exclusion of anything but opera, ballet, and spectacle; therefore, in the six preceding seasons of 1832-33, 1833-34, 1834-35, 1835-36, 1836-37, and 1837-38, the legitimate drama was played, under my management, *five hundred and sixty-eight nights*— nearly one half of the number of nights on which we had *any* PERFORMANCE. To prevent the possibility of any mistake occurring, to cast back into the teeth of those who have made such misstatements, their own unworthy assertions, and at the same time to maintain *my own* assertions by documentary matter, I subjoin the particulars of these performances, which can be checked by any parties sufficiently interested, who will take the trouble of referring to their files of playbills :—

" Number of nights in each of the following six " seasons, when the plays of Shakspeare were per" formed at the Theatre Royal Drury Lane and " Covent Garden, under the management of Mr. " Bunn, collated for the satisfaction of those who " have asserted that they were never played at all :

No. of Shakspeare's Plays.

In the season 1832-33 were given .   . 33

In the season 1833-34 were given . . 56
In the season 1834-35 were given . . 39
In the season 1835-36 were given . . 29
In the season 1836-37 were given . . 42
In the season 1837-38 were given . . 63

Total representations of Shakspeare . 262

In this number will be found almost every one of the poet's plays which keep possession of the stage; and that the reader may judge which were most run after by the people, I subjoin the list of them, with the stated number of times each was played in this period:—

		Times.
1. The *Tempest* was performed	. .	4
2. *Macbeth* —	. .	41
3. *Hamlet* —	. .	36
4. *Cymbeline* —	. .	1
5. *Antony and Cleopatra*	. .	3
6. *Midsummer Night's Dream*	. .	2
7. *Henry IV.* (first part)	. .	15
8. *Henry IV.* (second part)	. .	8
9. *Richard II.* . .	. .	2
10. *Richard III.* . .	. .	34
11. *Merry Wives of Windsor*	. .	8
12. *Othello* . .	. .	47
13. *Coriolanus* . .	. .	5
14. *Julius Cæsar* . .	. .	3
15. *King John* . .	. .	4
16. *Henry VIII.* . .	. .	7

17. *Romeo and Juliet*	.	.	. 5
18. *Henry V.*	.	.	. 1
19. *Merchant of Venice*	.	.	. 11
20. *Twelfth Night*	.	.	. 3
21. *As you Like it*	.	.	. 5
22. *Winter's Tale*	.	.	. 3
23. *King Lear*	.	.	. 14

Grand total of times . 262

Having shown how far, with the most anti-Shak-spearian set of actors that (save and except in an instance or two) ever crossed the London stage, a be-coming degree of homage was paid to the fountain head, the source of all the dramatic glory of the country, I will enter into the same minutiæ, as far as may be necessary, of the respect that was paid to the lesser, but still brilliant luminaries of the British drama,—after the following fashion :

Number of nights in each of the following six seasons, when pieces coming under the denomination of THE LEGITIMATE DRAMA, were played at the Thea-tres Royal Drury Lane and Covent Garden, under Mr. Bunn's management, with the names of the authors affixed to each :

IN THE SEASON 1832-33.

No. of nights performed.

The School for Scandal, by *Sheridan* . . 8

Jane Shore, by *Rowe* 1

The Revenge, by *Dr. Young*   .   .   . 2
Every Man in his Humour, by *Ben Jonson*   . 2
A New Way to Pay Old Debts, by *Massinger*   . 1
The Jealous Wife, by *Colman*   .   .   . 4
The Clandestine Marriage, by *Colman and Garrick* 3
She Stoops to Conquer, by *Goldsmith*   .   . 2
William Tell, by *Knowles*   .   .   . 4
The Hunchback, by *Knowles*   .   .   . 3
The House of Colberg, by *Serle*   .   . 4
Who Wants a Guinea? by *Colman*   .   . 2
Brutus, from *Cumberland* and others   .   . 1
Busy Body, by *Mrs. Centlivre*   .   . 1
She Would and She would not, by *Cibber*   . 2
The Hypocrite, by *Bickerstaff*   .   .   . 2
The Duenna, by *Sheridan*   1
Virginius, by *Knowles*   2
Way to get Married, by *Morton*   .   .   . 2
The Soldier's Daughter, by *Cherry*   .   . 2

49

By this first statement it will be seen that *eighty-two nights* (33 and 49) out of about TWO HUNDRED, were devoted, between Shakspeare and other writers of less renown, to what is looked upon as the legitimate drama. Perhaps, as we progress, we shall find that other seasons, directed to the same unfortunate object, went to a greater extent:—

IN THE SEASON 1833-34.

No. of nights performed.

The School for Scandal, by *Sheridan*	4
The Duenna, by *ditto*	2
Sardanapalus, by *Lord Byron*	23
Werner, by *ditto*	7
Virginius, by *Knowles*	4
William Tell, by *ditto*	3
The Stranger, by *Thompson* from *Kotzebue*	1
Jealous Wife, by *Colman the Elder*	1
Heir at Law, by *Colman the Younger*	1
Poor Gentleman, by *ditto*	3
Iron Chest, by *ditto*	1
Jane Shore, by *Rowe*	3
Venice Preserved, by *Otway*	1
Isabella, by *Southern*	1
Comus, by *Milton*	2
Alexander the Great, by *Lee*	3
Road to Ruin, by *Holcroft*	2
Belles' Stratagem, by *Cowley*	1
Hypocrite, by *Bickerstaff*	1
Speed the Plough, by *Morton*	1
Secrets Worth Knowing, by *ditto*	4
Wild Oats, by *O'Keefe*	2
Honey Moon, by *Tobin*	1
Minister and Mercer, by *Bunn* from *Scribe*	41

Times 113!

If the reader could but see the receipts produced by some of the foregoing bits of "legitimacy," es-

pecially the works of the elder and greater masters, he
would set me down as a bigger fool for having
played them, than perhaps the varlets considered me,
when they stated I never *had* played them ; but alas!
there is plenty more evidence to come :

IN THE SEASON 1834—35.

No. of nights performed.

A New Way to Pay Old Debts, by *Massinger*	4
Venice Preserved, by *Otway*	1
Cato, by *Addison*	3
School for Scandal, by *Sheridan* . . .	3
Rivals, by *ditto* . . .	1
Duenna, by *ditto* . . .	1
Revenge, by *Dr. Young*	1
Jane Shore, by *Rowe*	1
William Tell, by *Knowles*	1
Hunchback, by *ditto*	3
Grecian Daughter, by *Murphy* . . .	1
Clandestine Marriage, by *Garrick and Colman*	
the Elder	2
Hypocrite, by *Bickerstaff*	2
Wheel of Fortune, by *Cumberland* . . .	1
Road to Ruin, by *Holcroft* . . .	4
Poor Gentleman, by *Colman the Younger* .	3
Stranger, by *Thomson* from *Kotzebue* . .	3
Minister and Mercer, by *Bunn* from *Scribe*, .	3
Brutus, by *Payne* from *Cumberland* and others	1
Wild Oats, by *O'Keefe*	3
Bertram, by *Maturin*	2

Patrician and Parvenu, by *Poole* . . . 19
Werner, by *Lord Byron* 1
(Manfred, by *ditto*, 33 times, *not included,
for fear it should not be thought* LEGITIMATE
enough)

Times 64

The devil take such legitimacy, say I ! I wish I had,
for fun's sake only, the time to come over again ; my
assailants should squeak out to some purpose ! Now
for some more of it :

IN THE SEASON 1835-36.

No. of nights performed.

The School for Scandal, by *Sheridan* . . 1
The Provoked Husband, by *Vanburgh* . . 3
Clandestine Marriage, by *Colman and Garrick* 1
Wild Oats, by *O'Keefe* 1
Speed the Plough, by *Morton* . . . 1
The Stranger, by *Thompson* from *Kotzebue* . 1
Henriquez, by *Joanna Baillie* 1
Provost of Bruges, by *Lovell* . . . 8
William Tell, by *Knowles* 1
Virginius, by *ditto* 1
Road to Ruin, by *Holcroft* 1

Times 20

A comparative let-off, being the season in which
the JEWESS monopolised so large a portion of the
period ; and yet, with all this, Shakspeare was played
twenty-nine nights, and the other legitimates twenty
nights! O, dear! more yet, though :

IN THE YEAR 1836-37.

Jane Shore, by *Rowe* 2
School for Scandal, by *Sheridan* . . . 1
Gladiator, by *Dr. Bird* 4
Brutus, by *Payne* from others . . 1
Damon and Pythias, by *Banim* . . . 3
Wrecker's Daughter, by *Knowles* . . . 14
Virginius, by *ditto* 2
Hunchback, by *ditto* 1
                                        ——
                                Times 28

Shakspeare and the other legitimates were played
this season SEVENTY NIGHTS, being more than one-
third of the entire season; and if the people had not
enough of it, I can only say *I* had a great deal too
much. The last season of my management, when
anything of the kind was played, stands thus :

IN THE SEASON 1837-38.

No. of nights performed.

The School for Scandal, by *Sheridan* . . 1
The Duenna, by *ditto* 1
Caractacus, from *Bonduca*, by *Beaumont and
Fletcher* 11
New Way to Pay Old Debts, by *Massinger* . 6
The Poor Gentleman, by *Colman* . . . 3
The Iron Chest, by *ditto* 1
Belles' Stratagem, by *Mrs. Cowley* . . . 3
She Stoops to Conquer, by *Goldsmith* . . 4
Hypocrite, by *Bickerstaff* 1
Road to Ruin, by *Holcroft* 1
                                        ——
                                Times 32

In this last "legitimate" season we played Shak-speare " SIXTY-THREE TIMES," and other writers for the ear and not the eye" THIRTY-TWO NIGHTS, making toge-ther very nearly ONE-HALF THE ENTIRE SEASON. With what impressions must a man take up his pen, and state that " Mr. Bunn never played the legitimate drama," when the damning record, just introduced, was in existence? The writings of the party in question evince too much talent, generally, to admit for one moment the supposition that he could be igno-rant of the facts herein detailed ; consequently the perversion of them could have no other object than to degrade me in public opinion, and to do me essen-tial injury.

Having given a precise account, which any one has the power of checking who has filed the playbills of the time, of *two hundred and sixty-two* representations of the acting plays of the immortal dramatic poet, to-gether with *three hundred and six* representations of the writings of other dramatists, coming exclusively under the denomination of mental works, and as such classed under the title of legitimacy, I should very much like to know the opinion of this writer (and he is by no means singular in the assertion he has made) as to what constitutes the legitimate drama, if the pieces herein cited do NOT ? Is it not then perfectly monstrous that men of intellect should be found to propagate such unblushing falsehoods, merely for the purpose of sustaining their own argument, or of debasing him on whose actions they are founding it ?

As it would take me more time than I have either the heart or the inclination to devote, to give the receipts of the treasury on most of the evenings when this LEGITIMATE GAME was being played, I will content myself by observing that, beyond any question, ONE legitimate drama was played nearly as often as all the rest put together, and that was THE ROAD TO RUIN !

Another part of my stewardship, however, remains to be recorded, by which the representation of these pieces must after all be tested ; and as this forms the second part of the great charges against me, it must be met as boldly as the former one. After having so shamefully neglected the legitimate drama as to play it five hundred and sixty-eight nights out of about twelve hundred, (nearly one half the time,) let us see how wantonly I ill used the performers, by letting all the best talent slip through my fingers, and by placing my reliance upon quadrupeds and bipeds. In order to do this, I herewith subjoin an enumeration of the different principal performers, who, during the foregoing period, were engaged with me in the various classifications of the drama, and whose talents were called forth in support of the precious list of " legitimacy" with which the reader has just been regaled. They are arranged alphabetically, that no offence may be given, on the score of priority, to those who think themselves cleverer people than the world gives them credit for being.

" PRINCIPAL PERFORMERS engaged and introduced

" at various times at the Theatres Royal Drury Lane
" and Covent Garden, while under Mr. Bunn's ma-
" nagement :"—

IN TRAGEDY.

Messrs. Butler, Bennett G., Booth, Baker, Cooper,
Cooke H., Cooke F., Denvil, Diddear, Forrest (*of
America,*) Jones G. (*of America,*) Kean, Kean C.,
Knowles, King, Lee, Macready, Mathews, Perkins,
Powell, Paumier, Serle, Stanley, Ternan, Vandenhoff,
Wallack, Warde, Wood, Younge.

Mesdames Allison, Bartley, Clifton (*of America,*)
Faucit, Faucit H., Huddart, Hooper, Lovell, Phillips,
Phillips E., Placide (*of America,*) Sloman, Sharpe
(*of America,*) Tree E., Ternan, Vandenhoff.

IN COMEDY.

Messrs. Ayliffe Bartley, Bennett W., Burke, Balls,
Barnett M., Barrett (*of America,*) Buckstone, Blan-
chard, Brindal, Compton, Chippendale, Dowton,
Farren, Green, Harley, Hooper, Hughes, Hill (*of
America,*) Hackett (*of America,*) Jones R., Keeley,
Liston, Meadows, Power, Rayner, Russell S., Russell,
J., Shuter, Tayleure, Turnour, Vining F., Webster,
Yates.

IN OPERA.

Messrs. Allen, Anderson, Braham, Balfe, Bedford,
Cooke T., Duruset, Fraser, Giubelei, Giubelei A.,
Henry, Jones S., Martyn, Mears, Phillips H., Rans-

ford, Sinclair, Smith G., Stansbury, Templeton, Wood, Wilson, Yarnold.

Mesdames Atkinson, Albertazzi, Anderson, Bishop, Betts, Cawse, Cawse H., Chester, Forde, Hamilton, Healey, Inverarity, Newcombe, Poole, Penley, Pearson, Romer, Rainforth, Seguin E., Shirreff, Wood, Wyndham F., Woodham.

IN BALLET, PANTOMIME, MELO-DRAMA, AND SPECTACLE.

Messrs. Barnes, Cooke T. P., Ducrow, Ellar, Farley, Gilbert, Howell, Hatton, Mathews T., M'Ian, Marshall, Payne W. H., Southby, Sutton, Weiland, Wallack H., Van Amburgh.

Mesdames Ballin, Marshall, O'Brien, Vining, &c., exclusive of a host of minor performers, the largest and most effective chorus, and the most numerous corps de ballet ever produced upon the boards of the winter theatres.

THE ORCHESTRA

at various times has comprised the principal native talent, occasionally aided 'by such auxiliaries as Bochsa, Bonner, Cooke G., Distin, Dennan, Dragonetti, Eigstoff, Harper, Keilbach, Lindley, Nicholson, Puzzi, Price, Smart, &c.; and has been at different times conducted, and led, by Bishop, Balfe, Benedict, Cooke T., Costa, Eliason, Mori, Negri, Nadaud, &c.

THE SCENIC DEPARTMENT

has been directed and supported by Mr. Grieve, T. Grieve, W. Grieve, Stanfield, Marinari, Andrews, &c.

By an examination of this extensive list it will be perceived that scarcely an English performer, of any note, was known to, or connected with, the stage during that period, whose name is not to be found therein enumerated. I wish particularly to direct attention to this fact, because, amongst other high crimes and misdemeanours laid to my charge, that of totally neglecting NATIVE talent for the purpose of introducing FOREIGN talent has been included. A more impudent falsehood never was invented, as the previous statement will demonstrate. Having upon all occasions endeavoured to procure the best abilities of our own country, as soon as I had so done I made a point of introducing as much talent of other countries as was attainable : and as the reader has been regaled with the enumeration of the one, I will trouble him with that of the other :

PRINCIPAL FOREIGN ARTISTES introduced at various times at the Theatres Royal Drury Lane and Covent Garden, while under Mr. Bunn's management:

Messieurs Albert, Albert *fils*, Anatole, Arnal, Begrez, Bochsa, Bull Ole, Benedict, Catone, Curioni, Costa, Coulon, De Beriot, De Begnis, D'Angeli, Deshayes, Guerinot, Galli, Ivanhoff, Lablache, Lablache F., Mazilier, Mori, Paul, Paganini, Perrot,

Regondi, Rubini, Silvain, Tamburini, Taglioni père, Taglioni Paul.

Mesdames Adele, Ancellin, Angusta, Brambilla, Blasis, Chevigny, Celeste, Caradori, Cava, Castelli, De Meric, Duvernay, Dulcken, Dupont, Devrient Schroeder, Elsler F., Elsler I., Elsler H., Grisi, Grisi Carlotta, Giannoni, Giubelei Proche, Kepler, Leroux Pauline, Le Comte, Malibran, Noblet, Pasta, Stockhausen, Schieroni, Taglioni, Taglioni Paul, Vagon, Vertpré, Varin.

As this list comprises the names of nearly all the eminent performers of Europe who during the period have visited this country, I think it may not be considered a vain boast to state that, at all events, the good people had enough for their money. Will my contemporaries, whose partisans have been pleased to favour me with so much of their censure, or will my successors, now that I am beyond the censure of *any* partisans, have the goodness to display any such attractions as the names I have enumerated hold out? Impossible! and yet I have seen their various exertions held up as an example worthy of imitation, and described as being far beyond any that were ever made by ME!

Having given a detail of the legitimate productions during my period of office, and exhibited the names of those by whom such productions were sustained, it is necessary to enumerate the novelties, legitimate and otherwise, that were submitted for public approbation, and to show to what extent that approbation was carried.

Names of Pieces.	Authors or Adapters.	Composers.	No. of nights of their first season.
TRAGEDIES AND TRAGIC PLAYS.			
Sardanapalus - - -	Lord Byron		23
Wrecker's Daughter - -	Knowles		14
Provost of Bruges - -	Lovell		8
Gladiator - - - -	Dr. Bird		5
House of Colberg - -	Serle		5
Henriquez - - - -	Baillie		1
COMEDIES.			
Patrician and Parvenu -	Poole		16
The Minister and Mercer -	Bunn		41
Wedding Gown - - -	Jerrold		29
OPERAS.			
Gustavus the Third - -	Planché	Auber	100
The Red Mask - - -	Ditto	Marliani	26
The Challenge (*after Easter*)	Ditto	Herold	23
The Magic Flute - - -	Ditto	Mozart	19
Don Juan - - - -	Beazley	Ditto	20
The Siege of Corinth - -	Planché	Rossini	23
Guillaume Tell - - -	Bunn	Ditto	36
Maid of Artois (*after May* 27)	Ditto	Balfe	20
Lestocq - - - -	Ditto	Auber	41
The Bronze Horse - -	Ditto	Ditto	28
Maid of Cashmere - -	Fitzball	Ditto	28
Maid of Palaiseau - -	Bishop	Rossini	12
Siege of Rochelle - -	Fitzball	Balfe	73
Joan of Arc - - -	Ditto	Ditto	22
The Gipsy's Warning (*after Easter*)	Peake & Linley	Benedict	23
The Corsair (*after March*) -	Ball	Herold	13
Catherine Grey - - -	Linley	Balfe	4
Diadeste (*after Easter*) -	Fitzball	Ditto	16
Fair Rosamond - - -	Barnett	Barnett	17
Farinelli - - - -	Ditto	Ditto	22
SPECTACLES.			
St. George and the Dragon -	Bernard		63

King Arthur and the Knights	-	Pocock	69
The Jewess	- - -	Planché	84
Manfred	- - - -	Lord Byron	43
Chevy Chase	- - -	Planché	30
Charlemagne	- - -	Bernard	36

(*The Lions in this and other pieces were exhibited* 115 *times.*)

Caractacus	- - - -	Planché	12
Cavaliers and Roundheads	-	Pocock	9

BALLETS.

Revolt of the Harem	- -	Bunn	43
The Sleeping Beauty	- -	Ditto	17
Devil on Two Sticks	- -	Ditto	48
Fairy Slipper (*after Easter*)	-	Ditto	23
The Storm	- - - -	Ditto (*a mess !*)	3
Daughter of the Danube	-	Gilbert	47
The Spirit of Air	- - -	Ditto	32
The Little Hunchback	-	Peake	18

FARCES AND INTERLUDES.

Pleasant Dreams	- - -	C. Dance	12
Forget and Forgive	- -	Ditto	9
Petticoat Government	- -	G. Dance	11
Now or Never	- - -	Ditto	7
The Regent	- - -	Planché	17
Secret Service	- - -	Ditto	24
Reflection	- - - -	Ditto, Mrs.	8
Tam O'Shanter	- - -	Addison	37
The King's Seal	- - -	Ditto	12
Our Mary Anne	- - -	Buckstone	15
The King's Word	- -	Mrs. Gore	7
A Soldier's Courtship	- -	Poole	13
Mr. and Mrs. Pringle	- -	Trueba	21
Scan. Mag.	- - -	Pocock	26
Meltonians (*after Easter*)	-	Peake	21
The Nervous Man	- -	Bernard	10
Yankee Pedlar	- - -	Ditto	6
Chimney Piece	- - -	Rodwell	13

My Neighbour's Wife - - Bunn   68
Good-looking Fellow - - Bunn and Kenney   26

MELO-DRAMAS.

The Ferry and Mill - - Pocock   23
Child of the Wreck - - Planché   21
Travelling Carriage - - Ditto   8
Indian Girl - - - - Bernard   4
Hazard of the Die - - Jerrold   11
The Note Forger - - - Fitzball   12
Carl Milhan - - - Ditto   12
King of the Mist - - - Ditto   8

PANTOMIMES.

Harlequin and Queen Mab - Reynolds   34
Harlequin Gammer Gurton - Ditto   34
Harlequin Jack-a-lantern - Ditto   41
Harlequin and Jack Frost - Ditto   42
Old Mother Hubbard - - Farley   34
Whittington and his Cat - Ditto   24
Harlequin Traveller - - Peake   29

This list is exclusive of the enchanting opera of *La Sonnambula*, (by BEAZLEY,) *Fidelio*, (by LOGAN,) and *Norma*, (by PLANCHÉ,) produced for the first time in an English garb, to give the public an opportunity of witnessing the unsurpassed genius of Madame Malibran, and the extraordinary talents of Madame Schroeder Devrient. Neither is any notice taken in it of the various divertisements that were arranged, at various times, for the exertions of the eminent French dancers who so frequently contributed to the delight of the town. There might, moreover, be added to it three or four pieces of doubtful suc-

cess, the existence of which extended to no more
than two or three nights, and five pieces that were
particularly " well damned " off hand.

In looking thoroughly over the foregoing account,
the reader, I am vain enough to think, will find repeated traces of the dramatic enjoyments he experienced during the period to which it refers ; and as an
additional evidence of the popularity of many of them,
beyond the number standing against them, it may be
stated that most of the music which has become so
familiar and so pleasing to the people as to be conveyed to them day by day (on their own delightful
street organs,) belong to some one or other of the
operas herein enumerated. Beautifully and truly
indeed hath the modern Anacreon sung, in his own
unrivalled strain,

> Music! O how faint, how weak,
> Language fades before thy spell ;
> Why should language ever speak
> When thou canst tell her tale so well !

I think I have quoted right, at least I hope so.
Combining, therefore, the legitimate and the illegitimate accounts, it cannot be denied that every variety
was afforded to the lovers and followers of each. I
must not omit noticing another circumstance which
gave the snarlers an opportunity of showing their
teeth, indicative of their propensity to bite, if they
could. I approach this part of the business deli-
cately, because it is personal, and bearing in mind

that Shakspeare has put into the mouth of *Cæsar*,

" What touches us ourself shall be last served"

I have kept it back until worthier matter has been disposed of It will be seen that under the head of " authors and adapters," my own name figures pretty conspicuously; and it has been repeatedly charged against me, that I neglected the works of other far superior dramatists, for the purpose of stuffing my own goods down the throats of the suffering public. Though as daring a falsehood as any of the other fabrications " got up" against my management, it was not a bad lay for the malcontents to go upon, considering the repeated opportunities I gave them of indulging in their propensity. But I will explain my motives and my objects. I am quite as willing to admit my own inferiority to SOME, as I should be to maintain my superiority to MANY, if boasting were my trade; but that part of the business never once entered my head : but being rapid in the execution of what I *do* undertake, finding some others extremely slow, and knowing the urgency of our condition, I have over and over again, after rising at six, writing till eleven, attending rehearsals of three and four hours' duration, superintending the ordinary duties of management, such as answering letters, auditing accounts, going over the departments, conferring with the many seeking conferences, issuing general orders, and " orders for two," &c., had to sit up the greatest part of the night to complete a subject. Few other people will do for you what you will do for yourself; and as I never desired to have my effusions weighed in the standard-scales of dramatic literature, I cared little about the critics, so long as I could arrest the attention of the town. I must leave the town to determine how often I succeeded in so doing, while I attempt to vindicate myself from the forenamed unjust aspersion. I will dare any one to say that I did not avail myself, as frequently as possible, of the talent of all those worth availing oneself of—of our darling master, Knowles, whenever I could get hold of him; of my able, industrious, and zealous friend PLANCHÉ—of—of—but let us name them—" Name, name, if you please"—of those who worked for *our* treasury, and, with an exception or two, *their own*, at the same time: ADDISON, BEAZLEY, BIRD, BAILLIE, BALL, BYRON, BARNETT, BERNARD, BUCKSTONE, DANCE C., DANCE G., FITZBALL, FARLEY, GORE MRS., JERROLD, KNOWLES, KENNEY, LOVELL, LOGAN, LINLEY, MILLINGEN, POCOCK, POOLE, PLANCHÉ, PLANCHÉ MRS., PEAKE, REYNOLDS, RODWELL, SERLE, TRUEBA, WESTMACOTT R., &c.

If it had not been for the extraordinary terms demanded for the *Duchess de la Vallière*, previously commented upon, and for the assault committed by Mr. Macready, that led to the withdrawal of ION, (which was to have been brought out for that tragicide's benefit,) the names of Sir E. L. Bulwer and Mr. Serjeant Talfourd would have been added to this list;

M 5

and it is therefore not too much to say, that there was scarcely a dramatic author of any reputation, during my management of the London stage, whose works were not introduced on the boards of Drury Lane or Covent Garden Theatres; and while the finest music of such eminent foreign composers as Auber, Bellini, Herold, Halevy, Mozart, Marliani, Meyerbeer, Rossini, Weber, &c., was brought forward in rapid succession, the various contributions of Messrs. Balfe, Barnett, Benedict, Bishop, Cooke T., Loder, Lacy, &c., will surely bear out my assertion, that native talent was equally encouraged.

Of a verity these defamers, who have been so long trying to hold *me* up to ridicule, " cut a mighty ridiculous figure themselves ;" but they will cut a worse figure, as I follow them up, by every possible degree of COMPARISON.   Such a pompous and nonsensical parade has been hawked about of the mode in which Shakspeare's plays were represented, and were prepared, under the sublime management of Mr. Macready, that I take the liberty of questioning it again, as I have already so frequently done.   The hasty attempt of " *King Lear*, from the text of Shakspeare," he made before with me, both at Drury Lane and Covent Garden—consequently there was no novelty in THAT. The restoration of " the text of Shakspeare" in others of his plays was a mere joke, being resorted to only as it set off the hero of the piece to better advantage.   The *Macbeth*, about which such a flourish was made, claimed the blessing, to be sure, of his own performance, (and we claimed that of Mr. Forrest); but while its exquisite music was, comparatively speaking, shuffled through by a few voices at Covent Garden, I gave it the benefit of THIS SUPPORT at Drury Lane, by virtue of which the celebrated chorus of witches obtained the unprecedent honour of a nightly *encore.* Here are the names of THE VOCAL PERFORMERS:

Messrs. Balfe, Templeton, Wilson, Giubelei, Anderson, Bedford, Duruset, Henry, S. Jones, Seguin, &c.; *Mesdames* Shirreff, Romer, Poole, Forde, Taylor, C. Jones, Humby, &c., accompanied by A DOUBLE CHORUS AND THE ENLARGED BAND:

Altos.—Messrs. Miller, Lloyd, Rakes, Ashton, Lewis, Willing, Walsh, Healey, Chant, Hammond, &c.

Tenors.—Messrs. C. Tett, S. Tett, Birt, Morgue, W. Price, Goodson, Nye, Jones, J. Price, J. Taylor, &c.

Basses.—Messrs. Caulfield, Santry, Atkins, Barclay, Green, Butler, Caro, Field, Macarthy, Tolkien.

Soprani.—Mesdames Hamilton, Somerville, Allcroft, Boden, Perry, Goodson, Hughes, East, Barnett, Connelly, Butler, H. Bodon, Goodwin, Mapleson, &c.

Then again, while unable, by "the voice of the public press," to cram down the public gorge his own performance of *Hamlet,* we played that sublime tragedy TWENTY-ONE NIGHTS in the space of two months!

Then, as to *Othello,* can all the play-bills of the

gentleman who undertook to ADVANCE THE DRAMA AS
A BRANCH OF LITERATURE AND ART, produce such a
" cast" of its principal characters, as on two distinct
occasions was given by me at Drury Theatre?—
Read :

In 1833.	In 1835.
Othello ....Mr. Kean.	Othello ....Mr. Macready.
Iago ....— Macready.	Iago ....— Vandenhoff
Cassio...............— Cooper.	Cassio...............— Cooper.
Roderigo............— Balls.	Brabantio ....— Warde.
Desdemona ......Miss Phillips.	Roderigo............— Harley.
Emilia ....Mrs. Faucit.	Desdemona ......Mrs. Yates.
	Emilia ....Miss E. Tree.

Then, again, let us look at the announcement of
THE TEMPEST, about which such a trumpery fuss was
made, and see if we did not go as far towards THE
ADVANCEMENT OF THE DRAMA, even as " Shakspeare's
representative," which is surely saying a great deal.
His means of representing it shall be placed in JUXTA-
POSITION with *mine*:

THE TEMPEST.	THE TEMPEST
AT DRURY LANE IN 1833,	AT COVENT GARDEN IN 1838,
altered by Davenant and Dryden.	*from " the text of Shakspeare."*
Alonzo ....Mr. Diddear.	Alonzo .. ..Mr. Warde.
Prospero............— Macready.	Prospero............— Macready.
Antonio ....— Mathews.	Antonio ....— Phelps.
Ferdinand ....— Cooper.	Ferdinand ....— Anderson.
Hyppolito ....Miss Taylor.	Sebastian ....— Diddear.
Gonzalo ....Mr. Younge.	Gonzalo......... ...— Waldron.
Caliban ....— Bedford.	Caliban ....— G. Bennett.
Trinculo ....— Blanchard.	Trinculo............— Harley.
Stephano............— Dowton.	Stephano ....— Bartley.
Miranda........... Miss Inverarity	Miranda............Miss H. Faucit
Dorinda .... — Shirreff.	Dorinda ....*Not in the piece*
Ariel .. .. — Poole.	Ariel ....Miss P.Horton

Then, again, can he produce any " *cast*" of any one
of the finest plays of our olden masters, to be compared to the following distribution of characters in
Ben Jonson's *Every Man in his Humour*, played at
Drury Lane in 1833?

Kitely..................................	Mr. Macready.
Bobadil	— Power.
Edward Know'ell	— Cooper.
Brainworm............................	— Farren.
Justice Clement...........	— Dowton.
Master Stephen	— Harley.
Wellbred..............................	— Stanley.
Cob	— Bedford.
Dame Kitely	Mrs. Nesbitt.
Bridget	Miss Cawse.
Tib	Mrs. C. Jones.

Then, again, while I. can produce half a dozen
such instances of musical strength, I will content
myself by asking if the great restorator of the drama
ever " cast" an opera with the force by which *Don
Juan* was supported at Drury Lane in 1833?

Don Juan	Mr. Braham.
Don Ottavio	— Templeton.
Don Pedro	— Bedford.
Mazetto	— E. Seguin.
Leporello.............................	— H. Phillips.
Donna Anna	Madame de Meric.
Donna Elvira........................	Miss Betts.
Zerlina..............................	Mrs. Wood.

These be pleasant and useful recollections of a state
of things we shall not soon again see realised, and

afford a retrospect which I very much doubt if
"Shakspeare's representative," had he remained in
power three times as long as he did, would be able to
indulge in. True it is, I never made a set of un-
mea..ing promises, and took my own method of
fulfilling them : I did not exclude certain occu-
pants of the saloons — because they brought a
great deal of money to the treasury. I did not put
myself in all the principal characters, regardless of the
feelings or reputation of those who played the other
characters; and I did not, in fact, make "much ado
about nothing;" but I shall be perfectly content to
abide the decision of the public, on a dispassionate
comparison of our respective exertions, whether I did
not far surpass every effort of his, *to advance the
drama as a branch of literature and art!* The result
of our proceedings was, that, by a timely retreat, he
was enabled to demand £25 per night for his services
in another theatre, and I was—ruined! So would *he*
have been, had he toiled as many years at *his* undertaking, as I did at mine.

As respects the present management, which succeeded his, as far at least as it has gone during my
progress with these volumes, though I would not be
thought to disparage any effort of one claiming the
meed of approbation which beauty and talent are
always entitled to, nor to deny that great and praiseworthy energies have been bestowed by Madame
Vestris on her hazardous enterprise; yet I take the
liberty of saying, that one of the creditable perform-

ances which has distinguished her management, and won her " golden opinions," is not, at least, more entitled to public favour than a similar one given by me at Drury Lane—*ecce signum :*

THE SCHOOL FOR SCANDAL AT DRURY LANE IN 1833.	THE SCHOOL FOR SCANDAL AT COVENT GARDEN IN 1839.
Sir Peter Teazle...Mr. Farren.	Sir Peter Teazle...Mr. Farren.
Sir Oliver Surface — Dowton.	Sir Oliver Surface — Bartley.
Joseph Surface ...— Macready.	Joseph Surface ...— Cooper.
Charles Surface...— Cooper.	Charles Surface ...— Mathews.
Sir Benj. Backbite— Harley.	Sir Benj. Backbite— Harley.
Sir Harry ....— Braham.	Sir Harry ....— Binge.
Crabtree............— Ayliffe.	Crabtree ....— Meadows.
Trip ....— Balls.	Trip ....— Green.
Moses ....— Ross.	Moses ....— Keeley.
Lady Teazle ......Mrs. Nesbitt.	Lady Teazle ......Mad. Vestris.
Lady Sneerwell...— Faucit.	Lady Sneerwell...Mrs. Nesbitt.
Mrs. Candour......— Glover.	Mrs. Candour......Mrs. Orger.
Maria ....Miss Cawse.	Maria ....Miss Lee.

I think, without any disrespect to any party in question, that the comparison between these two " casts" must be considerably in my favour. But it is delightful to contrast the unpretending and admirable efforts of Madame Vestris with the bombastic froth and nothingness of her immediate predecessor: and even had she obtained no other advantage, the appearance of the theatre, under the respective managements, would be ample; for she may safely exclaim with *Augustus Cæsar* (I believe) that she " found her city brick, and made it marble."

Having now indulged the reader with a somewhat lengthened account of my legitimate and illegitimate performances, together with the names of the legitimate and illegitimate performers who were called in to support them; at the same time having furnished him with a compendium of the general nature of my humble efforts to manage the London stage, I should leave the very best and the very worst part of my task unfinished, if I did not add the result of it all. Having contributed my own slender means at starting, and having added from time to time my various subsequent gainings towards the general good of the concern; having never received salary but when others did, and often received with one hand ten times less than I advanced with the other; having toiled day and night, in winter and summer; travelled far and near, written and adapted, (bad enough if you please,) and done my best, (be it now deemed bad or good,) I can fearlessly insert the subjoined piece of documentary wretchedness; and while the high eulogium of the judge and the court is something to be proud of, I cannot deny that I wish it had pleased Providence that the opportunity of receiving it had not been afforded:

COURT OF BANKRUPTCY,

Basinghall Street, December the 17th, 1840.

[Before Mr. Commissioner Merivale.]

The bankruptcy of Alfred Bunn, late lessee and

manager of the Theatres Royal Drury Lane and Covent Garden.

The bankrupt appeared before the court to pass his final examination. There were but few creditors present at this sitting.

After proofs had been admitted from Messrs. Peake, Eliason, Fitzball, Dunn, &c., for services rendered,

Mr. Wryghte, the accountant, handed in the balance sheet of the bankrupt.

The following is the general sheet, which shows a clear and elucidating statement of all the bankrupt's affairs :—

IN RE ALFRED BUNN, A BANKRUPT.

From the 6th of December 1834 *to the 4th of November* 1839.

Dr.

On account of the theatres	-	£21,257	5	4
Money lent -	-	1,526	9	8
Private tradesmen	-	702	16	2
		23,486	11	2
Liabilities -	-	4,300	0	0
Capital, December 6th, 1834	-	250	0	0

PROFITS.*

Salary as manager, benefits, theatrical authorship, sale of musical compositions, country speculation of the Jewess, &c. as per statement	-	6,668	0	0
		34,704	11	2

* A curious fact occurred in the profits. One of the items is the sum of £40 enclosed in a parcel, and sent to the bankrupt by an unknown hand. He has never been able to trace the individual thus generously inclined towards him.

Cr.

On account of the theatres - -		2,276	3 8
Bad, and carried to losses - -	199 10 0		
Losses - - - -		23,252	1 5
Expenses - - - -		4,860	0 0
Liabilities per contra - -		4,300	0 0
Amount unaccounted for - -		16	6 1

34,704 11 2

The undermentioned statement shows the losses incurred throughout the theatrical management of the bankrupt, as exhibited in his balance-sheet:—

Losses by management of Theatres from the 6th of December 1834.

Season 1834—35.

(The bankrupt had both the patent theatres.)
Total xpenditure. Journal A, fo. 347 £51,526 15 10
Total receipts. Journal A, fol. 348 . . 49,876 9 1
————— 1,650 6 9

Season 1835—36.

(The bankrupt had but one of the patent theatres.)
Total expenditure. Journal B, folio 28   59,183 1 9
Total receipts. Journal B, folio 28 . . . 57,424 10 8
————— 1,758 11 1

Season 1836—37.

(The bankrupt had but one of the patent theatres.)
Total expenditure. Journal B, folio 69   44,282 5 4
Total receipts. Journal B, folio 69 . . . 40,638 19 2
————— 3,643 6 2

SEASON 1837—38.

(The bankrupt had the Theatre Royal Drury Lane.)

Total expenditure, Journal B, folio 108   39,066   3   2

Total receipts. Journal B, folio 108 . .   36,053 12   1

——————   3,012 11   1

SEASON 1838—39.

(The bankrupt had the Theatre Royal Drury Lane.)

Total expenditure, Journal B, fol. 143   44,211   6   3

Total receipts. Journal B, folio 143 . .   28,947   6   3

—————— 15,264   0   0

25,328 15   1

Rent and part of the above expenses payable by Cap-

tain Polhill   2,276   3   8

£23,052 11   5

Mr. Commissioner Merivale having examined the accounts, said, that if any person wished to address the court upon the bankrupt's balance-sheet, now was the time. He had heard from the official assignee that, as far as he was informed, there was no objection to his passing. Were the assignees present?

Mr. Mapleson replied in the affirmative.

Mr. Lewis, a solicitor to the fiat, said the accounts reflected great credit upon the bankrupt, and had entirely been made up from the books of the theatre, which had been uniformly and correctly kept. He also felt bound, in justice to the bankrupt, to state that his private debts did not far exceed £700, the remaining large sum having reference to the theatrical property, and in the liquidation of which, for a long period, he had been paying his own earnings. It was hoped that from £2,000 to £3,000 would be recovered for the benefit of the creditors.

Mr. Commissioner Merivale.—But I see that is under the head of doubtful debts.

Mr. Lewis.—Yes, your honour, because a lawsuit must be first commenced.

The Official Assignee.—It appears that in his private expenditure he has not been extravagant.

Mr. Commissioner Merivale.—That is highly creditable to him, and ought to be known, as it is a public business. The losses have been large in the theatrical management.

Mr. Mapleson.—Mr. Bunn is not an individual instance; managers before him have also suffered.

Mr. Commissioner Merivale.—I see there is a rapid falling off in the receipts in three seasons of Mr. Bunn's management, from £57,000 to £28,000, more than one half. I suppose that occurred in consequence of the reduction of prices.

Mr. Mapleson.—It was the reduction of prices and the loss of public inclination for the last two seasons.

Mr. Commissioner Merivale.—It also appears that at the time the receipts were highest, the disbursements were highest; the expenses must have been very heavy.

Mr. Mapleson replied in the affirmative.

Mr. Commissioner Merivale would make no further observations. Did any of the creditors wish to put any questions?

No reply being made, the bankrupt having been formally examined, *Mr. Commissioner Merivale* declared the bankrupt passed.

The court then rose.

This document does not refer, of course, to that part of my management when the pecuniary responsibility was on another's shoulders. Viewing, therefore, all that *has* been done, and foreseeing all that is likely *to* be done, we may, I fear me, safely say of the management of the patent theatres,

" To THIS FAVOUR it must come ! "

CHAPTER VIII.

Pains and penalties give way to rhyme and reason—A probable sus-
pension of both—Prospect of an epic poem overclouded—Spenser,
Leigh Hunt, and Southey—A change desirable, not ending in a de-
sirable change—Public meeting—Mr. Robins and Mr. Durrant—
Lots of fun, and a little mischief—A loud report, but a false one—
A slight mistake or two—How to draw up an advertisement—
Defence of Mr. Bunn by a proprietor—Opinions of the whole body
on Mr. Bunn for seven years—The chairman's individual opinion—
Eating one's own words sometimes a tough mouthful—Straight-
forward correspondence—Sale at the auction mart, and a sail at sea
—A good dinner and a bad speech—A grand finale.

HAVING overcome the painful and humiliating position of feeling bound, as a matter of honour, to give
additional promulgation to one's own indignities
and sufferance, on the principle adopted by *Lady
Townley*, of taking " a great gulp, and swallowing
it," I may more freely discuss all the petty miseries
which immediately preceded their consummation.
I had done with the theatre from the moment I
found that it was impossible to produce *The Fairy
Lake*, but I had not done with the embarrassments

in which it had involved me ; or, rather, some of the parties connected with them had not done with me. Any reference to private matters, now the affairs which gave rise to exasperated feelings on either side are disposed of, can answer no earthly purpose but molestation; and having no desire to annoy those who, perhaps under a mistaken notion, did their utmost to annoy me, I let my page do the duty of my goblet, and say with *Brutus*,

" In this I bury all unkindness."

I have shaken hands with two parties who shall be nameless ; and that sacred ceremony being performed, I regret if I have written even a syllable that may displease them, and for worlds would not repeat one here. My chief anxiety, on my retirement from the theatre, was to pay my debts and vent my spleen, as far as both were practicable. I found the first part of the business impracticable— the other part of it I turned over in my mind, and began it in, what I considered to be, a smart display of poetical merriment. It was originally intended to be an epic ! taking a view of the stage in verse, aided by copious addenda of notes and illustrations; and I purposed that it should be written as if spoken by Mr. Macready in his own person, on his abdication of Covent Garden Theatre. I had intended to give him full license of animadversion on *my* management as well as on *his* own, and to extend his remarks to the profession, and all in connexion with it. I began my sublime composition after the following fashion :—

1.

Now, worthy people, " going—going—GONE !"
　　As saith my neighbour-quack, the auctioneer ;
The best quotation I could pitch upon,
　　And so accordingly I use it here ;
Were there no other reason, it, to one
　　And all, beyond a question, must appear
That I've been " going" (it) these two years past,
As clearly as, that I am " gone" at last !

2.

Some sceptics who may envy me the pleasure
　　Which I derive from practising mine art,
Abuse my principle beyond all measure,
　　And that in terms, too, I take much to heart :
So having now again a little leisure,
　　All that I think and feel I shall impart ;
He who receives an injury resents it,
And if he has a fit of spleen, he vents if.

3.

'Tis wisely writ, " Whatever is, is best,"
　　And heaven forbid that I should e'er gainsay it ;
A precept simply, forcibly expressed,
　　And man is very prudent to obey it :
Though I heard one (I trust it was in jest,
　　And not as an example to display it,)
Say of the theatre, there was no doubt of it,
'Twere " best" for all that I at last was *out* of it.

I soon became of opinion, as the reader will easily imagine and readily join me in, that this promised to be a tremendous lot of rubbish, and I therefore abandoned the idea *in toto*. In the mean time my difficulties continued to increase, and rhyme and reason both threatened to take their departure. When Spenser was made poet laureate, he was awarded the yearly emolument, since handed down, and so ludicrously and admirably hit off by Mr. Leigh Hunt, in his amusing parody on Mr. Southey's *Carmen Triumphale*, wherein he describes the laureate's annual perquisites to consist of

" Wearing bag-wigs and other princely raiment,
Glory to kings his song, a hundred pounds his payment !"'

When this item of £100 came under the observation of the Lord Burleigh ; that prudent counsellor asked Queen Elizabeth whether she was in earnest in allotting so large a payment as that, MERELY FOR A SONG ? and, owing to Burleigh's remonstrance, the actual disbursement was a long time making its appearance. The suspense and the delay were vital to Spenser, who thus vented *his* spleen—at least so runs the story :

" I heard, that once upon a time
" They promised REASON for my rhyme ;
" But from that time until this season,
" I've had neither RHYME *nor* REASON !"

In some such dilemma as this did I find myself. I had no " *reason*," in Spenser's reading of the word, and my Pegasus could supply me with no rhyme. I tried all that I could, through the agency

of a host of kind friends, (being able, thank God !
to boast of as numerous an acquaintance as most
folk,) to effect some understanding, or arrange some
compromise, with those who had demands against
the theatre, all of which were of a professional nature, which probably accounts for the utter impos-
sibility that manifested itself of doing anything of
the sort. While these matters were in agitation, or
cogitation rather, the annual meeting of the proprietors of Drury Lane Theatre was held in the
saloon of the theatre, at which a statement of the
company's affairs was laid before the body by the
secretary of the committee. In addition to a feeling
of disappointment entertained towards me by most
of them, except the sub-committee who knew me
best, there was a spirit of dissatisfaction manifest
between each other—too often the case when men
are in a muddle, and do not clearly see their way
out of it. Of course *I* came in for a tolerable proportion of their flagellation. I am not certain if I
have said before, but if so, it will bear repeating,

" The evil that men do lives after them,
" The good is oft interred with their bones."

They had altogether forgotten how long I had worked
for their property, on my own as well as others' responsibilities—what monies I had been the means of
other lessees paying them, and what monies I had
paid them myself. They had forgotten the vast
improvements made in every department of their

building; in short, they had forgotten everything
but that paramount desire, always uppermost in the
human system, of seeking some change. They lost
sight of even their own discontent with one another,
in order to relieve themselves of the incubus they considered me to be upon their property—unmindful of
the ruin of my predecessors, and of the utter impossi-
bility their own experience had taught them of
finding a fit successor. George Robins was bent
on getting rid of me, for which he was quite right;
and, however annoyed at the time, I have been
thankful to him ever since. Mr. Durrant was bent
upon getting in Mr. Hammond, in which he was
quite wrong; and however flattered at the time,
Hammond will live to wish him at the devil for so
doing. Between ourselves, I think Robins would have
given a trifle if he could have got rid of Durrant at
the same time,—your committee and *ex*-committee
men not having, as I believe, any holy love for one
another. If men in such emergencies could but be
prevailed upon to do the right, even while they resorted to the expedient, they should have rejoiced
as long as they pleased in the glorious possession of
their new tenant; but the utmost expression that
should have escaped their lips respecting their old
and long-tried tenant, should have been a feeling of
regret. They might surely have praised a man of
whom they knew nothing, without abusing one of
whom they knew a great deal. Perhaps it may be
said, that is the very reason why they *did* abuse me.

N 2

No such thing: they were guided solely by a love of change, and it would seem, by their choice, that they considered *any* change would be for the better. What do they think NOW? If *I* brought their theatre into disrepute and *mauvaise odeur*, after seven or eight years' hard fag, what have THEY brought it to? If, after introducing upon their boards all the collective talent of this and other countries, and with the assistance of that talent introducing some of the most popular entertainments ever seen upon them, I brought their theatre into positive disgrace, as was alleged,—pray what has my successor, (the pet choice of one of their body, and cried up by the whole of them at the meeting in question,) without any collective talent, and without the aid of one popular entertainment, brought their house to? I should be truly sorry to say an unkind word against Mr. Hammond, who, it must have been known to all but the one or two who affected to patronise him into the lesseeship, was totally unfit for that position. I speak only of those casual superintendents over the sub-committee, who meet once a year to upset, or at least to question, all the proceedings of the past twelvemonth.

But mischief was altogether the order of the day at this assembly: for, leaving me out of the question, they were bent on the dismemberment of their own body, and were determined not to be satisfied until they had rid themselves of two parties—one as intellectual, and the other as strict a man of business as ever sat in council; and they placed in their stead one, and introduced another, of the greatest——but I shall wait until the new law of libel comes out before I finish the sentence.

Oh! but to think on the rare nonsense which, for two or three hours, some of them did indulge in, at a time when they ought to have lost sight of all personal feelings, and only have considered how they could best steer their vessel through the troubled waters in which she was then floundering. But the report of their proceedings, taken from a competent public journal, is the best authority that can be adduced of a scene of so much absurdity, and it is therefore subjoined :—

" DRURY LANE THEATRE.

" On Wednesday afternoon, July 24, 1839, a " meeting of the proprietors of Drury Lane Theatre " was held in the saloon to receive the report of the " general committee, and to elect a sub-committee, " &c. : the Earl of Glengall in the chair.

" Mr. Dunn, the secretary, read the report, " which stated that the delay in calling the present " meeting (which was usually held at an earlier period " of the year) was owing to the difficulties which " the committee had had to contend with in letting " the theatre. After stating the necessity of some " great reduction being made in the charges on the " property, and expressing a hope that some final " arrangement with respect to the rent-charge of

" the theatre would be made in the course of the
" present year, it suggested the propriety of coming
" to some arrangement with the new renters ; for
" which purpose some meetings of both parties had
" been held, but without any satisfactory result.
" The committee then mentioned the liberal con-
" duct of the ground landlord, the Duke of Bedford,
" (in reducing the rent by £ 500 a year,) adding,
" however, that it was a conditional surrender only,
" and liable to be recalled at any time, and added,
" that the rental of the theatre on which the poor-
" rate was assessed had lately been reduced by
" £ 2,165 per annum, and the other rates in propor-
" tion. The Report then stated, that the lessee, Mr.
" Bunn, finding the difficulties in which the com-
" mittee were placed with respect to letting the theatre,
" had last year again become the lessee. Had he
" not done so, either the theatre must have been
" closed during the past season, or been conducted
" by the sub-committee. After great delay and
" difficulty, the committee had again let the theatre.
" The new lessee was Mr. Hammond, who had
" taken the theatre for three years, and from his
" known talent the committee anticipated the
" greatest success. They had received other ten-
" ders, and taken them into consideration ; but
" some of them were not thought worthy of accept-
" ance, and as to others, the parties making them
" were not in a condition to keep the terms origi-
" nally proposed by themselves. The report con-

" cluded by stating, that an alteration would be
" made in the system of selling free admissions,
" which would tend to increase their value; that
" the accounts were audited and ready for inspec-
" tion, and that the theatre required some substan-
" tial repairs, the expense of which would be
" defrayed out of a fund that had been set apart for
" that purpose."

" On a motion that the report be received and
" adopted,

" Mr. Wells said, that a more meagre report he
" had never listened to in his life. He wished to
" have some information as to what were the duties
" of the general and sub-committee, and what were
" the dormant duties of the proprietors themselves.
" —(*Hear! hear!*)—He thought that a recently
" published pamphlet threw a considerable light
" upon the subject.

" The chairman trusted that no further notice
" would be taken of the pamphlet to which allusion
" had just been made, and that the meeting would
" at once proceed with the business for which it
" had been convened.

" Mr. T. Welch said, the present was the proper
" time for asking questions, which, if not put now,
" would not be answered at all. He complained that
" the proprietors were treated more like dependents
" than proprietors by the general committee, and
" said the business of the general meeting was
" always huddled through in a very hurried manner,

" and it was impossible to get any information
" whatever from the committee.

" Mr. Wells said, the pamphlet to which he had
" alluded was ordered to be printed by the last gene-
" ral meeting of the proprietors. He wished to
" know by whose authority its circulation had since
" been suppressed.

" The chairman said, that, on consideration, the
" general committee were of opinion that the pamph-
" let had better not be circulated, and they therefore
" caused its suppression.

" After some further discussion relative to the
" suppression of the pamphlet,

" The chairman said, that the committee were
" ready and willing to answer any question that
" might be put to them. He would admit that the
" affairs of the theatre were not in a satisfactory
" state, yet he could assure the proprietors that the
" committee had done everything that lay in their
" power for the benefit of the theatre, and all per-
" sons connected with it. It was but justice to Mr.
" Bunn to state, that he did all he could to sup-
" port the interests of the theatre.—(*Hear !*)—The
" committee, however, were in this position, when
" they let him the theatre last year, that they could
" not get anybody else to take it—(*hear !*)—and
" they delayed letting it to him until so late a period,
" that he had the greatest difficulty in getting a
" company of performers. If he had not come for-
" ward and placed himself in the gap, the theatre

" must have fallen into the hands of the grouhd
" landlord.

" Mr. George Robins begged to ask what rent
" Mr. Bunn had paid during the last three years
" for the theatre, and how much he was now in
" arrear? He believed that all he had paid towards
" the rent of last season was £1,350.

" The chairman said that was the fact.

" Major Naylor said, the rent Mr. Bunn agreed
" to pay was £6,000 a year. He now owed the
" proprietors £12,000, he having, during the last
" three years, paid altogether only £ 6,000.

" Mr. Robins observed, that when he came into
" the room, he intended only to get an answer to
" one or two important questions connected with
" the bygone season; but, after reading the re-
" port, he found himself compelled to travel out of
" his original intention, and make a commentary
" upon a document the most frightful and unsatis-
" factory that ever was presented to a public meet-
" ing. Mr. Robins assured Lord Glengall, that in
" the observations he should make, he intended no-
" thing personal; but he had a duty to perform,
" which he must and should discharge. His lord-
" ship had read the unfortunate statement, without
" receiving in his progress one smile or congratula-
" tory look. In bygone days things were different
" —something satisfactory could always be wedged
" in to save the report, but in this case the noble
" lord evidently foretold that nothing but one

" universal feeling of condemnation could exist in
" respect to the account they had just given of their
" stewardship, and the committee therefore substi-
" tuted a long useless commentary upon a real or
" supposed difference which existed with the new
" renters and the proprietors. But this could not
" avail them ; we must come to facts, and the figures
" before us left no doubt of the truth upon which
" he intended to speak. First, his lordship told
" them of the difficulty of letting the theatre; to
" that he rejoined, that he believed the committee
" in their hearts never intended or desired any
" other lessee except Mr. Bunn, or why put forth
" annually such an unmeaning advertisement ? He
" (Mr. Robins) took the trouble to write a more
" suitable one three years ago, and if they had the
" least intention that the theatre should change
" hands, they would have adopted it. But let us
" look at the facts as they stand before us, and
" which no sophistry of the noble lord's report could
" shake ! Has Covent Garden been without a
" tenant during this period ? Did not Mr. Osbal-
" diston pay £8,000 a year regularly for three years ?
" and has not Mr. Macready paid £7,000 a year
" with equal punctuality during the last two years ?
" At Covent Garden Theatre there is no arrear
" in the last three years ; they had received £22,000 !
" Now let us look at the sad reverse at Drury Lane :
" in three years £ 6,000 only had found its way
" into the treasury, although during the same period

" a minor theatre (the Haymarket) was actually
" paying £4,000 a year, and making great profits
" besides. But this is not all—' the worst remains
" behind.' The boards upon which the plays of the
" immortal bard have been represented for nearly
" a century have been disgraced by an exhibition
" worthy only of Bartholomew fair—wild beasts,
" monkeys, and horses, and asses, have polluted the
" fair fame of that once classic temple. But he had
" not yet done—the picture was not completed—for
" it had been visited by the additional indignity of
" becoming ' THE SHILLING THEATRE !' All the
" riff-raff of London let loose to congregate in
" Drury Lane Theatre—but to no purpose ; and all
" this was done and countenanced by the present
" MIS-managing committee ! It could not be pre-
" tended (as an honourable proprietor had just
" stated) that the drama could not support Mr.
" Bunn, because the legitimate drama never stood
" so high (since the lamented death of the illustrious
" John Kemble and his unapproachable sister Mrs.
" Siddons) as at the present moment ! Mr. Mac-
" ready had sustained the character and raised the
" reputation of Covent Garden, so as to show a
" painful contrast to the one in which he was ad-
" dressing them. Indeed, its reputation was raised
" so high under his superintendence, that the mo-
" ment he relinquished it, Madame Vestris became
" the lessee. Can the committee, after this, justify
" themselves for having continued it to be dis-

" graced by wild beasts, and at length shut up in the
" very heart of the season; yet, in the face of this
" frightful picture, the proprietors are now asked
" to respond to the *precious document* which had
" been read to them. He could only say, even if he was
" alone, he should hold up his hand against the pre-
" sent MIS-managing committee being re-elected.
" But that could not be accomplished, unless the
" 'general committee' (who annually are required
" to elect a sub--committee) would aid the cause of
" the unfortunate, the devoted proprietors. With
" their assistance, some hope of future success might
" appear.

" Lord Glengall then proposed that the six mem-
" bers of the general committee who go out by rota-
" tion should be balloted for. This being done,—

" John Ramsbottom, Esq., M. P., rose to state
" that he had been a member of the general com-
" mittee for five years, and he found the sub-com-
" mittee never called upon them except in cases (such
" as the present one) of great difficulty. Unless that
" system was altered, he must withdraw his name.

" The general committee was then re-elected.
" Lord Hardwick, it was stated, had never attended;
" upon which Mr. Robins proposed Mr. Wells, a
" barrister, as a substitute; but as his lordship had
" written a letter, promising to be a better member,
" Mr. Ramsbottom withdrew his amendment.

" The committee then retired to the saloon to
" elect a sub-committee. Now, it is not generally

" known to our readers that this had uniformly been
" a mere matter of form—they have always been
" re-elected by the 'general committee.' However,
" it soon became manifest A SCREW WAS LOOSE. Half
" an hour was occupied in an adjoining room, and a
" ballot taken, by which Mr. Spencer and Mr. Arden
" lost their seats at the board of control, and Mr.
" Ramsbottom and Mr. (somebody else) took their
" places. This seemed to give some satisfaction, as
" one of the gentlemen had become exceedingly un-
" popular with the proprietors.

" Lord Glengall esteemed and respected the names
" of the new committee; upon which Mr. Robins
" said, as they had weeded the committee a little,
" and promised to amend their ways in future, he
" should not oppose the vote of thanks to the
" chairman, although he should object to the con-
" firmation of the report.

" A proprietor said he rose to defend Mr. Bunn
" from the unwarrantable attack that had just been
" made upon him. Mr. Bunn had got together
" the best company he could ; he had engaged the
" most distinguished performers ; and if brutes were
" afterwards introduced upon the stage, that was
" the fault of the public, who chose to encourage
" such exhibitions.

" Mr. Wells wished to know the state of the
" accounts.

" Mr. George Robins said the debts were 17,706l.,
" to meet which there was 17,704l., which latter

" amount consisted of 5,000*l.* due from Captain
" Polhill, and 12,000*l.* from Mr. Bunn.

" Mr. Wells moved as an amendment, that the
" resolution, directing the pamphlet of Captain
" Spencer to be printed and circulated, be forthwith
" carried into effect.

" After a long discussion, the motion was nega-
" tived by a majority of thirteen to six. The meet-
" ing then separated."

This is a nice document, replete with taste, liberality, and as much good English as ever Lindley
Murray put together. The first bit of fun it contains is the announcement that Mr. Hammond had
taken the theatre for three years—(if they had said
three months, it would have been nearer the mark)—
and THE ANTICIPATION *of the greatest success from*
his KNOWN TALENT! I believe Hammond to be as
respectable and honourable a man as ever lived,
and when I told him, last November, where he
would be sure to go, (vol. ii. page 77,) it was as
far from my wish, as it was near to my conviction,
that go he must ; but " the known talent" of Mr.
Hammond not having escaped beyond the precincts
of the Strand Theatre, renders this part of the story
a burlesque. The pamphlet referred to is a compilation from the records of the establishment, by
one of the most assiduous gentlemen and ripe
scholars that ever formed part of a managing committee ; and the persons instrumental in the exclu-

sion of Captain Spencer on this occasion, will regret
it as long as the bricks of the theatre hold together.
The compliment paid to me by the noble chairman
breathes all the courtesy, as the abuse of others
betrays all the coarseness, to which I had been
accustomed.

With reference to George Robins's attack, the
joke of the thing is, that all the while he was a
member of the committee he was always foremost
in proposing any assistance or accommodation to
me ; but when he turned his back upon the building, he paid the lessee the same compliment.   His
sallies against the horses and asses, and the contrast he draws between their appearance and the
classical performances of John Kemble and Mrs.
Siddons, are diverting in the extreme, when it is re-
collected that they used all—horses, asses if you
please, John Kemble, Charles Kemble, and Mrs.
Siddons—to play *on the* SAME *evening,* some years
ago, at Covent Garden Theatre !   Then Mr. Osbaldiston only had the latter theatre TWO years, instead
of three as stated, and, being sick of his losses, relinquished it ; and as Mr. Macready did the same
at the end of the same period, it is fair to presume
that he was not particularly in love with his gains.
But, to use Robins's own words, " the worst remains behind ;" for the advertisement which he
took the trouble to draw up for the committee
three years ago, was shamefully disregarded. Such
a tidbit as that ought not to be lost to the public,

and though I have not been able to lay my hand
upon the identical document, I have no doubt the
subjoined is very near the valued original :

THEATRE ROYAL DRURY LANE.

MR. GEORGE ROBINS is honoured with the commands of the proprietors of this far-famed

MINE OF WEALTH

to submit to public competition the lease of it for
as many years as may be agreeablé, which a man of
any taste may think himself truly fortunate in possessing.

THE SCENERY,

consisting of some hundred pieces, described, in the
glowing language of the stage, under the head of
flats, wings, side-pieces, borders, sinks, flies, &c. &c.,
has been painted, if it be not rubbed out, by

STANFIELD AND GRIEVE,

whose unsurpassed genius has long since obtained
for them the enviable title of the

CLAUDES AND WILSONS OF THE DRAMA.

At the summit of one side of the building will be
found

THE MEN'S WARDROBE,

which consists, according to the Master Tailor's
latest report, of

THIRTY-THREE THOUSAND SEVEN HUNDRED AND FIFTY DRESSES,

from a king's jerkin to a peasant's jacket; while,
on the other side of the house, for the strict pre-
servation of moral rectitude, will be found

A BEAUTIFUL STOCK OF LADIES' ATTIRE,

from Queen Catherine's robe to Mrs. Bulgruddery's
best flannel petticoat.

THE PROPERTIES

are a valuable property indeed, as can be attested
by the evidence of Mr. Philip Stone, so many
years the eminent superintendent thereof. There
are

SIX-AND-THIRTY PRIVATE BOXES,

if you can but get a tenant for them; though it
must not be concealed that

HER GRACIOUS MAJESTY

is the only patroness who ever thinks of taking one.
To be sure

THE DUKE OF BEDFORD

has the best in the house, being able, as ground-
landlord, to pick and choose for himself, without
paying a penny for it. Then

MISS BURDETT COUTTS

is owner of one for life, in which no lessee can have
any interest. Then there are

THREE HUNDRED RENTERS' SHARES,

entitling the owner of each to a free admission;
and as those who don't use them sell them, the
theatre is subject to so many (and very many
more) nightly admissions.

THE SALOON,

in which so much nonsense is annually delivered by
some of the proprietors, is a spacious room capable
of holding

MORE THAN TWO HUNDRED LADIES,

and lined with sufficient plate-glass to monopolise
all the reflections that can possibly be made on it.

THE TREASURY,

upon the real Shaksperian principle of " safe bind,
safe find," is fitted up with a spacious iron chest,
desk, and counter, and wants nothing but a quantity of treasure to make it complete.

" A reform of the stage," which all will admit
has been long desirable, has been at length accomplished, for

A NEW STAGE

altogether has very recently been laid down and
perfected. To crown all, Mr. Robins is happy in
making it known that

A PELLUCID SPRING,

which has long given the title to Drury Lane, (and

likewise to a friend of his, resident in the neigh-
bourhood, who shall be nameless,) of

THE PUMP OF THE PARISH,

supplies the building with the purest water, and
was for years used by

THE IMMORTAL SHERIDAN,

Kean, and other " choice spirits," to mix with their
brandy and *other* choice spirits.

ITS REDOLENT LOCALITY

requires no observation, from its vicinity to Covent-
Garden Market; and its fashionable situation may
be best judged of when Mr. Robins states that it is
within a mile of

BUCKINGHAM PALACE.

*** Further particulars may be obtained at the
different libraries and hotels in Dunstable, Penzance,
Tadcaster, Sutton Coldfield, Moreton in the Marsh,
Crawley, Deptford, Gravesend, Droitwich, Ilford,
Middle Wallop, John o' Groats, Salisbury Plain,
and other well-known theatrical places; at the
celebrated establishments on Epsom Downs, Ascot,
Newmarket, and Doncaster, where " the play, the
play's the thing," and of Mr. George Robins, at
his Great Rooms, Piazza, Covent-Garden.

The proprietor, who " rose to defend Mr. Bunn
from the unwarrantable attack made upon him,"

was my much esteemed friend Mr. Wallace, a gentleman whose literary and social qualifications, whose excellent heart and general liberality, have made him as respected, beloved, and popular, since his return from India, as he was during his long residence there.

The reference in the foregoing report to the deficiency in the rent, made by Mr. Robins, led to the following correspondence in the *Times* newspaper, inserted here upon the principle, thus far acted upon, of giving all official documents, whether for me or against me :

No. 1.

To the Editor of the Times.

Sir,

Having read your report of the meeting of the Drury Lane Theatre proprietors, in which I am stated (in reply to a question from the garrulous ex-committee man, Mr. G. Robins,) to be indebted to that body in the sum of 12,211*l.* for rent, I solicit a small space in your valuable journal to say that such statement is a falsehood.

The theatre having been for the last three seasons let to me under such singular circumstances, and at such a period of the year as almost to preclude the possibility of forming a company and making the necessary arrangements to bring them into action,

I only consented to execute a lease on the express understanding that every indulgence was to be extended to me in the exaction of rent (considering myself rather as an agent than a tenant)—an understanding honourably acted up to by the sub-committee. No man in his senses would have taken the theatre on any other conditions.

At the same time, I beg to say, with reference to the difference in amount between the rent stipulated in my lease and what I actually did pay, that I transferred to the committee all the property I had introduced into their theatre, at a cost to myself of several thousand pounds.

I have the honour to be,
Sir,
Your obedient and obliged servant,
A. Bunn.

No. 2.

To the Editor of the Times.

Sir,

My attention has been called to a letter of Mr. Alfred Bunn's, written, I apprehend, while he was smarting under the severe lash created by his long continued Bartholomew * fair exhibition on the

---

* Contrasted with this mild rebuke may be submitted as good a bit of fun as can well be conceived, whereby it would seem that to carry their own purposes men sometimes eat their own words:

boards of Drury Lane. I pass by the falsehood
and the vulgarity of his notable production, and
content myself by observing, that the debt due to

*Copy of an announcement recently made by Mr. George Robins for the
sale of two renters' shares in the patent theatres.*

Particulars and Conditions of Sale of two renters' shares in the Theatres Royal Covent Garden and Drury Lane, held for about fifty-five
years, with annual free admissions, one to each share, which will be
sold by auction by Mr. George Robins, at the Auction Mart, London,
on Tuesday, 14th April, 1840, at 12 o'clock, in two lots, by direction
of the executor of Wm. Fraser, Esq., deceased. Madame Vestris is
the lessee of Covent Garden Theatre, which places beyond the possibility of doubt the fact that unapproachable tact and good taste have
prevailed in every department; and it is not too much to conclude
that triumphant success will reward a system of management which
she has constituted her own, and one not to be in dread of rivalry.

LOT I.—An annuity or rent-charge, secured upon the Theatre Royal
Covent Garden, denominated a renter's share, which originally cost
five hundred pounds. The income has been reduced from 25*l.* a year
to 12*l.* 10*s.* a year by the mutual consent of the shareholders; and
this sum is paid with the punctuality of the Bank dividends by the
respectable treasurer of Covent Garden theatre. The holder of the
share is likewise entitled to a free admission to any part of the theatre
before the curtain, which may be disposed of annually, and should
produce at least 5*l.* Upon this calculation the income may be estimated at 17*l.* 10*s.* a-year. Indeed, under such auspicious management
the free admissions will be greatly increased in their annual value.
The admission and income for the present season are both included.

LOT II.—An annuity of 25*l.* a year, secured upon the Theatre Royal
Drury Lane, reduced by consent, and upon the reliance of an act of
parliament, to 12*l.* 10*s.* a year. It is a first charge after payment of
rent and taxes, and is secured upon this splendid theatre and its ap-
pendages. The dividends upon these shares, so long as a healthy
management prevailed, were paid with the regularity of the Bank
dividends; and it must not be disguised that any expectation of im-

Drury Lane Theatre was stated by Lord Glengall and the secretary, at the public meeting, to be 12,211*l.*; and as I prefer their statement, I shall continue to believe he is a debtor to that amount, and I will add, I think it very probable he will never owe less.

I have the honour to be, sir,

Your very obedient servant,

GEORGE ROBINS.

Covent Garden, July 27, 1839.

provement will necessarily have reference to the hope that a committee will soon preside, who will adopt a better course of management. It may be well to add, that the difficulty of securing this annuity by levying a distress no longer exists. It needs only wise heads to let, and a clever man to take, the theatre, at a reasonable rate, to ensure a respectable dividend. Particulars may be had at the offices in Covent Garden.

Extract from the Morning Post of the 28th *November,* 1835, *relative to the very same subject.*

COVENT GARDEN THEATRE.—A rent-charge annuity of 25*l.* a year, payable half-yearly, without abatement, secured upon Covent Garden theatre, with a transferable free admission, held for sixty years. This lot, Mr. Robins said, had been sold, without his knowledge up to that hour, by private contract.

DRURY LANE THEATRE.—Next were submitted twenty shares, of 100*l.* each, in the joint stock company of the Theatre Royal Drury Lane. Mr. Robins stated that the shares he had to submit were very different from those of Covent Garden, where they *promised* to pay ; but at Drury Lane Theatre they were *bound* to pay 1*d.* and 3*d.* each night of performance : *and it was likely, from the astonishing success of* MR. BUNN *with the present pieces, the house would be open the whole year, and that it would be unnecessary to prepare either Christmas or Easter new entertainments. The money taken nightly was without precedent.*

No. 3.

To the Editor of the Times.

Sir,

Permit me to say, in reply to a letter in your paper of this day, signed " George Robins," that I desire no other testimony to the truth of my communication of Friday last, than that of the Lord Glengall and the secretary of the Drury Lane proprietors. Having, in the course of a long connexion with the London stage, brought before the public almost every performer of eminence my own or any other country could boast of, and having by their co-operation produced some of the most successful novelties known to that stage, I may smile at the vituperation levelled at me, as I do at the idle charge of falsehood and vulgarity, emanating from that exquisite sample of both, Mr. George Robins.

I have the honour to be,

Sir,

Your obliged and obedient servant,

A. Bunn.

Brompton, July 29, 1839.

I was told that Mr. Robins issued a rejoinder in some other paper, but I never read a syllable of it ; and if I had, I never should have replied to it. I really believe Robins is a good-hearted man at the bottom ; and if his fulminations against me either amused him or answered his purpose, I have not the slightest angry feeling for his having issued them.

The subject of thcse letters, viz. the actual arrear of rent, is easily disposed of. The committee proved under my estate, as their lease legally enabled them to do, for the said 12,21 1*l.*; but an equitable understanding, as will be perceived by their own official document presently to be submitted, was entered into, that an allowance was to be made for all the property introduced by me into the theatre; and from the mass of it, that allowance would have amounted to something considerable, had no arrear of rent existed. But such is the distinction between law and equity, that they were fully entitled to claim for the whole amount, being at the same time in possession of the said property as a proportionable security. That the reader, however, may judge of the position in which I stood for so many years with the sub-committee, general committee, and proprietors, I beg to subjoin the allusions to myself in each of the annual reports drawn up by the first, sanctioned by the second, and confirmed and passed by the latter body, during my connexion with them :

Extract from the Report on the Season, 1832-33, *made* 23*rd July,* 1833.

" The committee have re-let the theatre for a term
" of six years, at a rent of 8,000*l.* for the past three
" years, and 8,500*l.* for the last three years, but de-
" terminable at the end of the third year at the

" option of the lessee; and from the talent, in-
" dustry, and experience of Mr. Bunn, the com-
" mittee are sanguine in their expectations that
" that gentleman possesses the qualifications to
" render it successful. And the committee beg to
" add, that they have taken the most undeniable
" security for the payment of the rent and perform-
" ance of covenants."

Extract from the Report on the Season 1833-34,
made the 19*th July,* 1834.

" The committee have the satisfaction to report
" that the lease was executed, agreeably to their
" former report, on the stipulated rent of 8,000*l.*,
" which has been regularly paid by the lessee into
" the hands of the trustees for the proprietors.

" The experiment of uniting the two theatres
" under one management, (however hazardous the
" undertaking,) the committee have reason to believe
" has not only given satisfaction to the public, but
" afforded to the various persons dependent on these
" extensive concerns a security of receiving their
" salaries for the full complement of two hundred
" nights."

Extract from the Report on the Season 1834-35,
made the 4*th August,* 1835.

" Considerable difficulties have from time to
" time arisen during the progress, which claimed
" the best exertions of the committee to meet. It

" is a well-grounded belief that theatrical property
" at this time labours under a depression hitherto
" unknown ; yet by the extraordinary exertions and
" tact of the lessee, the season was brought to a
" close comparatively successful."

Extract from the Report on the Season 1835-36,
made the 4*th August,* 1836.

" The lease of the theatre having expired on
" the 5th of July last, the committee were called
" upon to exercise their judgment in fixing upon
" a future tenant of the property; and having sub-
" mitted it to competition in the usual way by pub-
" lic advertisement, and no opportunity presenting
" itself for otherwise disposing of it with advantage,
" from any tenders they received, they are again
" about to confide the property for three years to
" the lesseeship of Mr. Bunn, whose zealous and
" judicious management of the enterprise of the
" stage, during the past season, has evinced so much
" tact and knowledge in conducting an establish-
" ment of such magnitude and public interest."

Extract from the Report of the Season, 1836-37,
made the 17*th August,* 1837.

" The committee cannot omit this opportunity
" of bearing testimony to the zeal, industry, and
" talent of Mr. Bunn, under every trial and disap-
" pointment, and his anxious wish at all times to
" keep faith with the committee, who may fairly say
" that if success has not attended his exertions, all

" things considered in the preceding year, that
" they have no reason to complain, nor even under
" such unfavourable circumstances to withdraw their
" confidence from their lessee, who, it must not be
" forgotten, amongst all his other outlay, embel-
" lished and beautified the interior of the theatre,
" during the last vacation, at a cost of 1,500*l.*

Extract from the Report on the Season 1837-38,
made 8*th August*, 1838.

(A copy of which was officially sent me by the
sub-committee; and a reference to the memorandum at the bottom of it corroborates the statement
previously adduced, of the allowance that was to be
made for my addition to the company's stock.)

General Committee.   Resolution, 8*th Aug.* 1838.

" The theatre being now not only without a les-
" see, but without any prospect of one, and the
" sub-committee feeling the importance of not allow-
" ing the theatre to remain closed, came to the
" resolution of entering into some provisional ar-
" rangement with Mr. Bunn, subject to the sanc-
" tion of the general committee ; and Mr. Bunn
" having been called in, and having had the con-
" ditions on which the theatre had been submitted
" to public competition laid before him, (to the
" terms of which he signified his assent,) he agreed
" to continue his exertions as lessee of this property
" under the usual lease of the theatre, hoping, at

" the same time, that the committee would extend
" towards him their favourable consideration on
" the arduous undertaking in which he was about
" to engage.

" The lease was executed on the 9th of Octo-
" ber, and left in the *possession of the sub-committee*."

Mem. At the end of the report 28th July 1838:
viz. " Mr. Bunn also is entitled to an allowance
" for the increased amount of properties, scenery,
" and wardrobe, placed by him in the theatre, but
" not accurately estimated."

Extract from the Report on the season 1838-39
has already been given in the foregoing detail of the
annual meeting in July last.

No surreptitious means having been adopted, nor
indeed necessary, to obtain these extracts, they having been publicly read, and as publicly given in
most of the newspapers, I may be pardoned, I hope,
whatever vanity may attach itself to the dissemina-
tion of this compendium of them all, from the necessity, as it seems to me, of showing that the
scurrility I was on this last occasion subject to, was
at all events a novelty.

I have now recorded the opinion of the general
body of the Drury Lane proprietary ; and having by
letter thanked the noble chairman for the handsome
manner in which he was pleased to speak of me up
to the latest moment, my feelings were exceedingly
gratified by the receipt of the following letter from

that noble lord, which finally wound up my connexion with THE THEATRE ROYAL DRURY LANE :

"August 15, 1839.

" MY DEAR SIR,

" I assure you that I conceive I did you but an act
" of justice in making those observations which I felt
" myself called upon to express at our meeting; for
" indeed no one could have acted more honourably
" than you did, throughout your arduous manage-
" ment of Drury Lane Theatre ; and I only regret
" that you are not engaged at present in assisting
" in carrying on the business of the establishment.

" I hope sincerely that I may have it in my power
" to assist you in any of your future plans, and
" earnestly desire that they may be successful.

   " Believe me
    " Very sincerely yours,
     " &c. &c.
      " GLENGALL."

" To A. Bunn, Esq."

The Saturday preceding the Drury Lane meeting, a dinner was given to my late rival, to do justice, as the advertisements expressly stated, to " the
zeal, taste, and liberality," with which he had
managed Covent Garden Theatre for the two preceding years. His Royal Highness the Duke of
Sussex was coaxed into the chair, and, with his acknowledged good-nature, fulfilled the duties of it

SPEECH OF THE DUKE OF SUSSEX.

with his customary tact: but as his royal highness
(with deep regret be it stated) had been prevented by illness from entering Covent Garden
Theatre during the whole term of Mr. Macready's
tenure, it will be amusing to see to what an extent
his Royal Highness was impressed with a notion of
those exertions which, had he seen them, he must
have reported far differently. The following is the
report of His Royal Highness's speech, as given in
the newspapers of the time:

" The chairman said, he now rose for the purpose
" of performing a most pleasing duty, that of ex-
" pressing in the name of the meeting their high
" opinion of the merits of Mr. Macready, and the
" obligation which they themselves, and the public,
" were under to that gentleman, for his strenuous
" exertions in support of the legitimate drama. He
" felt great delicacy upon that occasion, inasmuch
" as he saw himself surrounded by men of the most
" eminent talents in this country, and who had
" most efficiently exerted themselves for the advan-
" tage of the stage. This was a circumstance
" which would have prompted him to say little;
" but when he perceived such a numerous attend-
" ance on that occasion, and when he recollect-
" ed the good materials he had to work upon,
" (a laugh)—he thought he should be enabled to
" say a few words more than he should otherwise
" have felt disposed to indulge in. In viewing

" many gentlemen then present who took their
" rank either as poets or in some other branch of
" the literature of the country, he would not give
" way to any flights of fancy, but would speak
" merely to facts, and leave to others the region of
" imagination. With respect to his (Mr. Mac-
" ready's) services to the drama, he thought they
" had a right to look at them in a twofold shape—
" first, the prominent figure he had always main-
" tained in his profession, and last, not least, his
" conduct as manager of Covent Garden Theatre.
" In the first capacity, his reputation was well
" known throughout this country, and in America
" also, where he at one time resided ; and when to
" this he added not only the talent of the individual,
" but the character of a gentleman* and of the
" honest man, he thought he conveyed the greatest
" compliment which it was in his power to bestow.
" The stage was an arduous task to undertake : the
" individual who entered upon that career, and
" who had worked his way up in the profession,
" well knew the difficulties he had to fight with,
" and the temptations to which he was exposed,
" the variety of calls upon him, either from af-
" fection, or friendship, or fellow-feeling ; and
" he also knew the thousand anxieties and vicis-
" situdes to which he was exposed in the per-

* Did his Royal Highness ever happen to be assailed and half
murdered in a dark room by a " gentleman," almost before he knew
who was his assailant ?

" formance of an irksome duty. When, therefore,
" having encountered and surmounted all these
" difficulties, they had arrived at the top of their
" profession, surely they deserved credit for their
" talent, and respect for the character which had
" carried them through all these trials. If that
" individual were a man of sense and reflection,
" such a career would teach him to give similar
" credit to others less successful, to excuse their
" follies, to assist their wants, and to give them the
" benefit of that compassion which existed in the
" breast of every honest man, and which he was
" satisfied held firm dominion in the breast of
" the gentleman whom he alluded to. After
" this preface, he need not add that such a
" school as the one he had adverted to was the
" very one which pointed out such an individual
" as the proper selection to be made for the
" management of a theatre. An individual im-
" pressed with such feelings would go to work in a
" very different way from vulgar minds. He would
" look upon his name as the last good thing to be
" considered. It was his duty to cater for the pub-
" lic, and to produce before them only such indi-
" viduals as were deserving of public attention. He
" had to bring before the public persons fitted to
" appear upon the stage, and pieces suitable to the
" taste, the feelings, and the morals of the country ;
" and he had to take care that the interests of
" those individuals whom he so engaged were pro-

" perly secured and guarded.   Having laid down
" that as a principle, let them look at Mr. Macready's
" exertions since he had presided for the last two
" years as manager of Covent Garden Theatre.   He
" had succeeded in reviving * no less than ten of
" Shakspeare's plays; indeed, he had not only revived
" them, but he had placed them upon a proper foot-
" ing, and· had caused them to be represented in a
" style worthy of the illustrious author of those
" works, thus inspiring an interest and giving an
" encouragement to the drama which every lover of
" this country would wish to see extended.   With
" the assistance of distinguished individuals then
" present, he had brought out two new plays which
" had ensured universal applause.   Need he name
" Sir E. L. Bulwer or Mr. Sheridan Knowles?
" Besides these, there were various others which he
" had revived—some of Lord Byron's, of Serjeant
" Talfourd's, and some of Beaumont and Fletcher's.
" It was a great exertion on the part of Mr.
" Macready to have provided such theatrical repre-
" sentations as merited the support of an enlightened
" and generous public.   In doing this, he had not
" sought his own advantage, for, on the contrary,
" he had made great personal sacrifices of his own
" income, in addition to having undergone great

---

* This is a somewhat curious term to apply to plays it is customary
to play, and which have been played every season, and far better " got
up " and acted, than under Mr. Macready's management—as hath
been shown.

" and heavy labour in conducting the theatre
" for two years—and why? because he was under
" the impression that it was possible to do good to the
" theatre, and even while paying others regularly,
" to raise the character of the national drama.
" He rejoiced that bankruptcy had not followed the
" experiment, which, on the contrary, had been most
" successful.   Mr. Macready paid a rental for the first
" year of 5,675l. for the theatre, and for the last year
" he had paid a rent of 7,000l., which rentals were
" actually paid out of the produce of the theatre in
" addition to 3,000l. for repairs.   Thus in the course
" of two years, under the management of Mr.
" Macready, nearly fifteen thousand pounds had been
" paid for rent and necessaries for the theatre.*
" Such an individual had a strong claim to the
" notice and attention of the company.   Having
" stated his claims on the ground of economy, he
" would now proceed to a more interesting part of
" his management—namely, the moral effects it had
" produced.   Mr. Macready had created such a
" sense of propriety in the theatre, that good fathers
" and mothers might now attend with their children,
" and not witness the scenes of confusion, idleness, and
" obscenity, which formerly prevailed.   He might go
" further, and ask what formerly was the state of con-

---

* In the two years I managed Covent Garden Theatre, the sum of
17,370l. was paid to the proprietors for rent, besides nearly 2,000l. for
taxes, and a large outlay on the building itself; but that's not worth
mentioning, because *I* was not' " Shakspeare's representative !"

" fusion in the saloon? It was now, however, of a dif-
" ferent character, and an honest woman and her
" husband might walk quietly through it. It was now
" conducted in a wholesome and proper manner, and
" was no longer calculated to shock the feelings of
" the public. They were therefore indebted to Mr.
" Macready, not only for his success in reviving the
" national drama, but for having provided a whole-
" some and pleasant amusement for honest people,
" where they were more likely to meet with sounder
" ideas of morality than if they had remained at
" home. He now came to a subject of much more
" delicacy. Matters of property should of course
" be decided by law, and he had no wish to excite
" an unpleasant feeling against any one. Yet he
" could not but regret that patent rights should
" exist as property. He had been always led to
" think they existed but for a certain number of
" years; but they were so far looked upon as per-
" petual property, that money had frequently been
" raised upon them. Under these circumstances,
" he would only say that the sooner a compromise
" was effected so as to get rid of them altogether,
" the better it would be for the public.* He
" saw his honourable friend (Mr. Sheil) near him,
" who had a greater facility than he possessed of
" addressing a public company ; but in good-will

---

* His Royal Highness is respectfully referred to the long account
given in these volumes of the said patents, by which he will find
they are worse than got rid of.

" to serve the cause no one could be more sincere
" than himself. He was delighted at having this
" opportunity of expressing his opinions and good
" feelings towards the theatre, his obligations to
" Mr. Macready for his services in reviving the
" legitimate drama, and his extreme pleasure at
" seeing so numerous a meeting. He was also glad
" to learn that the demonstration was not to be con-
" fined to a dinner, for he had heard that it was the
" intention of Mr. Macready's friends to present
" him with a more solid token of their approbation
" —a proposal he should follow with great pleasure.
" He begged to apologise for the length of time he
" had detained the meeting, and to add his acknow-
" ledgments of Mr. Macready's deserts for his exer-
" tions for the last two years; and whatever might
" be his (Mr. Macready's) future pursuits, he would
" carry with him the good wishes and kind feelings
" not only of that society, but of all friends to the
" prosperity of the drama."

Fresh from the perusal of this eulogium, I
went to sea—a sailing—a sailing—not in the capacity of those who have been " bound 'prentice to a
waterman," but in my worthy friend Allen's fine
yacht, THE OSPREY. A party of us dashed over
" the herring pond," and under the heights of Calais,
I dashed off a humble tribute, mediocre enough no
doubt, to our gallant little vessel :

> The Osprey! the Osprey !
> Oh, give us but a gale,

And none shall ride
Across the tide
With half as little sail!
We leave the world behind us—
  Its cares to hearts that weep :
  The surge of the sea
  And the melody
Of the winds which o'er it sweep,
Are the magic ties that bind us
To THE FREEDOM OF THE DEEP !

The Osprey ! the Osprey!
  Oh, 'tis a joy to mark
  On ocean's brim
  The gallant trim
Of that sea-worthy bark!
The storm may gather round us,
  Our vigils still we keep—
  The foam and the flash
  Of the waves that dash
O'er her deck, with angry leap,
Are the ties that long have bound us
To THE FREEDOM OF THE DEEP !

But as the object which had long been uppermost in
my mind stood very little chance of being disposed of
poetically, I at once directed my serious attention
to the composition of it, in its present form.

It is unnecessary to tell those who have been
obliging enough to peruse this work, that it aims at
no literary distinction, and is entitled to none. The
rapidity with which it has been " put together" will
convince the reader of all I wish him to *be* convinced of, that these pages present a cursory interpre-

tation of my own loose thoughts, at random strung, after the same fashion, and in precisely the same unpolished language, in which I *do* deliver, and *have* delivered, the same observations by word of mouth; in fact, they are but the familiar outpourings, perhaps, of a sanguine, but I hope a reflective turn of mind. There can be very little intellectual superiority manifested by the authorship of such a work as this, dependent as it is for its character principally upon the correctness of its statements, and the validity of its arguments. As I have neither aimed at, nor exhibited, a display of any vast mental acquirements, my ambition will be satisfied without the bestowal of praise, and my complacency will not be disturbed by that of disparagement. My labour has had no higher aim than

> " The colouring of the scenes which fleet along,
> " Which I would seize, in passing, to beguile
> " My breast, or that of others, for a while.
> " Fame is the thirst of youth—but I am not
> " So young as to regard men's frown or smile,
> " As loss or guerdon of a glorious lot."

I do not deny that I have striven throughout, with reference to those who have so wilfully or unintentionally misrepresented me, " to work mine end upon their senses;" but my staff being broken, I shall be perfectly content, without one feeling of disappointment, or one expression of annoyance, should it be the desire of my reader, and the gene-

ral pleasure of all-potent public opinion, to act upon
the conclusion which dissolved the spell of *Prospero,*

> " And deeper than did ever plummet sound,
> " I'll drown MY BOOK."

THE END.

LONDON:
PRINTED BY IBOTSON AND PALMER, SAVOY STREET.